Joeli Brearley founded Pregnant Then Screwed in 2015 after being sacked when she was four months pregnant. She writes for the *Telegraph* and the *Independent* and speaks about the motherhood penalty all over the world. She is one of *The Observer*'s 50 New Radicals of 2018, an Amnesty International Women Human Rights Defender, winner of the Northern Power Women 'Agent for Change' award, and in 2021 she took the Government to court for discriminating against women who had taken maternity leave. *Elle* magazine describes her as 'fearsome and funny'. A *Telegraph* commenter describes her writing as 'a massive pile of whiny nonsense'.

Praise for *The Motherhood Penalty*

'The thing I love about Joeli is that she doesn't just state the problem. She doesn't just give us the solution. She actually goes out and makes it happen. An infuriating, but also an inspiring read. What a woman.'
Caroline Criado Perez

'This book is f***king amazing. Practical help. Legal advice. Steps to take for anyone facing pregnancy or parental discrimination. This book is the sort of help pregnant folk and parents actually need.'
Hollie McNish

'It's the book that proves working mothers are shamefully mistreated.'
Daily Mail

'Brearley's book leaves no stone unturned in what needs to be done to remedy these problems going forward.'
Vogue

THE MOTHERHOOD PENALTY

HOW TO STOP MOTHERHOOD BEING THE KISS OF DEATH FOR YOUR CAREER

JOELI BREARLEY

GALLERY BOOKS UK

First published in Great Britain with the title *Pregnant Then Screwed* by Gallery Books,
an imprint of Simon & Schuster UK Ltd, 2021
This paperback edition published by Gallery Books, an imprint of
Simon & Schuster UK Ltd, 2022

1 3 5 7 9 10 8 6 4 2

Simon & Schuster UK Ltd
1st Floor
222 Gray's Inn Road
London WC1X 8HB

www.simonandschuster.co.uk
www.simonandschuster.com.au
www.simonandschuster.co.in

Simon & Schuster Australia, Sydney
Simon & Schuster India, New Delhi

A CIP catalogue record for this book is available from the British Library

Paperback ISBN: 978-1-3985-0804-0
eBook ISBN: 978-1-4711-9268-5

Typeset in Bembo by M Rules
Printed in the UK by CPI Group (UK) Ltd, Croydon, CR0 4YY

This one's for the mothers who survived a pandemic.
The pregnant women who attended hospital appointments on their
own, who gave birth without the support they needed, who spent
days or even weeks in a hospital bed broken and bruised and without
the people they love; those who went to work every day not knowing
whether they might catch a life-threatening disease; those who spent
their maternity leave losing their minds to loneliness; those who cared
for their children when the schools and nurseries closed, risking their
careers and their sanity while propping up society; those who have been
pushed out and pushed to the edge by a system and employers who
are incapable of recognising the extra load they carried to prevent it
all descending into total chaos. 2020 was the year we finally realised
that the needs of pregnant women and mothers are often sidelined and
ignored with sometimes disastrous consequences for families. Now
is the time we will demand recognition, respect and change.

So, yeah, this book is for the mothers. All of the mothers. Especially
my mother (try and ignore all the swearing, Mum. I love you xxx)

Contents

The Interview

It's a roasting-hot summer's day in July and my neighbour has agreed to spend an hour looking after my two boys. I ring the doorbell, deposit the kids on her doorstep, and excitedly scuttle back home. I'm greeted by the heavenly sound of silence, which I pause in the hallway to enjoy. The air is thick with a luminous heat, which briefly mingles with the sweet, sticky smell of suncream, causing my mind to flirt with the idea of cracking open a cold beer. I can almost taste that first, refreshing gulp; a sharp contrast to the scorching sunshine. But I resist. Once again, I have used the currency of friendship to leverage a childcare favour so that I can do some urgent work. This time it's a Skype interview with BBC Worldwide, due to take place in the next ten minutes from my cluttered kitchen table. The topic 'Why do so few women reach the top?' is one of my favourites, so I limber up eagerly in the kitchen, mentally flipping through the rolodex of facts in my brain, and pretending to passionately disagree with myself. It's my standard pre-interview ceremonial dance; I'm like Anthony Joshua with gender equality data for boxing gloves.

The jazzy sound of the Skype ringtone interrupts the excitable debate I'm having with myself, so I pull up a chair and click the phone symbol. In typical BBC fashion, they've found someone who has a view that contrasts with my own. This time it's an American author who is very confident she has the whole thing sussed. *'Clearly, it's all about choice,'* she says, sounding awfully pleased with herself and the utter nonsense she is spouting. *'Women choose to take time out of work to care for their children, or they choose to work fewer hours after they've had their kids because they want to spend time with them.'* There's a sharp intake of breath before she blurts out the punchline: *'Well, I'm afraid that if you're going to make those choices then unfortunately you are going to live with the consequences. How can women make it to the top when they work less than men? This isn't about the patriarchy, or whatever it is women are complaining about these days, it's about choice.'* My chin starts to ache from all the frustrated teeth-grinding I am doing. The goddam 'choice' argument again.

Interviews like this don't offer the opportunity to explore the nuances of an issue in detail. I think it's one of the reasons we've ended up in such political disarray. Problems are messy and complicated: you can't give a full answer as to why women have unequal access to the labour market in 90 seconds. It can't be summed up in a sound bite. But still, any opportunity to talk about how the labour market fails mothers is an opportunity I am going to take. Hold on, my bloody cat has just strolled in and jumped on the table. I quickly shove him off before I respond; specks of white fur hang in the air as he licks his lips and carefully calculates his next intervention. *'The notion that mothers have choice is absurd,'* I say, as the cat starts rubbing his furry back on my bare leg, purring loudly. *'Choice is a mythical unicorn to mothers. Instead a mother must make decisions within a very constrained framework, choosing between the only possible option for financial and mental survival, and total pandemonium.'* The American author sighs an audible sigh, but I continue undeterred: *'You may think I'm being melodramatic but ask any mother what choices she would make if she had complete freedom, and I can guarantee you that her imagined life would look very different.'* The presenter charges in: *'Are you saying women don't choose to spend time with their children, Joeli?'* I can feel my jaw clench again: *'What I am saying is that women don't make choices in a vacuum. Choices are influenced by a number of factors: culture, your family and legislation, in particular.'* I do a purposeful pregnant pause to ensure I don't sound too angry, even though I am. *'Let me give you some examples. In the UK, 54,000 women a year are pushed out of their jobs due to pregnancy or for taking maternity leave, and 77 per cent of working mums face discrimination – that's a lot of mums who have had their choice removed.'* I make sure they take note of how large those numbers are by saying them extra slowly. *'In the UK, parental-leave legislation favours mothers taking time out to care for children over fathers. In fact, thousands of working dads have no access to any paid paternity leave whatsoever. This means that, in nearly every family, the mother is the main carer, even though dads are desperate to spend more time with their children.'*

The American author tries to butt in, but I'm not feeling particularly hospitable so I confidently plough ahead: *'A mother's choices are limited by extortionately priced, inflexible, inaccessible childcare. A mother's choices are limited by maternity pay that is well below the national living wage. A mother's choices are limited by the rising cost of living, which means most families need two incomes to cover their basic costs.*[1] *A mother's choices are limited by a severe lack of part-time jobs and a working culture that demands long hours. A mother's choices are limited by the subtle and overt messages she receives from the media that tell her she should feel guilty for pretty much every decision she makes.'* I've forgotten to breathe and my lungs have run out of air. If breathing weren't actually required for me to continue, I could have carried on for at least another hour. I pause for breath, leaving a brief window for the American author to interject: *'But you don't know that changes to legislation would mean women make different choices; they have free will, and the women I know who have left their career to look after their children are very happy with their decision. Who are you to tell them otherwise?'*

I'm ready again. I managed to get a gulp of water down me while she was speaking, although some of it is now dribbling down my chin and the cat has started more or less head-butting me in an attempt to get my attention. *'I am in no way criticising parents who want to leave their job and look after their own children. It's the hardest, most important job there is. What I am saying is that the current system prevents many mothers from leaving their paid work to care for their own kids, and for those who want to work and continue their careers during pregnancy and early motherhood, they encounter unnecessary and impossible challenges. In both situations, women are disproportionately affected by a labour market and legislation that neither accommodates nor values care; and yet, without care, society falls apart.'* I wonder if I've gone off on a bit of a tangent, so I try to crystallise my point: *'If you look at other countries, which have very different legislative frameworks, women in those countries make different choices.'* The interviewer probes me further: *'What countries are you talking about, Joeli?'* I'm pleased she asked: *'Well, it's the usual suspects: Iceland, Denmark, Norway, Sweden. The countries where childcare is properly subsidised, where ring-fenced, properly paid paternity leave means dads are far more likely to take time out to care for their children, and flexible working is the norm for all employees. In these countries, mothers report far higher levels of well-being, they are more likely to work and more likely to work full-time. Children also have higher levels of well-being and they are less likely to live in poverty. I'm not saying that Scandinavia has entirely cracked the problem of mothers' unequal access to the labour market, but it is doing far better than the rest of us.'* The cat has given up on trying to get me to stroke him. He swivels around on his paws, proudly presents his bumhole and prowls out of the room. It seems the interviewer has given up, too: *'Well, I'm afraid that's all we have time for today. Thank you for speaking with me.'* The call goes dead. I stand up, stretch and head over to the fridge. I reach inside and grab an ice-cold beer. I'm sure my neighbour won't mind if I'm ten minutes late.

PREFACE

Do It All, Screw It All

Up until 2013, I was blissfully unaware of what it meant to be in charge of a child. I always knew I wanted kids, but I pictured my brood as sweet little angels who would giggle charmingly as I tickled them and tell me inadvertently hilarious anecdotes about their day at school. My heart, and my life, would be full. I'm a simple creature. I don't need much to feel content. I couldn't care less about fancy cars or expensive holidays; a satisfying job and a happy, healthy family was my idea of perfection. I had a vague, half-considered understanding that childcare might be tricky, particularly as I didn't have family close by, but I modestly considered myself strong and resourceful, so I was confident I could make it work. Sleep deprivation? Pah! I'd spent the late '90s raving, so I knew how to pull an all-nighter. I mean, how hard can maternity leave be?

Clearly, I was in for a shock, and a shock it was. As I write these words, I am surrounded by chaos. There's a cluster of milk-sodden Cheerios under my left arm. Whenever I go to the toilet, I have to navigate a Lego labyrinth, and I think I've got nits. Again. My children are four and six: two boys who spend an inordinate amount of time playing with their own penises and making statements you would expect to hear from

7

a university rugby team after ten pints of Stella. I love them with an all-encompassing visceral force, but, some of the time, I really don't love parenting. The depths of frustration, desperation and fury are beyond anything I ever thought possible. Of course, that's juxtaposed with joy, tenderness and pride, but, when the chips are down, life feels tough. Trying to balance parenting with my paid job leaves me exhausted, stressed and unkempt. The bills are high, and I worry about how we will pay them. I'm an atrocious friend and a rubbish partner. I sometimes hallucinate from lack of sleep, which can be somewhat disconcerting when I'm in a public place. There's a whiff of urine emanating from my son's bed, but it will likely be another week before I get around to changing his sheets. I've grown unwholesomely comfortable with that kind of thing.

And I am not alone. Modern-day motherhood is hard. Let's not pretend we've achieved equality and maternal bliss, because we absolutely have not. From the moment the stick turns blue, we face challenges and barriers we never previously knew existed − and most of them are entirely unnecessary. Our ability to procreate stands at the centre of centuries of gender inequality that's no different today, but frustratingly it feels like it's a challenge that is just too complex to solve, and, with such strength of feeling from pretty much all women (and some men) on anything related to motherhood, it can make the topic an intimidating one to address.

Did feminism forget motherhood? To date, it has mainly been skipped over by politicians, campaigners and even women's organisations. An afterthought when the main work has been done. More of an inconvenience, if anything. But mothers aren't an inconvenience; we are the foundation upon which society thrives, and it's about bloody time we lived in a society that worked for us. Brilliant, skilled, hard-working women are being pushed out and pushed to the edge by a system that ignores their needs and by employers who undermine their abilities. The rising cost of living, and a benefit system that doesn't consider caregiving to have worth, forces women into poverty for doing the most important job there is – raising the next generation.

Discrimination against pregnant women, mothers and women of childbearing age is rising sharply. Thousands of mothers are being forced out of their jobs, and hundreds of thousands more face other types of injustice such as demotions, halted careers or an impossible workload. We know that a third of employers avoid hiring women of childbearing age,[1] that 40 per cent of employers think women take advantage of their pregnancy in the workplace and that a third think women are less interested in their career once they get pregnant.[2] Trying to tackle this injustice as an individual, especially as a pregnant individual or one with a newborn baby, can feel impossible. The majority of those who try to use the legal system to protect themselves are either gagged by a non-disclosure agreement or they come to realise that everything is stacked against them.

We have the second most expensive childcare system in the world, after the Slovak Republic, which makes it prohibitively expensive for many parents to return to work.[3] Our own research of 20,000 mothers in 2021 found that a third pay more for their childcare than their mortgage, rising to almost half for respondents from a Black ethnic background. And in 2018 there were 870,000 stay-at-home mums who wanted to work but simply couldn't afford to do so because of childcare costs.[4] That's half of all out-of-work mums. Women still do almost three times as much childcare as fathers and 60 per cent more of the unpaid domestic work, [5] despite three-quarters of mothers being in paid work in 2020;[6] so I'm sure it's no surprise to hear that working mothers are 40 per cent more stressed than all other humans.[7] Same-sex couples have a much more equitable share of the unpaid labour ... until they become parents,[8] which shows that gender stereotypes are only part of the problem.

Many mothers look for part-time and flexible work so that they can manage all of this extra unpaid work, but only 10 per cent of jobs are advertised as part-time, with just 1 in 4 jobs specifying any type of flexible working,[9] so many women are forced to work in jobs that are well below their skill level. On top of this, part-time work is paid at an average rate of £5 less per hour than full-time work[10] – oh, hello there, gender pay gap. And then we wonder why women's pensions are 55 per cent lower than men's,[11] why women are more likely to live in poverty than men [12] and why there are so few women in leadership positions.[13]

Mothers are bombarded with incessant conflicting messages about how to do motherhood right. We must be selfless, never idle; we must constantly fill our kids' little brains with wholesome play, educational activities and creative stimulation. Ideally, our children should be baking cheese soufflés and reciting *War and Peace* from memory by the age of five. What many don't see is the severe impact this is all having on women – the damage of pregnancy and maternity discrimination on our mental health, the pressure to be perfect, the physical exhaustion of attempting to do it all, the struggle with the lack of power and control because the system doesn't work for us. It's all too much.

Throughout this book, I am going to show you how policy and culture conspire to either prevent mothers from progressing a career or to push mothers out of their jobs altogether and back to the kitchen sink. Even before the pandemic threw a microscope onto the inequalities experienced by pregnant women and mothers, our ability to progress had flatlined. We can see this from the gender pay gap statistics, a decline of only 0.6 per cent from 2012 to 2019.[14]

With political will and determination, this is an issue that could be solved, but it isn't a priority for those who have the power to make change happen; a rather odd outcome if you consider that solving it would benefit our economy and our collective well-being, not to mention the direct benefit for women and their families.

With the right changes to our legislation and labour market, genuine choices about work and child-rearing are possible. A quick poll I did before coronavirus (BC) showed how these choices have never been a reality: I asked working mums whether they wanted to quit their job, and 53 per cent said yes. I asked 'stay-at-home' mums if they wanted to do paid work, and 85 per cent said yes.[15]

We cannot solve any of this by continuing to shoehorn women into our current archaic structures; by replacing a handful of men with a handful of women. This will only ensure that mothers advance down the path of mental and physical burnout. When we asked, 'Can women have it all?', we didn't mean, 'Can women *do* it all?' Which appears to be where we've ended up. When feminists fought for women to be released from their caregiving responsibilities, that was all well and good, but clearly someone needs to care for the children and, strange as it may seem, a lot of parents actually like spending time with their kids. Without radical changes to our legislation, a restructuring of our labour market and a societal shift in how we view caring and the role of women, mothers will continue to work themselves to the bone, they will continue to feel like they are letting everyone down, and they will continue to be paid less for the privilege. How do we square that circle – and why should we bother?

This book – an accumulation of everything I've learned while building and growing the Pregnant Then Screwed campaign to combat pregnancy and maternity discrimination – will highlight some of the many impossible challenges mothers face in the twenty-first century. Using stories and quotes I have documented over the past six years, from the mothers (and fathers) I have spoken to and worked with, it will show how the systems and structures in which mothers create and raise new human life ensure they remain unequal to men and childless women. It will explore some of the specific challenges faced by mothers in same-sex relationships, adoptive mothers, single mothers, mothers of disabled children, Black, Asian and Minority Ethnic mothers. It will explore how we can fix the problem on a macro level and it will provide you with tips, tricks and tools to help you deal with those challenges when they apparently leap out of nowhere to smack you in the face.

And before you start frantically typing out a strongly worded email telling me it's also very hard for men: I agree. I'm not saying that men have it easy. They don't. The expectations placed on their shoulders can be deeply damaging. Many dads feel a sense of isolation and loneliness. Some are working themselves into a stupor affecting their mental and physical health, rarely seeing their children and feeling disconnected from the world. There are many wonderful men. Men who are striving for equality in the home. Men who champion working-women's rights. Men who adore their children and want nothing more than to spend more time caring for them. The conversation needs to be reframed. The majority of people want to do fulfilling paid work and they want quality time to see their family and friends as well as time to maybe do some exercise or something creative or self-indulgent. That's what we should all be working towards, and it is possible; other countries have managed to get far closer to such a reality than we have, and with no negative impact on their economy. We all need a better way to live and work.

Changing the working world is important to me, not just because of my own experience and my desire to create change for future mothers, but also for my sons. I don't want them to have children and feel that they cannot spend time with them; missing out on those precious years of their childhood, wondering where the time went and desperately wishing they could have that time again. I don't want them to feel the enormous, stressful burden of being the main breadwinner because their partner has been pushed out of their job or has been unfairly demoted to the point where they can't afford their bills any more. I want my sons to be in a relationship that is equal, where each person in that relationship takes their fair share of the domestic duties and financial responsibility, because I know (and research supports) that this can help to make a truly happy, stable relationship. Bronnie Ware, an Australian palliative care nurse, recorded the top regrets of people on their deathbeds, and among them, from men in particular, was: 'I wish I hadn't worked so hard.'[16]

Lastly, I have to admit that writing a book about motherhood and sending it out into the world feels like self-flagellation. It's such a personal, identity-shaping and emotional experience for women that to make any kind of statement about any of it ensures someone somewhere will passionately disagree with you. Every mother is an expert in mothering because they have literally invested blood, sweat and tears into birthing and raising a new human life. Every mother is different – strangely enough, we are not one homogenous group that speaks with one voice. Our experience of motherhood can be shaped by our background, race, income, class, sexuality, religion, relationship or disability. The stories I've collected and used in this book have been sent to me from a very diverse range of mothers, but, alas, there is no possible way I can speak for all mothers, and I would not dare to try. However, from my experience, there are common factors that bind us all, and if we work together we can fight for a world where care is valued and where women are enabled to make real choices about parenting and work.

I have dedicated the past seven years of my life to helping women who experience pregnancy and maternity discrimination. I have documented thousands of stories, read hundreds of books and papers on the subject and explored the solutions other countries have implemented. I've marched through the streets with thousands of mums to demand recognition, respect and change. This book will likely turn you off and turn you on (not in a sexy way) as you make your way through it. My hope is that reading it gives you a good understanding of what the barriers are for mums, and that it galvanises us to work together to demand better – with Cheerios proudly dangling from our sleeves.

1

How It All Began: Discrimination, Gestation, Creation

I am that girl. The one who did drama class and horse riding. If my bank account was bare, I could call my mum and £50 would appear out of thin air. Raised by an adoring mother and an ambitious father (albeit in Halifax, which back then was pretty grim), I was born into comfort and privilege. I had an excellent education and was repeatedly told I could be anything I wanted to be. My dad went on to make some pretty serious money in the rag trade and we swiftly moved to deluxe suburbia – a charming village just outside Leeds. I was 14 and furious. I rebelled by drinking 20/20 and listening to Nirvana at 140 decibels in my bedroom.

I know. THAT girl.

Now, I'm not saying it was all rosy, because it wasn't. There was bullying, sexual assault, a long, drawn-out divorce, and by the time I was 17 my dad had lost the money he had made and the business he had built. But still, if I was a sample in one of those 'expected life outcome' studies, I would be considered, you know, pedigreed.

After university, I used my privilege to grab the world by its lapels and started carving out a successful career. I was confident, qualified; I had everything going for me. Feminism was not a word I associated with. It conjured up images of joyless, angry women wearing comfortable shoes and large knickers. I liked drinking pints in the pub, dancing to drum and bass, and men – I really liked men, and I was their equal. Gender inequality was something that affected my grandmother, not me. I could be or do anything I wanted; I just needed to work really hard and prove myself to my employers, who, interestingly, were all men. When a male client placed his hand on my inner thigh under the table at an important meeting, I just thought he was a bit of a creep. When I applied for a job and was later propositioned by the interviewer – 'Have sex with me and the job is yours' – I felt violated and depressed, but still didn't resign my position as a wholly co-operative member of the patriarchy. Of course, I declined his grotesque proposition, and the role was then given to … a man (!!), but it was just a one-off incident, another bad apple – I was clearly very unlucky. You could surmise that I was a bit slow off the mark, rather unobservant, a little dense perhaps, and with hindsight I was. I have no idea how I excused these incidents or managed to ignore their broader connotation, but I did.

Do you know what finally ripped the blindfold off and brought everything into focus? Getting pregnant.

Fast forward to 10 April 2013. I could hear my phone buzzing in the kitchen as I brushed my teeth. Talking with a mouthful of white frothing toothpaste would risk permanently damaging my Nokia Lumia so I let it ring out. After rinsing my mouth and doing the obligatory *Wallace and Gromit* smile in the mirror, I pressed my phone to my ear so I could listen to the answerphone message. It was my employer, the CEO of a children's charity. I had informed her the day before that I was expecting my first baby. *'Hi Joeli. This is a really difficult call to make. I'm sorry to tell you that the board and I have decided to terminate your contract. It's not working out. Could you make sure you hand over all the project documents as soon as possible.'* My hand began to shake. As I let the news sink in, I began to pace the cheap lino of my rented flat: up and down, up and down. I was trying to force a thought, a reaction, an emotion, but my mind felt blank, like the hard drive of a computer that had been wiped clean by a virus. Not distressed, not angry, just empty. I called my partner, then my mum, then my father-in-law, a property lawyer who sadly knew nothing about employment law. The poor man had to painstakingly explain to me that the laws involved in selling a house are quite different from the laws involved in managing an employee.

The enormity of what had just happened started to sink in. I was four months pregnant and I had no idea where my next pay cheque was going to come from. Who would employ a visibly pregnant woman? I sat at my laptop and my eyes began to sting with tears, until finally the emptiness lifted – and terror kicked in. I sobbed uncontrollably. Hot, heavy, furious tears.

My phone beeped. It was a message from my partner, Tom: 'Try not to worry. We'll find a way to manage.' And with that the terror turned to anger. How could they do that to me when I was so vulnerable? What sort of person pushes a pregnant woman out of her job? I knew nothing about employment law but I was confident this was in breach of it. *They've made a big mistake*, I thought to myself, *they can't seriously believe they will get away with this. The law will protect me. I mean, what's the point in having employment law if it doesn't prevent pregnant women from being fired?*

I wiped away the tears and called a number of helplines, with mixed results. After hours of talking and researching,

I still didn't understand my legal position or what I should do next. A friend of a friend recommended an employment lawyer. They charged me £250 to write a letter to the charity demanding compensation. The letter was ignored. My bank account was empty. I had no idea how I was going to pay my rent next month but, if I wanted justice, the only option available to me was to take my employer to an employment tribunal. The solicitor estimated my legal fees to be in the region of £9,000 but he couldn't say for certain. I didn't have £9,000. Who the fuck has £9,000? 'What if I do it on my own with no legal support?' I asked the solicitor. 'Ha!' He scoffed. 'Well, good luck to you.'

Among the chaos, I attended a routine doctor's appointment where they suggested that I have my cervix checked as I had undergone surgery in 1999 due to Stage 2 cervical cancer. They scanned me and discovered that my cervix had almost vanished. The baby was hanging on by a thread: 'Your situation is dangerous,' said the doctor. 'If we don't act quickly, the baby might come, and at 20 weeks it is very unlikely it will survive.' They booked me in for a suture operation the following day – a delightful process where they would bolt my cervix together to force it into position. Their parting words were: 'Whatever you do, don't get stressed.'

Don't get stressed.

I was four months pregnant and unemployed. My confidence was in tatters and I thought my career was over. I had no idea how I would be able to afford the rent on our flat next month, let alone how I would survive maternity leave, and now it looked like my baby might die. Being stressed wasn't a choice I had the privilege of making. A strange ringing in my ears built to a crescendo and as the blood rushed from my head I collapsed in a crumpled heap on the floor. When I came around, I was lying on the crisp white sheets of a hospital bed with the concerned face of Tom staring back at me. 'Don't worry,' I said. 'I'm okay.' But he and I both knew that wasn't true.

The choice was stark: further risk the health of my unborn child and attempt to access the justice I clearly deserved, or drop the case. The law says you only have three months to raise a tribunal claim from the point discrimination occurs; I couldn't wait until my baby was born before I started proceedings. But I couldn't live with myself if I didn't do everything in my power to ensure I didn't go into labour prematurely. So, with a heavy heart, I dropped the case.

I was empty. The chance of justice had spurred me on. It wasn't that I'd wanted financial compensation; the idea of taking money from a charity that existed to support children left me feeling cold, but I had wanted some sort of vindication. I'd wanted reassurances that they would never put another woman through the same horrific experience. I wanted to hear someone in authority say that I'd been wronged. That had all been taken away. Now, there was just me, jobless and pregnant, wrestling with my hurt and fury inside my own head, praying my body would hold on to my growing baby.

I'm sure any women of colour or women with disabilities who are reading this are thinking, *What?! Seriously? This was the first time you experienced discrimination? This was the first time you realised that the systems and structures are set up to favour white, straight, non-disabled men?* And honestly, yes, it really was, and it knocked me for six. Before this happened, I had been comfortably gliding through the world. My sense of satisfaction and personal pride came from my paid work, which had now been snatched away, and, as the new life squiggled and squirmed inside me, my whole identity was thrown into question. This, combined with the knowledge that my baby might die and a fear that we may lose our home due to a lack of funds, meant my mental health took a turn for the worse. I am lucky to be surrounded by supportive people – a partner who sympathised but wouldn't let me wallow; friends who immediately rallied around with helpful words and affection; and my mum, who was comfortingly furious on my behalf. It all helped, but, as the magnitude of the situation dawned on me, I stopped eating and spent days rubbing my swollen belly, crying, begging my unborn child to stay put. I was crawling into a very dark place; left unmanaged, it risked sucking me in with such ferocity I would be swallowed whole.

Tom persuaded me to apply for a temporary position he had seen that started immediately. I was convinced they wouldn't employ a visibly pregnant woman, even though I was very well qualified for the role. But, with his help, I did it anyway, and to my bewildered delight I was invited to an interview. When I told them I was pregnant, they smiled and said, 'No shit, Sherlock,' and despite an imperfect interview they offered me the job and I whimpered with relief.

I was elated. Somebody *wanted* me. They didn't focus on my swollen uterus; they focused on my skill and my ability to do the job. I was the best candidate and impending motherhood was something they were prepared to work with. Their trust in me started the healing process, and very quickly I was back to scoffing cakes (after all, I was eating for two) and feeling much more positive about the future. My new employers and I both benefited from their trust. I gave that job everything I had: I was dedicated, productive, I wore their brand and vision like an expensive coat, and as my contract drew to an end they asked if I would be willing to return once I'd figured out how to keep a baby alive. The trust and faith we had in each other was mutual and it felt incredible to be respected for my skills and abilities again. That strength spurred me on to secure two further freelance contracts, so that by the time I went on maternity leave I was smashing that glass ceiling into tiny shards of amelioration. In the end, being sacked for daring to procreate had enormously benefited my career.

Despite this, the experience ate away at me. I thought about it every single day – the fact that it had happened, and then the fact that I was paralysed by an unfair system, unable to access the justice I deserved. My son remained in position, and after he was born I attended some parent groups and discussed my experience with other mums. To my horror, I discovered that, far from mine being an isolated incident, this was happening all the time. The majority of mothers I spoke with had experienced some form of discrimination. Their career had been, or would be, negatively affected in some form or other because they had started a family. I met so many bright, talented, brilliant women who had given up on their careers, not because they had freely chosen to, but because it had been made impossible for them to continue.

When two of my very good friends also lost their jobs for having a baby, I decided that something needed to be done. I couldn't bear how helpless and angry this whole situation made me feel; the waste of so many talented women whose confidence had been crushed, their career terminated because their status had changed to mother. I felt this deeply on a personal level, knowing what my experience had done to me, but I also began to calculate how nonsensical this was from an economic perspective. When the system in which we live and work isn't fully utilising the skills and competencies of women, then the system is broken. Did people even know this was happening?

Why would anyone want to live in a society where more than half its population were at serious risk of being bullied, ignored and undermined because they have the ability to birth a human? All I needed to do was prove that this was happening by exposing the problem. If people could hear the stories I had heard, then things would change, I had no doubt.

Then came the next major hurdle: these stories weren't available because many of the women who encounter pregnancy or maternity discrimination are gagged. Just like the victims of sexual harassment, we are silenced by power and money. The women who are able to challenge their employer usually sign a non-disclosure agreement (NDA), a legally binding contract that states that they are never allowed to utter another word about their experience again.

But NDA or no NDA, why would you speak out about a personal experience of discrimination when it's clear this will have a negative impact on your future career? Some of those who face discrimination still work for the same company, so they don't want to lose whatever is left of their job. Those who manage to find new employment don't want to be branded troublemakers – no one wants to employ a troublemaker, do they? Finding a job when you are pregnant or a new mum is hard enough without being labelled as the woman who is attempting to drag the good name of her previous employer through the mud. And who would even listen? Without a court ruling to show you were treated unfairly, it's just your word against theirs. The women who encounter this callous treatment keep it to themselves, like a dirty secret.

That creates part of the problem. Had I known the truth about how common this type of discrimination is, I would have felt less alone when it happened to me. Feeling isolated strips you of power, particularly when you are at your most vulnerable. There is a power in collective experience. A power in numbers. Defending yourself against a personal injustice is exhausting but doing it for the collective good can give you strength. It became clear that I needed to find a way for women to tell their stories of pregnancy or maternity discrimination without having to risk their job or break the law. Our voices had to be heard. I also needed a way to channel my own anger before it risked consuming me. I would daydream about revenge tactics I could take on the organisation, but in reality I knew that posting a dog poo through their letterbox wasn't going to give me the sense of solace I desired. Then one day, while my son napped upstairs, I asked my twitter followers for ideas on a campaign name. 'Beyond the Blue Line' and 'The Professional New Mum' were good, but not quite right. Then someone said: 'What about "Pregnant first, fucked second."' I could hear my son grumbling through the baby monitor so I shut my laptop and finished my cup of tea. As I scooped him out of his cot for a cuddle, he sleepily filled his nappy with hot, mustardy poo. *I've got it!* I thought. *Pregnant Then Screwed.* I chuckled to myself as I changed him. I was mothering like a pro while the campaign to end pregnancy and maternity discrimination started taking shape in my mind.

It was two months later, on International Women's Day 2015, when I sprang out of bed, whipped out my computer and decided that today was the day. I fed my son banana porridge with one hand and taught myself to use WordPress with the other. By 1 p.m., the website was live and Pregnant Then Screwed had been released into the world, a safe space for women to tell their stories of pregnancy and maternity discrimination anonymously. I documented my own experience; it was painful and cathartic in equal measure.

That day, over 2,000 people viewed the site but my email remained stubbornly quiet. I couldn't understand why the stories weren't flooding in when I knew how many women had faced this problem. I emailed everyone I had ever met to ask for their support, to spread the word or to link me up with useful people in the media. Within six weeks, I had ten stories, but each post had involved very sensitive and careful negotiation. These women were terrified. Even though the stories are completely anonymous, and no names of companies or colleagues are included, the process of writing the experience down had felt painful and they were extremely fearful that somebody might somehow identify them. For those who had signed a non-disclosure agreement, being caught talking about their experience would trigger a further legal battle.

It took four phone calls and eight email exchanges to convince one particular woman to share her story. She had been bullied and harassed so badly by her previous employer that she was on antidepressants and was barely able to leave the house. She wasn't a weak person. On the contrary, she had been a high-powered senior professional in a male-dominated environment, then her pregnancy triggered clients being removed and daily meetings where she was told she wasn't doing her job properly. She had felt like she was losing her mind, and simultaneously her colleagues made derogatory comments about her weight gain and 'baby brain'.

She had instructed a solicitor and threatened her employer with a tribunal. After a gruelling process, they made her sign a settlement agreement that included a gagging clause. This meant she would have just enough money to see her through maternity leave. It wasn't the justice she deserved, but when you're that vulnerable, you can only fight for so long. She was pregnant, jobless and her confidence was in tatters. Penning this traumatic experience meant reliving it when her coping mechanism had been to try to forget.

Those ten women only agreed to share their stories with me because I understood the mental torment they had been subjected to. The experiences varied dramatically: a woman who had hyperemesis[1] and was forced to vomit in the waste paper bin next to her boss's desk in an open-plan office of sixty people; a woman who had been refused a guaranteed promotion after she informed her boss she was pregnant because he had 'discussed things with his wife and they had decided that her priorities would change'; a woman who informed her boss she was pregnant and was told to have an abortion.

I wrote an article for Mumsnet, hoping that this would help to pull in a few more stories. One member commented that she was on a short-term contract that wasn't renewed due to her pregnancy; this had a catastrophic impact on her family, resulting in homelessness. Another member suggested that my experience of being sacked was the company getting rid of the 'dead wood'. A different member stated that many pregnant women take advantage of their pregnancy, leaving others in the lurch. My article and the energetic exchange with its respondents secured the attention of a BBC TV producer, Sarah Bell, who invited me to discuss the project on the *Victoria Derbyshire* show.

Appearing on live TV is terrifying. My only previous experience of being on television was as an extra in the children's programme *Just Us* and a rather dubious appearance on the late-night show *God's Gift* with Davina McCall in 1998, where I was chatted up in a launderette scene by an overexcited young buck wearing a T-shirt that said 'You've got to lick it.' Neither of these experiences had prepared me for a serious grilling about maternity rights by the queen of daytime TV.

Despite this, the appearance was a success and I managed to convey the messages I wanted to, though as soon as the cameras stopped rolling I burst into tears from the adrenaline. It was worth it: the stories came flooding in. By that evening, I had 200 personal tales of discrimination – everything from sackings to redundancies to employers making it completely impossible for new mums to manage their personal and professional responsibilities to demotions, bullying and harassment.

I read every single story that was sent to me. The anguish of the women who had penned these messages was evident. A number had encountered discrimination more than ten years earlier, yet the experience had never left them. They still thought about it every day, wondering what their life would be like had it not happened or had they felt able to challenge their employer's behaviour.

The messages weren't all stories of discrimination. Some were from nameless people who were furious at my audacity for even suggesting that this was a problem. Of course, I realised that some people would disagree with me – I had already had a variety of heated debates about the issue with members of my own family – but the anger within these messages was palpable. I tried to tell myself that they were just trolls; probably 40-year-old men who still lived with their mums, who penned hate mail while simultaneously eating a Pot Noodle and fondling themselves under a duvet with suspicious yellow stains on it. But it was clear that the majority of these letters weren't in keeping with an author of that description. The letters were written by educated and powerful people who were outraged. They pretended it was because they wanted to protect businesses, or they wanted to protect children, but their anger was deeper than that. I was messing with the status quo; I was messing with their privilege.

For the first time, I could clearly see how gender inequality is sewn into the fabric of our society in every sense possible. It is structural to its core. Thankfully, we have a rich history of women fighting for change, ensuring progress and driving us closer to equality. We can now vote, we are no longer the property of our husband, we can drink pints of lager in public without being burnt at the stake, and we have jobs that are protected through employment law (even if access to justice is almost impossible). But gender inequality is still very much alive; it is just better hidden than it was a few decades ago, and unless you are on the receiving end it is very easy to believe that we've achieved parity. In 2019, research by YouGov showed that one in three men think we have achieved gender equality and equal pay, so, when someone publicly disagrees with that perception, well, people tend to get their knickers in a twist.[2] Here are just a handful of the negative messages I received:

'Maternity leave is a joke. The idea of someone receiving full pay for no work makes me sick. I wish we had America's idea with two weeks and no pay.'

'Feminists like you make up this nonsense and give women a bad name.'

'Bogus statistics, false analogies, dubious claims, snide anti-male sneers, lashings of self-pity. If Brearley is paid less I am not surprised, if this is the usual quality of her work.'

'If women choose to have babies then they deserve everything they get. It's their problem, they should pay for it.'

And finally . . .

'I bet your idiotic disciples adore you, Joeli, but clearly you are unaware how many people out there despise you.'

Of course, some of these messages make me feel angry and confused, but in the main they remind me why this campaign is so important and how much work there is to do.

With the stories from these women etched on my mind and the negative messages lighting a fire within me, I made a commitment that Pregnant Then Screwed would be more than just stories. After a chance encounter with a kind-hearted and hilarious employment lawyer called Danielle Ayres, who specialises in pregnancy and maternity discrimination, I wanted to find a way of providing women with free legal advice. Danielle and I agreed to meet in a café in Manchester while our other halves wandered around the city centre with the kids. Somehow I convinced Danielle to set up a free legal advice service for the women who contact us. (I still wonder to this day if she had perhaps drunk too many strong coffees and was high on caffeine, causing her to get a bit carried away.) It has since become a lifeline to thousands of women, and, indeed, a fair few dads.

It was only a few months later, in July 2015, that the Equality and Human Rights Commission released its eagerly anticipated report into pregnancy and maternity discrimination.[3] The report had been commissioned by the Government. It had taken three years to conduct and cost £1 million. The headline figures caused a press storm.

The research found that 54,000 women a year lose their jobs for daring to procreate[4] and 77 per cent of working mums encounter negative or discriminatory treatment in the workplace.[5] What's more, those figures had almost doubled over the previous ten years.[6] As suspected, the situation for working mums had not improved; in fact, it had drastically deteriorated.

I couldn't help but break the numbers down further. Fifty-four thousand women being pushed out of their job every year: that's a woman every ten minutes in the UK; one in nine pregnant women losing her job. All those brilliant, talented women who spent years nurturing their career, investing their heart and soul into something they were absolutely committed to. The late nights, the social sacrifices, working for a pittance to get experience. Just for it all to be snatched away in the blink of an eye. Then there are the women who don't see themselves as having 'careers'; the women who have jobs, the women who need their job to feed themselves and keep a roof over their head, the women who are on zero-hours contracts or in more precarious types of work. WHAT ABOUT THEM? WHO IS LOOKING OUT FOR THEM? Well, not their employer, that's for sure, because the research showed that these women are also far more likely to be pushed out of their jobs if they have a baby.

What I found particularly horrifying about the statistics was how few women were able to access justice. Just 1 per cent of women who encounter pregnancy or maternity discrimination raise a tribunal claim.[7] When the same report was conducted in 2005, that figure had stood at 3 per cent, so, while the number of women encountering this type of discrimination had almost doubled, the number of women able to access justice had decreased significantly.[8]

After speaking with a few women who had been through the tribunal process, I understood why. The challenges they had faced were colossal. The impact on their mental health was enormous. Jen Jones had taken her employer to tribunal at a personal cost of £40,000. She lost her case and then they threatened to sue her for costs. She could have lost everything and would have had to file for bankruptcy. In her fragile state, she called me and suggested I set up a mentor scheme where women could support each other through the legal process; and so I did. I then went on to establish a flexible-working helpline staffed by volunteers from the HR sector. I then set up Pregnant Then Screwed in Spain, Sweden and the US, because no country is immune from pregnancy and maternity discrimination. Next, alongside other brilliant women, we began lobbying MPs for legislative change. We organised a protest called March of the Mummies that encouraged 2,000 people from six cities across the UK to dress up as the walking dead and demand recognition, respect and change for mums, and we started running festivals to help women rebuild their confidence and find work that works for them.

Out of despair came hope: a bunch of women fused together by frustration and rage were challenging the status quo. We've made a start, but there's so much more to do.

2

How Did We Get Here?

'Men have broad shoulders and narrow hips, and accordingly they possess intelligence. Women have narrow shoulders and broad hips. Women ought to stay at home; the way they were created indicates this, for they have broad hips and a fundament to sit upon, keep house and bear and raise children.'

Martin Luther, 1531[1]

You would expect most women to burst out laughing if they were told that they earn less money than men do because they have broad hips, or their brains are smaller, or perhaps because they have a 'fundament' to sit upon; but, just like Martin Luther in 1531, Ernst & Young delivered training sessions for their female executives in 2019 where the women were told that their brains are 6–11 per cent smaller, that they should always look 'fit' and they must never make eye contact with men. Attendees had to rate how 'masculine' or 'feminine' they were before the training. Masculine adjectives included 'ambitious' and 'has leadership abilities';

feminine adjectives included 'shy' and 'childlike'.[2] 'Women's brains absorb information like pancakes soak up syrup so it's hard for them to focus,' the attendees were told. 'Men's brains are more like waffles. They're better able to focus because the information collects in each little waffle square.'[3]

Unfortunately, most of us pancake-brains have had one or two experiences that don't sound too dissimilar to the Ernst & Young training. In 2018, almost a third of young women reported sex discrimination while working or looking for work,[4] while three-quarters of pregnant women and mothers have experienced negative or discriminatory treatment in the workplace.[5]

Our perception of women and mothers as being less able, less committed, less ambitious has a long and somewhat painful history. We may have moved on intellectually (thankfully, we no longer believe that you can cure any illness with a tobacco enema) but it is clear that fragments of our past have impacted the way we view pregnancy and motherhood today. It is also clear that women's ability to procreate has been central to centuries of female oppression, though there is plenty of evidence of women fighting back, often with a baby strapped to their breast, to demand freedom and rights or simply to resist their imposed servitude. Examining the experiences of the women who came before us can help to put things in perspective, so let's have a look at how we got here.

A quick rewind to the fifteenth century shows us that a mother's role was very different to what it is today. Families were people flung together because of work, and work would mostly be conducted on farms. Wealthier mothers would send their babies off to a wet nurse from birth until they were two to three years old so that they could crack on with the work that was deemed more important, such as buying and selling at market, dairying or brewing;[6] for those with high status they might use this time to do a spot of hunting, dancing or playing games; which, you know, sounds just like my maternity leave. If the child returned (many died), a servant or older sibling, rather than the mother, was likely charged with their care. Although early-modern Britain was undoubtedly patriarchal, many women were self-reliant, and they had a core role to play in industry. They were able to start and run businesses, own property, and divorce their husbands for a variety of reasons (including if their husband failed to 'perform in the marriage bed'). There were notable women writers, scholars, warriors and business owners.

But things started to change for women at the close of the fifteenth century. Workplaces began to move away from the home and, for a variety of reasons, women found themselves at a disadvantage in this new organisation of industry. Foreign trade had brought great wealth to a group of merchant capitalists, but England wanted more, and so it embarked on three centuries of war in a bid to establish a colonial empire.[7] Slowly but surely, women were stripped of their rights, forced out of industries, and their work became associated with low pay.[8] Women's ultimate subservience meant that the men could get on with killing each other and striving for world domination, while married women were relegated to domestic labour, low-paid work and baby-making, something they had to do with extraordinary regularity.[9]

The First Industrial Revolution (which kicked off around 1760) meant that work was now mainly done in the mills, factories or mines that were springing up all over the place and, as most families needed two wages to survive, mothers were a key part of the labour force, as were children, some as young as four. It was around this time that two male philosophers – John Locke and Jean-Jacques Rousseau – triggered the nature–nurture debate, which had a profound impact on the way mothers were viewed. Her new role was not just to procreate and keep a child alive, but to mother, to parent, to ensure her children were the image of perceived perfection; now it was clear that the moral well-being of society rested on her shoulders – 'he' said.[10]

'In all cases of dwarfishness or deformity, ninety-nine out of a hundred are owing to the folly, misconduct or neglect of mothers,' wrote William Buchan in 1804, which reminds me of a few headlines I've read in the *Daily Mail* recently. Ultimately, a woman's worth was reduced to motherhood alone: 'Womanliness means only motherhood,' wrote Robert Browning in 1875, conveniently ignoring the fact that 80 per cent of women were labourers and ensuring childless and unmarried women were considered an aberration.[11]

As part of this colonial empire, the British began trading in slaves from 1562. African slave women, owned by British people, were forced to birth their children into a world of abject horror. The women were raped and their reproductive systems industrialised. The children were brutally ripped away from their mothers to be sold separately. Some slaves fought against their oppression by going on reproduction strike, using cotton root as a form of birth control. A number of these women were forced to play the role of mother, but for the children of their slave-owners, rather than their own offspring.

In 1866, Millicent Fawcett and other campaigners started to fight back against women's oppression, and they handed over a petition for women's suffrage to Parliament. Then, in 1903, Emmeline Pankhurst, with her daughters Sylvia and Christabel, kick-started their mission to get the vote for women with the Women's Social and Political Union. They were renamed by the *Daily Mail* (who actually supported women's suffrage – I know, I know) as the Suffragettes. Their efforts were interrupted in 1914 by the First World War, which changed a mother's role in society again.

As men left the country to go and fight, women were required to fill their jobs; yet the women were paid a lot less than the men had been paid to do exactly the same work. But women weren't prepared to just accept this blatant discrimination and so they went on strike to demand pay equal to men, and in 1917 a committee was established by the War Cabinet to examine whether they should increase women's wages. The report endorsed the principle of 'equal pay for equal work', but their expectation was that, due to women's 'lesser strength and special health problems', their 'output' would not be equal to that of men. By 'special health problems' we can only assume they meant periods and pregnancy.

When the recession hit in the 1920s, employment was hugely limited, so the remaining jobs were kept aside for the men. Any woman who dared to remain employed was brutally slandered by the press for taking up the jobs of ex-servicemen. The Marriage Bar was brought in during this economic recession to protect men's paid work. It meant that when women who worked in teaching and clerical positions got married, they would be forced to leave their jobs. It remained in place until 1946 for the Civil Service, but for some other professions it was still in existence in the 1970s.

Then, on 1 September 1939, the prime minister of Great Britain, Neville Chamberlain, declared war on Germany. Now that the men were needed to fight, women were needed to fill the men's jobs again. By 1943, 80 per cent of married women were working in factories, on the land or in the armed forces.[12] These were jobs that previously had been considered unsuitable for women. It would not have been possible to win without the invaluable work of mothers, so flexible working hours became the norm and the number of nurseries rapidly increased.[13] State funding was provided to establish 1,345 wartime nurseries by 1943, a huge increase from the fourteen such nurseries that existed in 1940.[14] When the survival of the country depended on ensuring the workplace worked for women, structures and systems were quickly established so that the country could benefit from their skills and labour. Those structures dissolved as the war came to an end, and, despite the majority of surveyed women saying they wanted to keep the job they had been asked to do, most were forced out to make way for the returning servicemen.[15] Only the women who worked in industries that weren't unionised were able to keep their jobs, mainly because they were much cheaper to employ.

Both my grandmothers (born in the 1920s) had to get creative during this period so that they could generate a much-needed income for their family. From a young age, my paternal grandmother, Sally, had run a corner shop, which she was forced to give up when her second child was born, but, after the war ended, her family was so desperately poor that she went door-to-door selling cleaning products and clothing out of a suitcase to try to make ends meet. She was very successful at it, so much so that she eventually got her own clothing shop and became the main breadwinner, while my grandad took on many of the caring duties for their three children.

My mum's mum, Joyce, who was raised in an orphanage, made bombs at Thorp Arch during the war and would later regale me with tales of the camaraderie and pure joy she found in that type of hard graft. When the war came to an end, she trained as a hairdresser, and continued working until a few years before she died, in her seventies, though, by then, her eyesight was clearly deteriorating, and elderly ladies would stagger out of her house having divulged all of their gossip, with a brandy aperitif, and hair that looked a slightly odd shade of green.

In contrast to the First World War, the 1950s was a period of sustained economic growth so the Government was keen to expand the labour force. It ran campaigns to get more women into work and encouraged the migration of workers from British colonies. The jobs were strictly segregated by gender, with women shoehorned into routine, repetitive work and clerical or caring roles. Black and Asian women, brought to the UK as a source of cheap labour, were concentrated in the lowest-status positions; they were also more likely to work full-time, as little consideration was given to all the unpaid work (caring, cooking, cleaning) these women had to do in the home.[16] White mothers were more likely to work part-time, and, if they had young children, were discouraged from working at all, with the Marriage Bar still in operation by many employers.[17]

Until the 1960s, a married woman took her husband's name, promised to 'obey' him and, unless she had property in her own name, became economically and financially dependent on him. But then, between the late 1960s and the 1980s, things started to really change for mothers. They could buy a house, go on the pill, legally have an abortion, get social housing and, finally, divorce their husbands. Hurrah! In 1970, the Equal Pay Act came into force, thanks to a hard-fought battle by thousands of tenacious women, including 850 female machinists who worked at the Ford factory in Dagenham. By the early 1980s, there were more than 17 million mothers with children under the age of 18 in work, a whopping 44 per cent more than there had been in the 1970s.[18]

But this economic and social freedom for women had seemingly gone too far for some. In a speech at the 1992 Conservative Party Conference, Peter Lilley, Secretary of State for Social Security, included single mums on his list of fraudsters and benefit offenders. He suggested that women were getting themselves pregnant just to jump the housing queue. Yep, that old chestnut. As if women were going around begging men to impregnate them, then tossing them aside, just so they could get a shitty little maisonette in a tower block. John Redwood, another Conservative MP in the '90s, suggested single mums should put their children up for adoption if the father couldn't be found (the irony being that he later made his own wife a single mother when he left her for an ex-model). Single mums were being stereotyped as scroungers, leaching money off the state, and giving nothing of value in return.

Maternity rights were first introduced to the UK in 1973 but there was no legal protection for the women who took this leave, so once they had given birth they were inevitably out on their ear with their new babe, making the notion of 'maternity leave' redundant. The right to take maternity leave and keep your job wasn't introduced until 1975, and you had to have worked for your employer for a minimum of two years – or five years if you were employed part-time – so many women didn't qualify. At the same time, the Sex Discrimination Act made it illegal to discriminate against women in work, education and training. In 1992, following the introduction of a European directive (thanks, EU), all working women in the UK became entitled to Statutory Maternity Leave and pay for 14 weeks, with the right to return to their previous jobs. If they had two years' service, they could access 28 weeks' maternity leave.[19]

It wasn't until 2006 that the Work and Families Act extended maternity and adoption leave to 52 weeks and pay to 39 weeks. Later, the 2010 Equality Act listed pregnancy and maternity as a 'protected characteristic', making it illegal to discriminate against someone because they have a bun in the oven or because they have taken time away from work to birth and care for a new human. In 2003, male employees received paid Statutory Paternity Leave for the first time, and, in April 2015, Shared Parental Leave was introduced. More on that 'progressive utopia' later.

The right for all working women to take paid maternity leave has only come into existence in my lifetime (and probably yours), so when you hear those wearisome words 'It's the twenty-first century, for God's sake' in response to incidents of pregnancy and maternity discrimination, we have to remember that maternity rights are a relatively new phenomenon and, as this chapter outlines, a mother's role and how she is perceived by society is many centuries old.

Our history makes for bleak reading: for 270 years, African women were forced into slavery, beaten, raped and made to do gruelling work, their children removed from them and sold. It wasn't until the latter part of the twentieth century that women were allowed to own land or any other significant assets. Our laws and welfare system ensured wives were dependent on their husbands, and any work women did outside of the home was very poorly paid. Their worth was measured only by their ability to procreate, keep house and care for their offspring; unless they were extremely poor or unmarried, in which case they had no worth at all. As a result, until around sixty years ago, all capital was controlled by men.

These issues are still present in the twenty-first century, though much diluted. Men still dominate the high-paid sectors and CEO roles; women are still expected to do the lion's share of the housewifery and parenting; single mums are left in an awful mess by an ineffective welfare state that means, in 2019, 45 per cent were living in poverty;[20] women are still cast aside because they dared to use their uterus; and 36 per cent of mums feel they are judged negatively by friends and family for working.[21] Black, Asian and Minority Ethnic mothers encounter a toxic combination of racism and sexism that ensures their ability to succeed within a capitalist framework is very much hindered.

Mothers are told to 'lean in', as if it is somehow our fault that the labour market isn't working for us; we clearly aren't confident, ambitious or assertive enough. The thing is, we *are* 'leaning in' – to a structure that was not built for mothers. If we look back at all the difficult and tenacious women who've stood firm and changed the system, from the Suffragettes, who changed the voting rights of women, to the Dagenham machinists, whose strike triggered the formation of the Equal Pay Act, to MP Harriet Harman, who pushed hard for childcare provision and the 2010 Equality Act, we can see that it is going to take a bunch of difficult and tenacious people to now change the working world for parents. And so it is here we find ourselves.

3

The Guilt Will Gobble You Up If You Let It

It's a Sunday afternoon in mid-February, and, instead of entertaining the children with wholesome and educational activities, I am stuffing my face with chocolate Hobnobs and ignoring them. I don't think they mind; why would they? They're sprawled across the sofa with their beloved screens, although one of them has just sat on the other one's head and farted. The youngest erupts into a fit of laughter, while the eldest lazily indicates that he is not amused, his eyes still firmly fixed on his iPad. I pay little attention and begin to nibble on my third Hobnob; my high-alert radar is only provoked by blood-curdling screams or prolonged periods of deathly silence – and anyway, how else am I meant to have time to gormlessly scroll through social media? You've all done it. Don't pretend you haven't. I know you use the TV as a babysitter sometimes. I know you linger in the bathroom with the door locked, pretending you're doing the longest poo in history. It's perfectly normal and no one is going to die or develop any long-term mental health issues as a result, no matter what the media will have you believe. Stop feeling guilty about it immediately.

Guilt is an all too common emotion for mothers. Particularly for those of us who work. According to a survey by the baby product manufacturer NUK, 87 per cent of mothers feel guilty at some point.[1] But guilt is not an emotion that we needlessly self-generate because we relish a good bit of self-flagellation. It's an emotion triggered by society's view of how mothers should behave. The problem is that this guilt can have a really detrimental impact on a mother's mental health, her time, her parenting and her confidence to progress in her professional work. Guilt is a key contributor to the motherhood penalty.

The saying goes that 'guilt arrives with the baby' – but the truth is that it arrives sooner than that. From the moment our bellies start expanding and the stretch marks scar our skin, attitudes towards us change – dramatically – and we're subjected to the rest of the world telling us exactly what they think of us. 'Advice' is dished out with unsolicited abandon: we shouldn't drink this, we mustn't eat that, we most definitely shouldn't have gone there, and in our condition we certainly shouldn't be wearing that. Our bodies, now mere vessels for new human life, are no longer our own.

One weekend in Manchester, when I was six months pregnant with my first baby, I went for a drink in a craft ale bar with some friends. They all drank overpriced pints of cloudy bitter; I ordered a refreshing mint tea. As I perched on a stool sipping my brew, a bald Mancunian bloke approached us. As he leered over me, his hot, thick breath reeking of ale, he checked the contents of my porcelain mug before asking: 'What are *you* doing in here?' When I queried his interrogation, he looked up at my friends and said: 'You should be looking after this one. Take her home.' Surely my 'situation' precluded me from anything resembling entertainment and I should have locked myself inside my house to bake cakes and fluff up cushions for eternity, or at least until I gave birth. Pregnant women, in this man's mind, were to be kept at home, neither seen nor heard. My friends and I decided to move on, but it became clear that this wasn't going to be an isolated incident. The small, stocky bouncer at the next bar point-blank refused to let me in: 'We're not insured for pregnancy,' he told me, staring into the middle distance. Who the hell *is* insured for pregnancy?

It's not just in pubs and clubs that pregnant women and new mothers are told by strangers exactly what we should and shouldn't be doing. And what we should or shouldn't be feeling, planning, or be on the verge of thinking. Receiving unsolicited advice from strangers is a common feature of pregnancy and early motherhood. Most of us just accept it, too exhausted and confused by this sudden identity shift to argue back, though there are some who do.

Jaclene Paolucci was seven months pregnant when she popped into Starbucks and ordered herself a regular latte. She was rudely interrupted by a stranger who suggested she should switch to decaf. Jaclene wasn't in the mood, and coolly responded by telling the stranger she wasn't pregnant.[2] Of course, this led to a very awkward apology, the stranger presumably now a shade of beetroot red.

In addition to an onslaught of unsolicited advice, pregnancy and the gruelling process of making a baby is undermined by the language we regularly use. The word 'miscarriage' literally implies that the mother simply screwed the whole thing up and failed to follow the instructions properly. 'Morning sickness' trivialises the absolute-hellish experience of incessantly vomiting your guts up, not to mention it's entirely inaccurate to suggest pregnancy sickness only happens in the morning. Some folk use the term 'fell pregnant', as if we have absolutely no control over it, we're just lazy passengers in the procreation process. My all-time favourite is: 'WE are pregnant!' No, you're fucking not; you might both be having a baby at the end of it but there's only one of you doing all the hard work. Credit where it's due, lads; and, for the love of God, don't get me started on 'baby brain' or 'geriatric mum'.

Meanwhile, scientists studying the ultimate limit of human endurance found that being pregnant is akin to constantly running a marathon due to the strain it puts on our bodies: 'Pregnancy is the most energetically expensive activity the human body can maintain for nine months,' said Professor Herman Pontzer, who co-authored the study.[3] And if a man says it – well, it must be true.

In contrast, dads breeze through their partner's pregnancy barely noticing any change to their experience of the world whatsoever – apart from, perhaps, the odd frustrating trip to Mothercare, where they're asked to help make decisions about nappy bags and teething rings and are then sold a pram as if it is a Formula One car, and some attend the antenatal classes. But no random stranger tells them they shouldn't be in the pub, or questions their commitment and ability at work, or advises them to rub some weird gel on their perineum every day so as not to damage their undercarriage during childbirth. It must be bliss to be a passenger in your child's prenatal development, offering the odd sympathetic noise or occasionally rubbing a lower back until, one day, a fully formed baby is plonked into your arms while your exhausted, dishevelled partner has her vulva sewn back together.

I know I'm being flippant and making sweeping generalisa-tions here. I don't underestimate the role that fathers play, and many dads are incredibly dedicated to their partners and the raising of their children. I'm just not sure it's possible to ever fully understand what it feels like to experience such a rapid change to your body and your identity, and encounter the public policing that goes with it, unless you are a mother-to-be. Essentially, gestation is an elite training camp for the guilty mother.

Once the training is over and the baby has arrived, mothers are the ones held accountable by society for how children are raised. Until relatively recently, traditional gender stereotypes were even commonplace in psychoanalytic thought. Take, for example, the 'refrigerator mothers' of the 1950s, whose supposed coldness apparently triggered autism in their children.[4] In 2019, a study blamed 'helicopter parenting' in the toddler years for causing behavioural problems later in life; in examining the impact of over-controlling parents on their children's characters and futures, the study appears, interestingly enough, to have used only mothers in its research.[5] Mothers are targeted and blamed for mental illness, school truancy and even serial killers. *The Sun* published an article in 2017 subtitled 'These are the three types of mums most likely to raise a murderer ... is yours one of them?'[6] It's no wonder, then, that we feel guilt at every turn.

Over the past six years, 'guilt' has been the word I've heard most frequently from the women I have worked with. Even if they don't use that exact word, they will explain, through gritted teeth, how they believe they have failed as a mother because of work pressure. I can empathise. On a pretty regular basis I use sweets and trashy TV programmes as an opportunity for me to crack on with some work. During lockdown, my kids gorged themselves on so much American TV that my son asked me if he could have a 'garage sale', equipped with a pitch-perfect American accent. When I explained that wouldn't be possible because we are not American and we don't own a garage, he tutted loudly and said: 'Ahhh, maaaan, that sucks.'

Of course, my kids still attempt to distract me while my head is buried in a laptop, but I discovered that the best way to achieve maximum productivity is to agree to every request without interrogation. The latter once resulted in my darling children squirting washing-up liquid into our fish tank to 'see if the fish would get really clean'. When I discovered the chaos – fish flapping around for breath amid the thick green Fairy liquid – I lost my shit. They both cried hysterically, saying I had told them they could do it, and I probably had – who knows? And then I feel guilty. I feel guilty because I ignored them, I feel guilty because I shouted at them, I feel guilty because my distraction has cost six fish their little fishy lives, and I feel guilty because I've got a whole fuck-tonne of work to do, and it feels like I am failing at it all.

Even the places we use as an escape from the daily pressures of motherhood contribute to our feelings of guilt. A study that surveyed 500 Canadian mothers found that Instagram, Facebook and Twitter are making mothers feel insecure about their parenting. Sixty-nine per cent had insecurities stemming from these apps, even though 53 per cent knew that what people posted wasn't a true reflection of the realities of motherhood. I know from personal experience that comparing yourself to others on the internet can only lead to feelings of complete inadequacy.[7] It's sometimes hard to remember that social media isn't real, and that those with a large following carefully craft and curate what they want the world to see.

Working mothers are an easy target for public shaming. The media often implies, or explicitly says, that many of the problems in today's society are due to the consequences of mothers who go out to work, offloading the responsibility of looking after their children onto their partner, a grandparent or a qualified childminder. In 2019, the *Mail on Sunday* published an article with the title 'Scientists blame working mothers for Britain's childhood obesity epidemic after study of 20,000 families'. In the article, journalist Michael Powell states: 'Researchers could not find any significant effect of a father's job on his children's weight.'[8] I took the time to read the actual paper the scientists, from University College London, had published, and, although they had focused on the impact of maternal employment on a child's weight, they made it very clear that women still carry too much of the burden of childcare and men need to play a larger role in their child's health if this situation is to change.[9] This was disregarded by several newspapers reporting on the study, including the *Mail on Sunday*,[10] *The Sun*[11] and *The Times*,[12] who chose to shift that blame and place it squarely on the shoulders of women who dare to procreate and do paid work so that they can keep a roof over their family's heads. Journalist Rhiannon Lucy Cosslett rectified the headline in a tweet: 'Lazy dads leave burden of healthy home cooking entirely to women.' And Sophie Walker, founding leader of the Women's Equality Party, tweeted: 'Still waiting for that study on the impact of poorly thought-through research reported by misogynist media outlets.'[13]

Among other recent headlines published is 'Working mothers risk damaging their child's prospects'. This article, written by a man, claimed that a study had proven a link between mums working full-time and their children doing less well in the education system, having mental health issues and being unemployed when they are older.[14] Then there's 'Children of working mothers lag behind'[15] and 'Psychotherapist warns that working mothers are producing mentally ill children – and claims the problem is at an "epidemic level"'.[16] My absolute favourite, though, is 'Stay-at-home mothers have the most worthwhile lives', an enthusiastic piece on the joys of fastening oneself to the kitchen sink rather than heading out to work, written by – you've guessed it – a man.[17]

Funnily enough, a groundbreaking Harvard Business School study from 2015 that used data from twenty-four different countries demonstrated quite the opposite: daughters of working mums have more equal relationships, better careers and higher pay than daughters from stay-at-home mums. Sons also benefit, growing up to be more involved at home, taking more time to care for their own family, and holding significantly more egalitarian attitudes than sons from stay-at-home mums.[18] Did the *Mail on Sunday* publish that study? No, but they did print this: 'Outdazzled by our daughters! Three mothers candidly talk about their "looks fading" as their teenage girls bloom.'

During the past six years that I have researched this topic, I have not found any research that categorically proves a link between mothers working and severe issues for children. Emily Oster published the book *Cribsheet* after having her first baby and being overwhelmed with all the conflicting information and advice she was given. As an economist, she wanted to understand the facts, what data and research existed, and what it was really telling us. She concluded that, in the argument of working parents, 'The weight of the evidence suggests the net effects of working on child development are small or zero. Depending on your household configuration, these effects could be a little positive or a little negative. But this isn't the decision that is going to make or break your child's future success.' Instead, Emily tells parents that it is much more important to do what makes the most sense for your family – 'if you need to work, then work, if you want to work, then work'.[19]

Happiness, for me, comes from achieving a balance of parenting and working. I need to earn money so we can pay our bills, but I get a kick out of it, too. Having children has made me better at my job and having a job has made me a better mother. That's not the same for everyone – some mothers despise their job, others desperately want to spend as much time as they can with their children and outsourcing any of the caring work seems inconceivable. There isn't an ideal set-up here; one is not better than the other. There isn't a hierarchy of mothering perfection, with working mums wearing the crown and stay-at-home mums wallowing in the lower rankings. The optimum set-up is the one that makes everyone the happiest. I love my kids with fierce, uncompromising devotion, but they benefit from having a mum who is happy and who relishes her time with them, rather than a mum who feels forced to give up on her own dreams because that is what she feels is expected of her. There have been plenty of times when I have felt forced to relinquish what I want because the barriers have been overwhelming and the guilt all-consuming. If I were for some reason forced to choose between my job and my kids, I would give up my job immediately. But I know that my kids benefit from me working; they get the best of me for around three hours a day plus weekends. It is a perfect balance and one I feel our whole family is lucky to have.

Yet, despite striking my ideal balance, why do I still feel like I am failing? The challenge for many working mums is that the examples we are fed by the media of 'women who have it all' make us feel like we must be a disappointment. They are those intimidating, pristine types who've smashed down all the chaotic-and-unreliable-working-mum stereotypes by being enormously successful, having a gazillion children and not turning up to work with fossilised Weetabix in their hair. Dame Helena Morrissey is one such impressive individual. The mother of *nine* children, she is one of only a handful of women to have been the CEO of an investment bank. Dame Helena is earning the megabucks and seemingly never has a hair out of place. I haven't had the opportunity to get up close but, from the many pictures of her in the media, I am always astounded by how unbearably rested she looks. Though I hugely admire her for achieving the seemingly impossible, I can't help but think that her achievements just make the rest of us feel and look a bit shit. She is dubbed as the woman who has made 'having it all' a reality, but let's just remember that Helena has a stay-at-home husband who performs the traditional role of a wife, and she has bags of cash to throw at any problem that might come her way.

The fact remains that for most working mums, their partner (if they have one) will be working full-time and between the two of them they will be just about staying afloat financially and mentally. But, while the mother is working, the expectations placed upon her to be the perfect mum have not changed. Most mothers feel continuously trapped between the burden of housework and rearing the perfect child while trying to earn a living. But this isn't something many women feel able to talk about publicly for fear of losing their job or looking like a terrible mother, unable to cope with the demands of modern-day life, so instead the conversation is dominated by the likes of Dame Helena Morrissey, Sheryl Sandberg (Facebook), Sarah Friar (Squarespace) or Marissa Mayer (Yahoo!), women who are indeed inspirational but likely don't remember what life was like before they had staff to fold the laundry and cook the kids their dinner. Meanwhile, the genuine challenges faced by everyday mothers go largely ignored by the media, and if your experience is at odds with everything you are reading and seeing then it's no wonder you feel it must be you who are doing something wrong.

And so the guilt sits on mothers like a bad toupee, sliding around from time to time, revealing itself to onlookers and constantly reminding us of our faults. This guilt drives women out of the workforce, particularly when it's combined with discrimination. It is a toxic mix that inevitably leads to new mothers retreating from their personal ambitions.

The guilt that we working mums experience is not our fault; it's a product of the inherent sexism in our society coupled with a labour market that wasn't built to accommodate caregiving. Society tells mothers that it's their choice to have a child and to work, but the same isn't said to fathers. This also ignores the fact that, for many families, it is a financial necessity: the cost of living largely requires two salaries for the average family household. In 2015–16, 43 per cent of children living with one working parent and one non-working parent were in relative income poverty, compared with 11 per cent of children in two-earner households.[20] A mother's role is no longer clear-cut, leaving us in a role vortex, where we are damned if we do and damned if we don't.

In 2019, in almost half of two-parent households (with kids under the age of ten), both parents worked full-time.[21] And with the average full-time working week in the UK being 42 hours 18 minutes (the longest in Europe), not including commuting time, this potentially leaves very little space for parents to spend quality time with their kids.[22] Yet research by *The Economist* says that, on average, middle-class parents spend double the amount of time with their kids than they did fifty years ago.[23] In fact, all parents are, on average, spending much more time with their offspring. We are all working longer hours in our paid jobs, and we are spending more time on childcare, which begs the question: are there really enough hours in the day? Are we trying to achieve something that is physically impossible? When are we meant to find some time for ourselves? It's not the kids we should be worried about here, it's the parents – and, in particular, the mums. How on earth do we fit all of this in without going absolutely crackers?

All this pressure is creating anxiety and depression among mothers. In 2016, the journal *Brain and Behavior* found that women are twice as likely as men to suffer from severe stress and anxiety.[24] The pressure causes many women to fall out of their careers altogether, while others struggle along, grabbing their career with one shaky hand and stroking their child's tired head with the other, feeling like they're failing at both. More than a third of mums have experienced mental health issues as a direct result of parenthood, with 17 per cent of dads saying they have experienced similar challenges. The fact is that the pressure on both mums and dads is now far more intense than it was fifty years ago. Workplaces are expecting us to work longer and harder, and when we get home it's almost impossible to switch off with our devices merrily chirping for attention, reminding us that we have a billion urgent things to do.

'My children call my iPhone by my boss's name. I can't decide if that's funny or not, but it does make me feel awfully guilty.'

'I'm starting to realise this pressure. This unattainable view of motherhood is just another load of shit we are being screwed over by.'

'I feel guilty that I love my job and want that time to be "me" and not "Mummy". But I also feel guilty for only working three days a week, which seems to have completely halted any progress I can make in my career. My workplace won't even consider having someone in a management position who works part-time so it looks like I'm stuck for the time being feeling guilty for half-doing both jobs.'

'I feel guilty that I love my job and want to do well in it. I'm doing compressed hours for a global bank; they are absolutely brilliant at flexible working, but my head feels like it's in a vice and I feel agitated and unable to give 100 per cent wherever I am. Guilt makes me be a martyr.'

Guilt ensures we slog our guts out doing our paid work, and then we come home and slog our guts out trying to make our house look perfect, and then we slog our guts out on a healthy nutritious dinner because the kids absolutely must get their five a day, and then we slog our guts out reading and cuddling and tickling and listening and tucking into bed, but we still feel guilty that none of it was enough. When I contacted Christine Armstrong, author of *The Mother of All Jobs: How to Have Children and a Career and Stay Sane(ish)*, to pick her brains on the topic of guilt, she had this to say: 'Parents all over the land are staring at each other and their kids and feeling like failures that they can't make this work. They are buying slow cookers and bigger whiteboards in the desperate hope that being better organised will solve the problem of two parents working 14-hour days and not having time for their kids. And wondering what they did wrong. Even though they did nothing wrong – they just tried to work and pay the bills and be parents.'

God forbid we should find some time for ourselves. Then we really do feel guilty. Yet the *Harvard Business Review* published research in 2018 that showed that mothers spending time on themselves, rather than on housework, was good for children.[25] The report says: 'Mothers spending time on themselves – on relaxation and self-care – and not so much on housework, was associated with positive outcomes for children. It's not just a matter of mothers being at home versus at work, it's what they do when they're at home with their non-work time.' The point here is that the amount of time spent with your children is not a measurement by which you should decipher whether or not you are a good parent. Your kids benefit from you being happy, calm and fulfilled. I hate the phrase 'self-care' – it's totally overused, just another thing to add to your to-do list, and for some reason it just makes me think about masturbating – but there's clearly a lot to be said for prioritising your health and well-being where you can. Yet the mothers who dare to take the afternoon off to hang out with a friend, or to watch *Gogglebox* and eat crisps in bed, can be made to feel horribly guilty, as if they aren't fulfilling their duty as a parent. A 2014 study found that the average mother only gets 17 minutes of 'me time' to herself in an average day and more than half of respondents said they don't get any time for hobbies or interests since having a child.[26]

You would expect the superhero single parents who raise their children on their own to be excused from the constant guilt-slinging, considering the enormous pressure they are under, but instead it is far more pronounced. The words 'single mum' have been weaponised by some parts of the media to conjure up an image of someone scrounging from the system, despite the fact that most are not single by choice and they are the ones who have dedicated their life to raising this new human rather than dumping their responsibilities on someone else. Single dads are held up as heroes, but not single mums.

Two separate studies confirmed that many people put single dads on a pedestal while hyper-policing single mums.[27] One report concludes that 'many of the beliefs about single parents stem from the view that single fathers have admirably risen to the challenge of parenting by choice, while single mothers are assumed to be parenting out of a necessity resulting from bad judgment, accidental pregnancy or the failure to maintain a relationship'. The researchers also determined that negative views about single motherhood tend to stem from a conviction that there is something inherently wrong or damaged about a single mother as a person. During the study, single mums were described as 'neglectful, irresponsible, immature, stressed out, depressed, prone to making bad choices, promiscuous, hopeless, and/or insecure'. Single fathers, on the other hand, were perceived by those surveyed as individuals in a challenging situation who had to worry about complications of solo parenting like finding childcare and balancing their dating life with raising kids.

Mothers are held to an entirely different standard from fathers – standards that are, in the main, entirely unattainable, thereby raising our stress and anxiety levels and ensuring we question our actions and our abilities. It's no wonder that comments made by work colleagues and employers cut deep. Societal expectations are so unrealistic for working mothers that we inevitably feel as though we are failing, that we aren't good enough, that we are somehow damaging our children. This guilt has an impact on the decisions we make about our paid work. We sacrifice our own dreams and ambitions because of this guilt; we accept the pay cuts or demotions because, deep down, we believe the narrative that we shouldn't be working if we have kids. The guilt keeps us in our place, but what *is* a 'mother's place'? Do we even know? She is primary caregiver, nurturer, holder of small hands and reader of stories. She is cleaner and cook and organiser. She is breadwinner and professional adult. Her identity clashes fiercely with everyone who interacts with it – employers dismiss her commitment because she leaves on time to collect the kids; children shout and scream because they are not getting the undivided attention they want; the house is a pigsty because it's way down the priority list; and caught in the middle of it all is a mother just trying to do her best.

The experiences, situations and backgrounds of the mothers I speak to are wildly different, but the one thing that seems to connect them all is ... guilt. Whether they're a stay-at-home mum or a freelancer, whether they work-full time at an investment bank or part-time at a garden centre, whether they're a single mum, a mother of an adopted child or a mum on a career break, the pejorative feeling of guilt, and its best friend, shame, are relatively indiscriminate, and they can drive mothers over the edge. The standards set for us are unattainable and this pressure is a trigger for unhappiness and mental health issues. It is a form of female oppression, preventing us from rising up, and it ensures we continue to adhere to the status quo, where women take a back seat in careers and scoop up the majority of the unpaid labour.

Let go of that guilt – forgive yourself for not achieving what is physically and mentally impossible. You're doing your best and your best is definitely good enough. When you feel the urge for self-flagellation, try to talk to yourself as you would talk to a friend in the same situation. Let's spend less time trying to measure up to the expectations of others, and more time working out what it is we need and want – and then let's fight for it. Stop punishing yourself, give yourself a great big pat on the back, stick two fingers up at the bullshit we are subjected to. Let's stop judging other women for the decisions they make for their families, and let's work together to call out the mum-shaming that attempts to trample on our identity and encumber our spirit. Until we tame the mum guilt and recognise it for what it is – a form of oppression – then we will never be free.

Worth knowing

Employees in the UK are legally entitled to 18 weeks of unpaid parental leave, per child, until their son or daughter is 18. You can use this for pretty much any reason – maybe you need to settle your child into a new childcare setting or want them to spend more time getting to know family who live abroad. Perhaps there's something personal going on that you want to spend some time together addressing. Or maybe you've just realised that, although your children can be massive dickheads from time to time (or, if they're between the ages of two and five, most of the time), they can also be bloody good company and you want to make the most of them before they turn into stroppy teenagers who tell you every five minutes that they wish they'd never been born. Whatever the reason, your employer is legally obliged to give you this time off, up to a maximum of four weeks per year, as long as you give ample notice. They can ask you to reschedule the time off if there is something very important happening at work, but they must allow you this allocation. Being unpaid, it's a law for the privileged, but, if you can afford it and you need it, then it's yours for the taking.

These 18 weeks of unpaid parental leave are in addition to your legal entitlement to 'Time off for family and dependants', which is for emergencies. This doesn't need to be booked in advance. (Lucky that: it'd be pretty tricky to do if it is an emergency.) Unfortunately the legislation around this is pretty vague: there is no limit to how much time you can have off (it's left to your employer's discretion) and your employer doesn't have to pay you, but, if you encounter any detriment, such as a demotion or being placed at risk of redundancy, as a result of taking this time off, then you could have a legal case against your employer.

If you can't help but scroll the pixelated, social-media world, then try to curate your own feed to reduce those feelings of inadequacy and guilt. Get rid of the accounts that project fake perfection and make you feel as though you have to live up to a certain standard. Delete them and never look back. It's all a load of hogwash and fairy tales anyway.

———

4

The Motherhood Penalty

'It is often the case that mothers are held to a higher standard than others in the workplace, and they are penalised if
they cannot meet that standard.'

**Emily Martin, Vice President for Education and
Workplace Justice, the National Women's Law Center**[1]

Before you get your knickers in a twist, I am not saying that
motherhood is a penalty. Sure, parenting can sometimes be
a total pain in the arse, but being a mother isn't (always) a
punishment. It's a wonderful, joyous, noisy thing, and most
of us wouldn't want it any other way (if we could just have
an extra hour in bed). This isn't about motherhood being the
problem. This is about a system that shuts mothers out, and
assembles participation barriers, because some employers see
procreation as messing up all of that capitalism stuff.

The 'motherhood penalty' is a term coined by sociologists.
It sums up the disadvantages women encounter in terms of
earnings and career progression when they have children.

Let's start at the beginning. Right the way through their

life, girls and women are given subtle and not-so-subtle messages about how they should behave and what their place is in society. You know, all that crap about how girls are told not to be bossy, or that he's only tormenting you because he likes you, or how girls are expected to do more of the tidying and are valued by how they look much more than how they think or act. However, amazingly, these messages don't affect their performance – in fact, on average, girls and women leave the education system with better grades than boys and men, and this is true for most of Europe. In 2018, 44 per cent of women in Europe aged 30–34 had completed tertiary education or higher, compared with 34 per cent of men.[2] The data on this is undeniable: at every level of the formal education system, girls outperform boys, and in almost every subject, not just the ones you would expect; they outperform boys in the subjects we consider to be the domain of boys – maths and science. This is true for 70 per cent of all countries – even in states like Qatar and Jordan, where there is 'relatively low' gender equality, girls leave the education system better qualified for careers.[3] In England, according to secondary school league-table data, boys have had worse exam results than girls for the past thirty years.[4] It's when girls leave the education system and enter the workplace that things start to go awry.

But wait – it's not just the education system where girls and women are showing off their skills in greater numbers. Women also take up work-based training and community learning in much greater numbers than men do. In fact, the ratio for community learning is 3:1 in favour of women.[5] According to Tom Schuller, author of *The Paula Principle: Why Women Lose Out at Work – and What Needs To Be Done About It*, 'Women in every age group are more likely than men to have taken part in some form of training at work within the last three months – anything from basic Health and Safety, to how to build better teams, or learning the latest technology.'

So, women are outperforming men in the education system, and they are doing more training as adults. We get better grades, and then we continue to hoover up as much knowledge as we can to improve our skills. Does it then make sense that we are paid less and are vastly under-represented in the boardroom?

What more can we do to improve our chances of being promoted? Sitting on the boss's knee wasn't working out too well, and women who attempt to emulate masculine behaviours to get to the top are ultimately disliked; paradoxically, if they adopt a stereotypically feminine style then they are not respected, so who knows where we are meant to go from here.[6] This constant challenge for women, combined with the lethal infusion of childbearing, packs a poisonous punch in our earning potential. In 2021, the UK gender pay gap for full-time employees was 7.9 per cent while the gap among all employees was 15.4 per cent; this takes into account part-time and full-time workers but is based on an hourly rate of pay.[7] Most people who quote the gender pay gap tend to state the first figure because they think it is fair to compare full-time with full-time, like for like. But I don't. Why are we ignoring the 8.7 million people who are working part-time?[8] Do they not matter? If we want a true picture of how fairly people are paid and how gender influences that, then it should cover all employees – and, of course, it just so happens that the majority of people working part-time are women. Saying you are only interested in the gender pay gap between full-time employees is just another way of ignoring women and the specific challenges they face in accessing the labour market.

The gender pay gap is the difference between men's and women's average earnings per hour, regardless of job or sector. The reasons women earn less money than men, and are less likely to reach senior positions, are complex and nuanced, but the key ones are:

1. Women are more likely to work part-time because of caring responsibilities. Part-time work, even if it's the same type of job within the same sector, does not pay as well as a full-time job. An average hourly rate for part-time work is £9.36 compared with £14.31 for full-time work.[9]

2. Women are more likely to take time out of the workplace to care for others. This is due to outdated gender stereotypes about what role women should be playing in society, and legislation that encourages women to do the caring, despite men being just as capable of caring for others as women are (more on this in Chapter 10). Now that the mother has become the main carer, if she does return to work, she is more likely to take a wage cut as she looks for family-friendly employment or perhaps employment closer to home so that she can do the drop-offs and pick-ups more easily.

3. Women face a negative bias and discrimination due to pregnancy, maternity and parenthood (more on this in Chapter 5). Research conducted by KPMG in Australia shows that two-fifths of the gender pay gap can be attributed to discrimination.[10]

4. Despite equal pay legislation existing for more than half a century, some women are still paid less than men for doing work of equal value.

5. The industries women work in tend to command lower salaries.

The gender pay gap can have dire consequences for women. This isn't just about female executives being unable to go on more holidays to Barbados; the gender pay gap is an indicator of how many more women than men live in poverty. In 2017, women made up 62 per cent of those earning less than the living wage.[11] Since the pandemic and corresponding recession disproportionately impacted women's jobs and earnings, the likelihood is that this figure has increased.

If you're still with me, great. If you've got bored and started thinking about what you're going to have for breakfast, then I get it – you're knackered and you've got a million things buzzing through your brain – but here's the kicker: all of this is relevant because the gender pay gap is only marginally to do with gender. Most of the gender pay gap is really a motherhood pay gap. The gap between men's and women's earnings is 3.9 per cent for ages 22–29, then 11.8 per cent for ages 30–39, and then it does a pole vault to 21.3 per cent for ages 40–49 – just as the impact of all the challenges mothers encounter with balancing work and childcare soccer-punch them right in the wallet.[12] If you compare the wages of women and men as they enter the job market, working in the same sector, in a similar role, being similarly educated and both working full-time, the pay gap is negligible.[13] It's from the moment the woman gets pregnant that things start to go awry.

Studies have shown that women's wages fall when they give birth to their first child, and they fall further with each child that she has; whereas men's wages do not fall when they have children – in fact (according to some studies), a father's wages *rise* with each child that he has, so, while mothers encounter a penalty, the dads receive a parenthood premium. The TUC estimates that full-time working dads earn 20 per cent more than childless men, while a full-time working mother's wages fall by an average of 11 per cent compared with her childless colleagues.[14] According to a University of Columbia Study, this is because men seem more dependable once they've had children.[15]

One of the best – and by best I mean absolutely appalling – stats to demonstrate the impact that childbearing has on a woman's career is that, according to the Institute of Fiscal Studies, by the time a woman's first child is 12 years old, her hourly pay rate is 33 per cent behind a man's[16] and the *European Sociological Review* found that British women who have children earn up to 45 per cent less than women who do not have children.[17] By and large, women who do not have children continue to grow their earnings at the same rate as men – as long as you are white and able-bodied, of course. Most people expect the pay gap to be due to mothers working fewer hours than the hours worked by women without children, but in 2016 the TUC calculated that there is also a pay gap of 7 per cent between mothers and non-mothers working full-time and with similar personal characteristics, such as education, region, occupation and social class.[18]

When we hear those treacherous words 'the gender pay gap', we think of the difference in pay between men and women, but in actual fact the pay gap between mothers and childless women is more than the pay gap between men and women without children.[19] Research conducted in Denmark, which has a gender pay gap of 15 per cent, shows how dramatically motherhood affects earnings. The study concludes that childbearing is the cause of 80 per cent of the gender pay gap.[20]

Same-sex couples also experience a motherhood penalty. Research with Norwegian parents found that, in lesbian couples, both mothers experience a penalty for 12 months after the birth of their child, with the pay penalty of the birthing mother being double the size of her partner's. Five years after giving birth, the child penalty for both women has largely disappeared. The fact that the partner who gives birth initially experiences this larger penalty does suggest that biology plays a role in the motherhood penalty, but only in the first year after giving birth. It's also interesting to note that the non-birthing mother encounters a pay penalty, when in heterosexual couples the father receives pay rises and promotions. Mothers in both heterosexual couples and same-sex couples experience a motherhood penalty, but it is only heterosexual couples where it persists beyond the child's fifth year, and it is only dads who financially benefit from parenthood.[21] Of course, the Norwegian system is very different from the UK's (they work fewer hours, have heavily subsidised childcare, and fathers receive 15 weeks of non-transferable, properly paid paternity leave), so we can't directly compare like with like, but what this strongly suggests is that gender stereotypes play an important role in the motherhood penalty.

Meanwhile, in the UK, it is quite evident that raging discrimination towards pregnant women and new mums is having a serious impact on their earnings:

'I was on track for area manager, got pregnant and suddenly everyone stopped talking about it. I came back from maternity and my area had been taken over by someone else, thus blocking my promotion.'

'I was being promoted almost yearly, I had been given a reporting line that went straight into director level, I was involved in all senior management meetings and discussions. Before going on maternity, I was told they expected me to progress to a head of department. After maternity leave, I returned to work and a "restructure" occurred and now I have two levels in between me and my old director. I see no career growth unless someone leaves, I am no longer in the same meetings or discussions and my role has reduced in responsibility drastically.'

'I was a highly skilled engineer who was designing circuitry for Silicon Valley companies and I had been nominated for awards. After I had a baby, my employer was completely unsupportive and kept doing unreasonable things like cancelling my leave at short notice, which I just couldn't manage with a baby. I felt forced to leave and I'm now teaching physics in a school. I took a pay cut of about £20,000.'

This type of discrimination is part of the maternal wall that women find themselves headbutting from the point they get pregnant. Some large and well-known companies have specific policies that purposefully discriminate against mothers, ensuring women either leave their jobs due to motherhood or receive a lower rate of pay.

In 2019, Alysia Montaño, a two-times world-champion athlete, spoke out about her experience of becoming a mother while under contract with Nike. The multinational corporation was penalising female athletes by not making any allowances whatsoever for pregnancy or maternity. They made their female athletes sign contracts to waive their right to any paid time off after giving birth. If a pregnant or recently post-partum athlete wasn't winning highly competitive races, she would face performance-related pay cuts, with no consideration for her physical or mental condition. It was all wrapped up with a strict non-disclosure agreement that prevented Nike athletes from talking about these disadvantages.[22] Thankfully, Alysia's courage to break her NDA paid off and Nike agreed to protect an athlete's pay during pregnancy. Another athlete, Allyson Felix, was dropped by Nike after she got pregnant.[23] Despite this, she found a new sponsor and went on to beat the Usain Bolt record for world titles in 2019, ten months after having a C-section. So, up your bum, Nike!

It was reported in the *Financial Times* in 2019 that UBS bank had been using maternity leave to impose long-term cuts on the bonuses of their female staff in the UK. When women returned from maternity, they found their bonus had been rebased and reduced by 30 per cent or more; in some cases it remained this way for three years. One woman was told it was a 'lifestyle choice' to have children, when she challenged the policy. Another was told to concentrate on her baby.[24]

Meanwhile, the chair of UBS, Axel Weber, has repeatedly called for more women in executive and leadership positions within the finance sector, saying he wants UBS to be less pale, male and stale.[25] Well, Axel, you might want to have a look under your own bonnet before playing the gender-equality hero in public. UBS responded to the allegations in March 2019 with a statement from its head of diversity and inclusion (Carolanne Minashi), promising that the issue would be addressed with a thorough review of the bonus policy, but some women are claiming that they continue to be affected by cuts.[26]

A senior member of staff at Sony spoke out against the company for taking maternity pay from departmental, rather than central, budgets. The money for maternity cover would come out of their own staffing budget, which meant covering just one maternity leave was enormously problematic. This resulted in managers being reluctant to hire women of child-bearing age, and sometimes women altogether. Speaking to Lucy Tobin at the *Evening Standard*, the whistle-blower said: 'At Sony, it's easier to hire men. If you've got two equally good candidates, one male and one female, are you going to go with the man because you then won't potentially face this problem?' The whistle-blower said that he raised this issue three times with HR and board-level managers, 'but I was told it's difficult to change things at Sony'.[27] Sony refused to comment on its maternity policies but says it 'embraces diversity and the working contributions of women'. Oh, and apparently they provide 'opportunities for career development and assisting the professional growth of women'.

Many women have also told me that, when they went on maternity leave, their employer decided to save some cash by not recruiting a replacement; instead they distributed the work to current employees. This inevitably creates resentment and puts returning mums on the back foot while reinforcing a workplace culture that blames and shames mothers. 'When I returned to work after nine months' leave, my colleagues just seemed thoroughly pissed off with me,' said Sarah, a digital marketing manager, when we met for a cup of tea in my local library café. 'I couldn't understand what I had done wrong. We all got along swimmingly before I left and now they could barely look me in the eye.' After a month or so back at work, Sarah realised the problem. 'My boss had told me he was going to distribute some of my work among the team and bring in two new people at a more junior level to deal with most of the day-to-day admin to relieve the pressure, but he didn't do that; he just expected the staff to take on all of my work without any support or any additional pay. They were overworked and totally stressed out, and blamed me for leaving them in the lurch.' The atmosphere was so toxic when she returned that she quit her job a month later.

The impact of the motherhood penalty isn't a temporary issue. It is felt throughout a woman's life, leaving her scrabbling around for cash when it comes to her pension. The gender pension gap means that the average pot of cash a 65-year-old woman has to live on for the rest of her life is a total of £35,800 – a fifth of what the average man has at the same age.[28] Black, Asian and Minority Ethnic women and disabled women receive a lower pension as they are more likely to work in low-paid sectors and face other types of discrimination, which reduces their earning potential.[29] The double whammy is that women need more money than men if they are to live comfortably in their old age. Women, on average, live for longer but are more likely to have higher care costs due to ill health. The sacrifices women make throughout their life to care for others result in hundreds of thousands of elderly women living in poverty.[30] It's no wonder the WASPI (Women Against State Pension Inequality) women have been campaigning so hard after the state pension age for women increased by five years, giving the women affected little to no notice and leaving thousands of elderly women in a terrible financial mess.

The good news is that, when the Government legislated for companies with more than 250 employees to publish their gender pay gap statistics on an annual basis, there was a flurry of interest in the specific barriers women face in the workplace. Employers couldn't continue to hide their lacklustre approach to gender equality, and an extreme gender pay gap would have a negative impact on sales and the companies' hiring ability. Finding ways to reduce their gender pay gap therefore made good business sense. The bad news is that there appear to be very few companies, or employers, who have really got to grips with what causes the gender pay gap in the first place. Until companies stop shelling out cash on free manicures to demonstrate their commitment to gender equality, or putting women through resilience workshops when it's the workplace that needs to change, not women, we will continue to experience a penalty because we dared to procreate.

Hot tips to reduce your motherhood penalty

If you're in a relationship when you have a child and you decide that you're to take on the lion's share of the caring responsibility, work out what this means for you in terms of missing contributions to your pension and ask your partner to split their pension contributions with you as well as the income from their paid work. It's only fair, and, although you might feel like you're blissfully in love and will continue to share everything for eternity, please remember that divorces do happen, and you need to protect yourself. If your partner refuses, then work out exactly what you'll be missing out on in pension contributions and perhaps suggest they take Shared Parental Leave so you can split the hit on your finances. If they still refuse, then I would probably refuse to do anything in the house that helps them (like making dinner or doing their washing) and I would definitely deny them sex. They don't deserve it, and there are many high-quality, battery-powered solutions to solve that particular issue for you.

The only real way to reduce the impact on your career is to

grit your teeth during those early years and go back to work after maternity leave, even if it actually costs you to do so, and as long as you are privileged enough to take that temporary financial hit. The long-term impact on your finances will be positive as you'll have more chance of moving up the career ladder, you'll be contributing to your pension and you'll be making your National Insurance contributions. Admittedly, this is playing by the rules of the boys' club, but under the current system we are left with the choice of shitty option A, or even more shitty option B.

When considering childcare costs, don't compare them with your wage. If you're in a relationship, compare the cost with your combined income. If you want to consider arrangements so your children aren't in full-time childcare, don't take it for granted that it will be you who requires flexibility from your work, unless you are solo-parenting. Have the conversation with your partner; he or she has just as much right to flexible working and just as much responsibility for your child's welfare.

Be a voice for change: if you work within a company that has a large gender pay gap and they seem incapable of understanding what should be done, set up a women's group. Invite female colleagues to band together to discuss the challenges they have faced at the organisation and then, as a collective, lobby your company for change. If they ignore your requests, then there's an excellent organisation, aptly called 'Organise' and run by the marvellous human that is Nat Whalley, that will support you in your lobbying efforts.

5

I Had a Baby, Not a Lobotomy: Pregnancy and Maternity Discrimination

'I wish I had known five years ago, as a young, childless manager, that mothers are the people you need on your team,' said Katharine Zaleski, an ex-manager at *HuffPost*, in an apology letter she penned for *Fortune* magazine. 'I secretly rolled my eyes at a mother who couldn't make it to last-minute drinks with me and my team,' she wrote, adding, 'I didn't disagree when another female editor said we should hurry up and fire another woman before she "got pregnant".'

Then Zaleski had her own child and realised she had been perpetuating a workplace culture that revolves 'around how men bond' and she had failed to recognise the unique strengths of working mothers. 'For mothers in the workplace, it's death by a thousand cuts – and sometimes its other women holding the knives.'[1]

We are told time and time again that companies are working hard to recruit, retain and promote women in their workplaces. CEOs and managers proudly launch their fast-track leadership courses for women, fantastic maternity packages, lactation rooms with free gourmet chocolates, and even a ladies' on-site steam room (I kid you not). But these fancy gimmicks mask a much more serious issue for women: whether we work at Asda, Apple or the local zoo, getting pregnant can be the kiss of death for your career.

According to the Government's own records, 1,814 tribunal claims were brought against employers due to pregnancy, parental rights and maternity issues between 1 February 2019 and 3 November 2021.[2] The majority of these cases have since been withdrawn, usually because the employer doesn't want their dirty laundry to be aired in public so they pay the claimant to keep their gob shut (more on this in Chapter 7). The companies listed include Santander UK, Network Rail, Goldman Sachs, IBM and Balfour Beatty, all of whom shout about their pioneering programmes to support their female workforce. Network Rail's website states: 'We are encouraging and supporting more women to get involved in the railway as a career.' Which is all very well and good but, with five cases of pregnancy and maternity discrimination brought against it between May 2018 and April 2020, it seems its ability to encourage and support women doesn't apply to those who use their uterus. According to research conducted by the Equality and Human Rights Commission, fewer than 1 per cent of those who experience discrimination raise a tribunal claim, and *The Times* has reported that 60 per cent of cases raised are dropped before they make it to tribunal, so the five cases against Network Rail are likely just the tip of a very deep discrimination iceberg.

In 2017, Zainab brought a successful discrimination claim against Network Rail and did so without any legal support: 'I started working at Network Rail and got pregnant quite quickly,' she told me.[3] 'It wasn't planned, so when I started to feel unwell I didn't realise there was a new life growing inside me. I asked to work from home because I was feeling terrible, and thankfully they agreed. All was going well until I became so unwell I had to go to hospital and as a result I told my employer in confidence that I was pregnant. He immediately retracted my ability to work from home and said that any time I took off work would be classed as sick leave. From that point on, everything changed. They put me under an enormous amount of stress, they kept telling me that I wasn't doing my job properly and they purposefully made my life very difficult. I was then hospitalised for two weeks due to complications that were causing me immense pain. I was told that by taking time off work I had negatively affected my colleagues. They suggested I shouldn't bother returning.'

Zainab did return to work, but her employer refused to make any reasonable adjustments for her, despite her explaining that she was extremely uncomfortable. 'This meant I started having contractions. I was terrified I was going to have a miscarriage. My manager said I wasn't fit to work but both my doctor and my midwife said I was, as long as Network Rail made the adjustments necessary for me to be comfortable. I continued to go to work and they started performance-managing me; they even told the man who sat next to me that he had to monitor my hours and report back to my employer. The whole experience was horrific.' She raised a grievance, which was ignored, and when she issued legal proceedings against Network Rail they wrote to her twice demanding she drop the case and stating that she would be forced to pay all of their legal costs when she lost. This could have been hundreds of thousands of pounds.

Zainab is able to speak publicly about her experience because she took her employer to tribunal and she won. She's a rare case as so few women are able to get this far in the proceedings, and, even if they do, they are usually coerced into signing a non-disclosure agreement preventing them from speaking publicly. When I spoke to her on the phone, it was clear the whole process was painful to remember. I asked her whether it was worth it and she sobbed. 'No, it wasn't worth it. I didn't do it for me; I did it because I wanted them to know that what they did was wrong. I wanted to be sure no other woman will be subjected to the same horrific experience that I was. But they broke me. I feel broken.'

It's not just private-sector companies that discriminate. Cases related to pregnancy and maternity rights have been brought against the Department for Work and Pensions, and the Ministry of Justice.[4] Those are the people who are in charge of ensuring our justice system works (it doesn't) and ensuring fair distribution of benefits; this includes the benefits that mothers are forced to apply for because they have faced discrimination – oh, the irony.

The period from pregnancy until approximately 12 months after a new mum returns to work is fraught with challenges. From the moment a woman announces she is pregnant, she is viewed differently by those around her while she simultaneously navigates the mind-blowing concept that she is growing a new human life. She is forced to watch helplessly as her career slips through her fingers. She is left out of important meetings, she is unable to attend the after-work drinks, she is relegated to basic tasks and no longer called upon for future planning, because the future doesn't include her; she is being replaced.

'I had been in my job two months when I was promoted to a more senior position,' said Michelle, a care worker. 'I was repeatedly told by my manager that I was the best employee they had and that I excelled in my work.' She then got pregnant, and after she announced the good news things started to deteriorate. 'The management team called me into their office three times (I had never been called in once before). They fabricated lies and said I had done things that I knew I hadn't. I started receiving emails daily with complaints and accusations. I was then demoted back to my previous position, and, when I raised concerns about manual handling, I was told all they could offer me was a cleaning job.' This started to have a significant impact on Michelle's mental health. 'I had never been under so much stress or felt so intimidated in my life. I stopped sleeping, my appetite vanished, and I felt completely alone and helpless.'

If you've experienced pregnancy or maternity discrimination, you know how deeply and permanently it scars. The fallout can have a ripple effect on those close to you, impacting your relationship and your ability to bond with your new baby. You can feel unbearably lonely; the anxiety pounds on your chest so hard you feel like you're suffocating. If you experience pregnancy or maternity discrimination, there is one thing for certain: it will play a defining role in your future.

Part of the reason it cuts so deep is because you are so vulnerable. Battling any kind of injustice is an isolating experience that takes enormous courage and tenacity; when you're pregnant, the stress triggered by this injustice can have serious consequences for an unborn child and its mother. The negative impact of stress on a foetus is well documented: it can affect your baby's brain development or immune system and can trigger early labour causing lower birth weight. A study published in the *Journal of Applied Psychology* in July 2020 revealed a worrying connection between pregnancy discrimination and the health of mothers and babies. The study, led by Baylor

University in the USA, revealed that pregnancy discrimination indirectly relates to an increased likelihood of post-natal depression, and it can also affect a growing baby, both in the womb and outside of it – lower birth weights and premature labour are more likely, as are increased doctor visits for babies.[5] I have spoken to thousands of women over the past six years and far too many went into labour prematurely, had severe complications during pregnancy, or have miscarried, as a result of the stress caused by pregnancy discrimination.

> 'I had worked in my sales team for two years when I told my boss I was pregnant. From that point on, I was bullied and harassed so viciously by my employer and my colleagues that I went into labour 12 weeks prematurely. When I was in the neonatal clinic with my baby, who could have died, my boss called me and made me redundant.'

Thousands of women are forced to contend with discrimination while on maternity leave. When you've just had a baby, making a cup of tea every day can feel like climbing Mount Everest; confronting discriminatory behaviour can feel nigh-on impossible. The unadulterated infatuation you can feel for your baby, the overwhelming exhaustion, coupled with the mind-numbing, spirit-sucking ordeal of early motherhood (particularly with your first child) is all-consuming. Navigating this mental and physical roller coaster while simultaneously being pushed out of your job can play absolute havoc with your mental health and ability to bond with your new child. It's like challenging someone with no arms to an unremitting custard pie fight.

Pregnancy and maternity discrimination takes many different forms, including sacking, redundancy, stagnating career, demotion, ignoring your Health and Safety needs, refusing a flexible-working request without a valid reason, bullying and harassment. Discrimination is not usually overt; it is often insidious. It takes place in meeting rooms with the blinds down; documents are shredded; witnesses are blackmailed into silence. Those who hold the power conspire with one another, while your confidence is salami-chopped into submission until you feel dizzy with bewilderment.

When considering ways to tackle pregnancy and maternity discrimination, what is often overlooked is that it doesn't only occur when someone is employed. It is highly likely that, if you are of childbearing age, you have also encountered discrimination in the recruitment process, without ever realising it. And, if you have ever tried applying for jobs while you're visibly pregnant – well, I won't bother explaining to you why you didn't get the job.

According to research by law firm Slater and Gordon, a third of employers avoid hiring women of childbearing age.[6] Just to spell it out: this means that if you are aged 24–40 (I realise you can get pregnant when you are younger or older than this, but this age bracket is the 'danger zone') then you will be rejected by one in three employers from a job you are probably very well qualified to do, simply because you have a uterus and you might actually use it. To many employers, a woman is a walking womb. Maternity is viewed as such a burden to business that thousands of employers will do whatever they can to avoid it.

Sometimes you will be rejected even before you get to an interview. Employers are just as nervous about hiring women with young children, and gaps in a CV can be very telling. If you've got a year missing from your professional experience, there's little doubt what you were up to. I was once contacted by a male recruitment consultant who told me that 80 per cent of his clients say they don't want him to put forward for interview women with young children or women of childbearing age. He said this happened across the recruitment sector. The recruiters themselves are powerless in this situation as their job is to enact their client's wishes. It's one of the reasons some people have started referring to the gaps in their CV as 'CEO of the household' as a way to demonstrate that this wasn't just a year of wiping bums and watching *Homes Under the Hammer*.

A 2007 American study gave a panel a bunch of CVs to assess for a job. The applicants' skills and experience were pretty much identical; the notable difference between them was the parental status, which was detailed on the CV. Let me tell you what happened – you're going to be truly shocked. The panel judged the mothers as less competent and less committed when compared with other types of employees. They offered the mothers a starting salary that was, on average, $11,000 below the other potential recruits' – all because their CVs said 'mother' on them. Fathers, however, were not affected.[7] A further study by Shelley Correll, a Stanford University sociologist, presented hundreds of real-world hiring managers with the CVs of two equally qualified women. One of the CVs stated that the candidate had a child. The managers were twice as likely to call the apparently childless woman for an interview.[8]

It is illegal to not hire someone because they are pregnant, are considering having a baby in the future, have young children or have taken maternity leave, but how can you prove it's the reason you didn't get a job? There has never been a single tribunal case on pregnancy or motherhood discrimination during the recruitment process, because candidates are powerless in this situation. This, despite women being asked inappropriate questions on a regular basis:

'I went for an interview with a law firm and was asked whether I planned to get married and have children. I was only 20 at the time and didn't have the courage to query why they needed to know this, so I said nothing.'

'A friend of mine recently received an email by accident about her interview, which stated: "Don't offer her more than £xxx. She's a mum, she needs the job, she won't ask for more." My friend was too scared to whistle-blow and she took the job.'

'I was grilled by the CEO about how I would manage a senior role with kids and a husband to take care of.'

'Last year, having returned from maternity leave and deciding I would like a new work challenge, I was asked in two separate interviews whether I had children, what my childcare arrangements would be and how I felt (as a mother) leaving my child to travel to work. I was also asked what my husband does for a living and whether I was with the child's father.'

'I went for my first postgraduate job interview with two kids at home and was asked: "Two kids ... So, do you think you'll have any more?" I replied: "You offering? Well, it's a bit early for an office romance, but I suppose we can see how it goes." Needless to say, I didn't get the job.'

Once employed, the pressure to remain childless can be extraordinary. One woman told me about the time she was called into her employer's office. He beckoned her to take a seat opposite him while he was on the phone. He proceeded to say, very audibly, 'She knows she'll get fired if she dares to get pregnant while working for me.' Another woman told me how she and her female colleagues were forced to take a shot of vodka every morning before they started work to prove they weren't pregnant. Another said her female boss would joke that they were going to put birth control in the water cooler.

'I'm sorry, I'm pregnant' are the words no working woman should ever have to say to her employer. It should be a joyous occasion, but, even if you work in a company where derogatory comments are not made about pregnancy or motherhood, announcing a pregnancy can fill women with dread, and with good reason.

> 'My boss shouted at me: "You're a fucking idiot. Why have you gone and done something so bloody stupid? You know your career is over now, don't you?"'

> 'I was asked if I knew who the father was and was then told I better get an abortion if I wanted to keep my job.'

> 'A colleague in my male-dominated agency once said, "Have you ever thought about getting a coat hanger for that baby?"'

Such responses are more common than one might hope, though the usual response is much more subtle and insidious. On the face of it, an employer can look like they are taking the news in their stride, happy for you, even; but behind the warm smile and congratulatory hug, a negative bias towards your ability and commitment starts to creep in and affects your chances of promotion and your experience at work. When I explain this to some employers, they look at me like I've just grown another head. People don't like to believe they hold deeply ingrained biases towards particular types of people, but they do. We all do.

Many women complain that their personal-development reviews go from 'excellent with serious chances of progression and promotion' to 'substandard' within the blink of an eye. The pregnant employee knows she is performing just as well as she was before; it's the perception of her ability that has changed.

'When I was pregnant, I lost out on a promotion to do a role I had essentially been doing for free for six months. I was told the person they had chosen was more suitable because they had older children so would be able to commit to the role.'

'I worked for a women's organisation but was advised to keep my pregnancy secret as I was up for promotion. At 18 weeks pregnant, I presented my report in a loose-fitting dress and my promotion was confirmed and announced. A few months later, I was constructively dismissed.'

'The headmaster at the school where I teach refers to all pregnant women and women with young children as "half a teacher".'

One in five mothers reported a financial loss as a direct result of their pregnancy. The most common reason is that they miss out on an expected promotion, but many also experience a reduction in their salary or their bonus.[9] Six in ten mothers experience discrimination during their pregnancy.[10]

Please make me safe

When you're pregnant and your body is being pushed to the limit of human endurance, it's only right that your employer makes sure you're safe and comfortable while doing your job – but you would be amazed by the number of employers who either barely give it any thought or clearly couldn't care less. Entering stage left: Health and Safety – the topic that makes many of us immediately glaze over but, for pregnant women, is paramount. In the modern-day UK workplace, numerous women find themselves left with a choice between protecting the health of their growing babe and keeping their job.

If you've been pregnant, you know what it feels like to have a growing human playing baseball with your kidneys and bladder. Pregnant women can be in a tremendous amount of pain, even if they are not doing strenuous work, and ignoring their needs can be an act of physical torture:

'I worked for a large engineering company when I was expecting my first child. During my third trimester, I suffered with excruciating back pain when I sat down, to the point I was often reduced to tears. I saw my GP, who recommended I sit on a birthing ball and ask my employer for a risk assessment. My employer declined the birthing ball on the grounds of 'safety' and I was told to do the risk assessment myself and send it to HR. I didn't know what else to do so I just took the pain.'

Health and Safety issues affect two in five expectant mothers at work. Pregnant women are forced to carry heavy objects, work with dangerous chemicals or, during a global pandemic, are forced to have direct contact with people who could have a deadly disease. Research from 2015 found that 4 per cent of expectant mothers leave their job because the risk to them and their baby is so severe – that's 21,000 mothers each year.[11]

During the pandemic, the specific needs of pregnant women were not prioritised, with tragic results. We know that in May 2020, 25 per cent of pregnant NHS workers were continuing to work with patients who could have Covid-19. That figure rose to 31 per cent for Black, Asian or ethnic-minority pregnant NHS workers.[12] The Pregnant Then Screwed helpline was awash with women saying that if they objected or kicked up a fuss because they were scared for their safety, they would be suspended with no pay. Previous respiratory diseases, including SARS, had demonstrated that pregnant women were more likely to become severely unwell should they become infected, and by the end of 2020 we had research to prove that this was the case with Covid-19: babies were more likely to be born prematurely, end up in NICU, and tragically to be stillborn. Mothers were more likely to end up in ICU, particularly in the later stages of pregnancy, and we know that in the first wave nine pregnant women died with Covid-19.[13] But still, by April 2021, less than half of pregnant women said their employer had done a risk assessment to evaluate their safety at work. The number of pregnant women who felt forced to leave their job as a result of this is still unknown.

It is the job of the Health and Safety Executive to act as the enforcement body where safety regulations are breached, but *The Observer* found that in January 2021 only 0.1 per cent of the 97,000 Covid safety cases reported had been issued with an enforcement notice.[14]

The dangerous positions pregnant women are placed in can be extraordinary:

'My employer said to me: "I am meant to do a risk assessment but you're just pregnant so what more is there to say? I'll just make it up."'

'I asked my boss for a risk assessment and she said: "I didn't need a risk assessment when I came into work after I had broken my leg, so you don't need one when you're pregnant."'

'I work as a scientist in a lab. I had to fight for a Health and Safety assessment. In a meeting with the boss, I was told I needed to think about the business and what I am employed to do. I kept fighting and printed out Health and Safety documents to say it wasn't safe for me to be in the lab. Finally, they did an assessment, but it said I was fit to carry on working with all the chemicals, even though the chemicals warned that they could be harmful to my unborn child. Thankfully, the doctor signed me off work.'

'I was working in events – no risk assessment was ever done, and I had to stand at a helpdesk for up to 16 hours a day in boiling-hot weather with only a 30-minute break. They would make me work 18–20 hours a day, four days a week, and then I would get home and have to lug my heavy suitcase and laptop up the steps to my house while my boss watched me struggle. I had the most horrendous swollen elephant-ankles. I would cry when I got home as I was in so much pain and the stress was too much to cope with. I had a bleed at 36 weeks and went on to have a very poorly baby who had "IUGR" (a serious growth issue). The doctors told me it had been caused by stress. It was such an awful time; they were so horrid to me – my boss even called my bump disgusting.'

'I worked for a well-known coffee chain. My boss never did a risk assessment and just expected me to carry on as normal. He expected me to carry the heavy chairs and tables outside each morning. He left me on my own, so I was expected to lift the 5kg bags of coffee. I ended up being admitted to hospital with reduced movements at around 32 weeks.'

Employers sometimes use Health and Safety as an excuse to either belittle their pregnant employee or as a way of covering up discrimination:

'I was working on a casual basis as an office manager when I got pregnant – I didn't have a contract but there was a verbal agreement that I would work at least 25 hours per week. The day I told my employer I was pregnant, they did a risk assessment and decided that I was unsafe to have in the building! As I didn't have a contract and was working on zero hours, they just asked me to leave, and that was that.'

British scientist Dr Samantha Decombel was invited to speak at a conference at the European Commission. She accepted and started working on her speech. However, the offer was retracted when they discovered she was seven months pregnant. Their email said: 'The European Commission are not very enthusiastic for you to take the risk for your health by making you travel to Brussels at such a late stage of pregnancy.' Dr Decombel posted her response to the European Commission on a blog, stating: 'As I am sure you are aware, one of the key hurdles facing many women in science and entrepreneurship is the desire to start a family, and how this will fit in with their career plans. Turning away a pregnant speaker, who is in excellent health and has voluntarily agreed to travel to voice her opinions at this event, seems to me to be the perfect demonstration of why this is still such an issue for many, and the absolute opposite of what I would hope the European Commission would want to convey.'[16]

Dr Decombel added that she would like them to reconsider their decision to withdraw her speech. They didn't. Nor did they respond to her email. Her post sent Twitter into a spin, and a friend of Samantha's invented the hashtag #7monthsawesome, which women across the globe started using to state all the incredible things they had achieved while seven months pregnant.[17]

'While pregnant, I gave ten talks in five countries, built a new lab, and spoke at the White House. #7monthsawesome,' said Christina Warinner.

'Painted almost every damn room in our remodelled house

while setting up a new lab at 7–9 months pregnant with baby number 3. #7monthsawesome,' said Dr Tara C. Smith.

'I attended a five-day conference, chaired a session, gave a talk at another session and slept in a dorm on a tiny cot. #7monthsawesome,' said Andrea Kirkwood.

Some pregnancies can be straightforward; others can be debilitating. All pregnant women should have a workplace risk assessment done, and if something is unsafe or is making them uncomfortable then it needs to be fixed immediately – but employers mustn't use Health and Safety as another way of condescending women with paternalism to the detriment of their career, and we can't allow pregnant women to be placed in situations that are clearly unsafe for a growing baby, thereby forcing women to choose between the health of their unborn child and their pay cheque. While outside the workplace pregnant women are regularly told what they mustn't eat and what they mustn't do, and they are judged negatively by onlookers for partaking in such dangerous pastimes as eating a soft-boiled egg or drinking caffeinated coffee, inside the workplace the safety of pregnant women is rarely considered, and, when it is, sometimes it is used as a way to patronise and undermine pregnant employees, rather than to keep them safe.

Pregnancy loss

One in five women will experience pregnancy loss in her lifetime.[18] Nothing can prepare you for the moment a midwife says the words 'I'm very sorry but I can't find a heartbeat,' or the moment your stomach clenches tight and you feel the hot, damp stickiness of blood between your legs. The little life you have named and spent days/weeks/months imagining abruptly ends. Pregnancy loss is not only mentally and emotionally ago- nising, it is also physically painful. Your body has to go into labour with severe cramping that can last for days – sometimes it can last for months. Alongside this all-encompassing ordeal, women sometimes experience challenges with work. Though employers may appear sympathetic, telling an employer about pregnancy loss alerts them to the fact that you want to have a baby, and that can have a catastrophic impact on your career.

Laura was a senior manager in a recruitment company. 'I loved my job,' she told me when we met for a coffee at King's Cross train station in London. 'I was given loads of autonomy compared to previous roles and I really felt like my opinion and experience were valued.' Laura unexpectedly discovered she was pregnant at six weeks. 'I had been married for a few years and we really wanted kids, but I had been told by the doctors that I wouldn't get pregnant without IVF, so when I started to get all the pregnancy symptoms it was the last thing I'd expected.' She had awful morning sickness and says she looked and felt like death, but tried to keep it together at work. She was called into the boardroom by her boss and was asked if she had a drinking problem. 'I couldn't believe it – he was angrily accusing me of being an alcoholic.' To defend herself, she blurted out that she was pregnant. Other than her husband, her boss was the first person she told, which wasn't exactly how she had planned things. 'My boss was really surprised. He had never had a pregnant employee before. I explained the circumstances – that I, too, was shocked as it was totally unexpected.'

Her employer seemed generally supportive, so she was pleased. He recommended she go home that day to rest up. Then, about four weeks later, she was in a meeting and started to get some severe cramping. She went to the toilet and realised she was bleeding. 'I knew that I was probably miscarrying. I was hysterical. I went into his office and panicked. I called my husband and he came to get me and took me to the hospital, and they confirmed that my baby had died.' Laura told her boss the devastating news, and again he was sympathetic. She was signed off work for two weeks. 'That was on the Tuesday, but then the next day I got a text message from him saying "When are you coming back?" That happened every single day that week.'

She was bombarded by text messages and emails with questions and tasks her boss wanted completing immediately. She responded as she felt a sense of responsibility for her team, even though she was struggling, but the messages didn't stop, even at the weekend, and that was when she realised this wasn't at all fair. She asked him if she could deal with the work when she returned to the office. 'He didn't seem to understand what I was going through. It wasn't just the mental impact of losing the baby; it was an incredibly physical process. I was having contractions; I was in a lot of pain. I was bleeding heavily.'

Still reeling from losing her baby, she went back to work after two weeks. On her first day, her boss called her into a meeting room at 9 a.m. 'It was a glass meeting room in the centre of the office so everybody could see in. He asked me how I was feeling, and I said that I was managing. He then said that he had a business to run and people had targets to hit, and if I was going to be sad and was going to start bringing the whole office down that I should just leave.' Suddenly she felt enormously self-conscious; it became clear that everyone knew her personal business. She just wanted to get her head down and get on with her job but it was obvious that her card was marked. 'He assumed I was going to try for another baby, so he recruited someone to replace me and expected me to train them up. I was being replaced even though having another baby hadn't even crossed my mind. I was still recovering from losing the first.' In front of Laura, her boss started commenting that he didn't want to employ any other women in case they got pregnant, so he was only going to employ men from now on. 'I told him I felt uncomfortable with this new person starting, but my pleas were ignored.'

The culture of the organisation grew more and more toxic. Laura wasn't invited to meetings any more and her duties were slowly removed. She became more and more ostracised. 'I was crying every day on my way to work. In the end, I decided I had to resign.' She asked her boss for a meeting and told him she was giving him a month's notice. 'He exploded, shouting at me – he was determined to make me cry. He said he wouldn't pay me my notice and told me to pack up my stuff and to leave today.' Laura tried to argue back, and, as she left the room, he shouted after her, 'Make no mistake, I will destroy you.' The whole experience was so stressful that Laura decided she had to change career – she couldn't bear the thought of anything like that happening to her again.

Many women go through the horrific process of a miscarriage and tell no one. Louisa Pritchard talked about her haunting experience of miscarriage at work in an article she penned for the *Telegraph*. 'A week later, at my desk, feeling the cramps get worse, I knew I'd lost our baby. Huddled in the ladies' loos – the lunchtime rush had luckily just finished – I sat in stunned silence. All I could see was blood. I didn't even cry; that came later. Instead, after 20 minutes spent struggling to compose myself, I walked silently back to my desk. In hindsight I don't know how I didn't break down.

Luckily it was a frantic day in the office, so no one even

looked up. I know my colleagues would have been incredibly supportive, but how do you tell someone you've had a miscarriage when they didn't even know you were pregnant? That's the ironic thing about waiting to 12 weeks. If something goes wrong, it becomes a heavy secret you carry around by yourself.'[19]

Women can feel like they have no one they can confide in, but they also worry about the impact it will have on their career. 'The reason I think that it's so taboo is you're doubly failing,' said Elizabeth Siler, Associate Professor of Management at Worcester State University, during an interview on CNN. 'The reason you're failing is because you're pregnant, then you're failing at being pregnant. The idea that the workplace is neutral is not true. We pretend it's neutral, but it's male.'[20] Obviously, pregnancy and pregnancy loss are not about failure at all, in any form, but that's how we are made to feel. Company culture makes us feel like pregnancy is letting the side down as we have another priority besides work.

Another challenge with pregnancy loss is that the law is pretty flimsy. Amy McKeown was told at her 12-week scan that her baby had no heartbeat. She opted to let nature run its course and to give birth to her stillborn baby rather than undergoing a medical procedure, but Amy bled heavily for ten weeks afterwards, causing her frequent blackouts where she would come around on the floor in a pool of blood. When she returned to work, she was made redundant by her employer, Ernst & Young. Believing this was discrimination, she tried to start a legal claim but soon discovered that her vulnerable state wasn't protected under employment law. In fact, you are protected against discrimination on the grounds of pregnancy, or pregnancy-related illness, for a period of only two weeks from when the pregnancy ends. In legal terms, the end of pregnancy is when the baby has sadly died; however, in medical terms, the end of pregnancy is when a woman has passed the foetus. Amy has been tenaciously campaigning for the legal definition of pregnancy to match the medical definition.[21]

These boobs were made for milking

If you are breastfeeding and returning to work, things can get a little tricky. When I returned to work after the birth of my second baby, he absolutely refused to take a bottle. I re-mortgaged our house to buy different kinds of teats in the hope they might trick him into giving it a little suck, but he was, and remains, a wilful little human. Nothing compared to my boobs, and, as I was unable to detach them from my body, this left me with two choices: leave the poor little thing to starve all day or negotiate time with my boss so I could visit my son's nursery to feed him. Thankfully, my boss didn't hesitate and he agreed that I could cycle the five-mile round trip twice a day to ensure my little person could eat his dinner. There's nothing like the sound of contentment and comfort when your baby finally nestles back into his milk source. It was definitely worth it, and I was so grateful to my employer for his flexibility and understanding. Of course, I didn't have to do this for long, a couple of months at most, but it meant I felt so much happier about my return. If I had been forced to choose between my job and feeding my child, then I would have walked out on my career in a heartbeat.

Many mums continue to express milk when they return to work but more than a third of breastfeeding mothers have had to express in the work toilets – forced to make their baby's lunch where their colleagues have done their 11 a.m. poo.[22] Half of working mums said they had to express in an unsuitable place, such as the staffroom or in their car. Many women understandably feel ridiculously awkward strapping a great big cacophonous pump to their nipple in a public space – or, worse, in front of their colleagues. It's weird enough trying to milk yourself in front of your own family. So, understandably, 30 per cent of mums have felt forced to stop breastfeeding earlier than they would have liked.[23]

Half of breastfeeding mothers said their boss didn't know what to do – there was just pure bewilderment at the very concept a mother might need to provide food for her baby while at work.[24] They said their employer had no facilities at all, despite the law stating that breastfeeding mothers should have a place to rest. Some employers would do their best to avoid the conversation, feeling unbearably awkward because a woman said the word 'breast'. I mean, *how embarrassing!* Perhaps the solution is to round up all the men and shout 'BREASTS!', 'VAGINA!', "VULVA!', 'PERIOD!' at them until they can repeat without blushing.

'I had to sit on the floor of the disabled loo looking at pics of my baby girl to try to get the milk flowing while ignoring the questionable odours and people constantly trying the door.'

'I was forced to work 12-hour overnight shifts when I went back to work. I explained that I was still breast-feeding, but they didn't care. There was no time for a break to express. Eventually I was hospitalised with severe mastitis.'

Women are still thrown out of professional conferences for taking their breastfeeding baby with them, even if they are not at all disruptive. In 2016, a woman was kicked out of TED Women, the conference created to champion powerful working women and girls, for bringing her breastfed baby with her.[25] In 2015, mothers were told they couldn't breastfeed at a Scottish Government-backed event aimed at 'removing the barriers to breastfeeding' – I kid you not.[26] In July 2019, airline KLM told a customer on Twitter that if another passenger was made to feel uncomfortable by her breastfeeding then she would be told to cover up,[27] making it clear that they prioritised the perplexing discomfort of another passenger over the needs of a starving baby and its mother. It seems extraordinary to me that we still need to explain to people that breasts exist to produce milk for babies and that babies need milk to survive.

The UK has the lowest rates of breastfeeding in the world, according to data from 2016, with only 0.5 per cent of babies still being breastfed after one year, compared with 62 per cent in Sweden, 23 per cent in Germany and 27 per cent in the USA (and that's despite the USA having no paid parental leave).[28] The needs of breastfeeding mothers being ignored and undermined by employers undoubtedly has an impact on this low statistic.

However, there are a handful of companies that recognise that they have a role to play in really supporting mothers who are returning to work and are still breastfeeding their child. Goldman Sachs has adopted a family-friendly image in recent years, despite the brutal hours they expect people to work. One of their perks for mothers is to have breastmilk couriered straight from the office to their child's nursery – from boob to baby in a matter of minutes. I love the thought of thousands of milky mopeds zooming around the country, a Deliveroo just for babies (a Delivermoo, perhaps?).

Maternity absurdity

The Government often states that the UK's maternity policy is 'one of the most generous in the world', which it certainly is in terms of time but definitely isn't in terms of money, and you need both for maternity leave to be viable (and, in the Government's own words, generous!).[29] According to Unicef, the UK is the third-worst-ranking country in Europe in terms of paid maternity leave (number twenty-nine out of thirty-one countries, with only Switzerland and Ireland fairing worse).[30] I can't tell you how often I hear people say 'But maternity leave is so expensive for companies. Why should they pay for you to have a baby?' Well, here's the thing: companies don't pay for your maternity leave – you pay for your own maternity leave. The money new mums receive, in the form of Statutory Maternity Pay (SMP), comes from their own National Insurance contributions. Your company pays you the money, but then they claim it back. Small companies receive 103 per cent of what they pay you (this gives them a little bit extra to cover administration costs) and they can also apply to receive the money upfront so they're not forced to wait for a rebate. Larger companies reclaim 92 per cent of your maternity pay from the Government.

Some employers choose to top up your SMP, even though they have no legal obligation to do so. This is called 'enhanced maternity pay'. They do this because it has a direct benefit for the business; it means they attract more brilliant women to work for their organisation and they improve staff retention after maternity leave. There are no stats on the percentage of women who receive enhanced maternity pay but I think it's safe to say that the majority do not, and, in 2020, during the pandemic, Pregnant Then Screwed received numerous messages from women saying their company had removed this benefit from their contract. Without enhanced maternity pay, financial survival during maternity leave is very difficult. How do you survive on £151 a week if you're a single mum without any savings? Well, you struggle – a lot – and, with a quarter of new parents saying they got into debt during maternity leave and 300,000 parents using credit to manage their costs, things can get pretty hairy.[31]

But let's get back to discrimination. If you are currently on maternity leave, I don't want to worry you, but you're more likely to be pushed out of your job during this phase than when you are pregnant, or when you return to work after parental leave.[32] And wrestling with sleep deprivation and the complexities of keeping a new human alive leaves little physical or mental energy to challenge any shitty behaviour from an employer:

'I started my job in 2000. I was a national account manager and was really successful, doing that job for fifteen years, earning about £55,000 per year. I had my baby then went on maternity leave, having trained up my maternity replacement. While I was on maternity leave, they called me in for an urgent meeting and said my job was no longer available and offered me a demotion. They said I had to make the decision there and then as to whether I wanted it. I was confused but took them at their word and accepted the demoted job. When I returned, my maternity cover was still there – it took me six months to realise I had been taken for a ride and they had kept my maternity cover in my job. By then it was too late to do anything about it. Five years later and I am earning half of what I was earning before. The knock to my confidence and mental health has been awful and I can't imagine it will ever recover.'

It's pretty hard for us to expect better from employers when our own government is guilty of maternity discrimination. In 2018, Jo Swinson was a Liberal Democrat MP. She had given birth to her second son, Gabriel, three weeks before a crucial Brexit vote was due to take place in Parliament. As she was breastfeeding and still wading through the early days of fug and fatigue, attending Parliament for the vote without her baby would have been enormously challenging, so she agreed to a 'pairing process'. This is a long-standing Parliamentary agreement that pairs up two MPs who would be voting differently from one another; neither MP is allowed to vote, thereby cancelling each other out. Yet the MP who Jo was paired with, Brandon Lewis, was told by his chief whip to ignore the agreement and vote anyway, which he did. Thankfully, this was spotted by a journalist, who informed Jo Swinson that the deal had been broken, and Jo took to Twitter to show her outrage. It was a perfect example of maternity discrimination brazenly committed by our own Government for all the world to see. It may not have cost Jo in terms of money, but an MP's capital is their voting ability and that was purposefully removed. A mother with a brand-new baby was side-lined and consciously undermined as the two men involved patted each other on the back for a job well done. Obviously, when they were caught out and publicly chastised for their behaviour, they were forced to immediately apologise and claimed it was all a big misunderstanding.[33]

We don't like the mums

In the days I lovingly refer to as Joeli BC (Before Children, or rather, Before Chaos), I was your typical job-swot. I would be the last to leave the office, I internalised every work-based decision and I would respond to emails at literally any hour of the day. If other members of the team didn't behave like me, then they clearly weren't as committed. My bias against colleagues who worked part-time was conscious and overt. It's not easy to admit this, but it's really important that I do, because I get it: it's ingrained in us, and, unless we start to question that bias and use facts to counter it, it will endure and it will continue to affect the progression of mothers in the workplace – particularly Black, Asian and Minority Ethnic mothers, young mothers and mothers with disabilities.

The Equality and Human Rights Commission (EHRC) did some research on how pregnant women and new mums are viewed in the workplace and found that 40 per cent of employers claim to have seen at least one pregnant woman 'take advantage' of their pregnancy. The idea that any woman gains some sort of workplace advantage from pregnancy is utterly ridiculous. I'm not entirely sure what 'take advantage' means in this context but it's definitely not a compliment. Perhaps she just wanted to, you know, sit down for a bit, or maybe she spent too long in the toilet because a growing baby was using her bladder as a punchbag; maybe she had to attend a prenatal appointment to make sure her baby was still developing, or maybe she had to leave a meeting to get some food as her blood sugar was plummeting – a bit like the heavily pregnant MP Tulip Siddiq, who was then told by Eleanor

Laing, Deputy Speaker of the House of Commons, that she had made 'womankind look bad'.[34]

The EHRC also found that a third of employers believe that pregnant women and new mums are 'generally less interested in career progression' when compared with other employees. What these chumps don't realise is that, for many new mums, their career becomes *more* important to them after they have children. Sure, their kids are their top priority, but, when you're spending time away from your child, you want to make it matter, and amazingly it is possible to care about more than one thing at once. For many mums, going to work is much easier than looking after kids; it's a break from the nonsensical tantrums about the way you sliced a piece of toast, or the saint-like patience required to teach your child to read/walk/wipe their bottom properly. When you go to work, you get to engage with other adults, achieve goals you have set for yourself and feel fulfilled as a result. Hopefully without anyone shouting: 'Mummy! Will you wipe my bottom?' (If this does happen, I would definitely suggest lodging a complaint and calling our free advice line immediately.)

What some women might experience (and men, too, if their social programming is a little lax and they have managed to separate themselves from patriarchal expectations) isn't a lack of interest in their career but a rearrangement of values, a desire to work flexibly, perhaps part-time, to occasionally hang out with their children rather than 'lean in' to work 24/7. That's not a giving-up mentality or a not-caring-about-your-career mentality, it's a wanting-to-be-'all-in'-with-every-aspect-of-your-life-without-reaching-burnout mentality.

The EHRC also found that four in ten (41 per cent) employers agreed that pregnancy puts 'an unnecessary cost burden' on the workplace. Which demonstrates that the vast majority of people don't realise that, as above, your maternity pay is covered by your own National Insurance contributions, and that, if you receive extra money, it is the company's choice to give you that. It's probably a good idea that we each get this tattooed on our face.

And they found that half (51 per cent) of employers agree that there is sometimes resentment among employees towards women who are pregnant or on maternity leave. This is something most of us who have been pregnant at work will have noticed, but to have it spelt out like this is pretty devastating. Imagine dealing with the intensity of growing a new human life, then experiencing discrimination from your employer and your colleagues resenting you, all at once.[35]

We know that successful mothers are seen as significantly less likeable than otherwise identical fathers because studies have proved it.[36] We see time and time again that dads are not affected by the conscious and unconscious bias that affects mothers. Dads get off scot-free – well, actually, it seems men are viewed even more positively by employers and colleagues once they have children. But then there's also the really worrying research that shows mothers just cannot win, no matter what they do. In a study by the University of Exeter, mothers who took their full maternity leave to care for their babies were seen as less competent and not as committed to their jobs, while those who continued working, rather than taking their full maternity leave, were viewed as being less caring. According to the study's lead author, Dr Thekla Morgenroth, 'This is a no-win situation for women.' Perhaps this is why the EHRC found that around a third (36 per cent) of employers disagree that it's easy to protect expectant or new mothers from discrimination in the workplace.[37]

The number of women forced out of their jobs because

they dared to procreate, and the number of working mums experiencing discrimination, almost doubled between 2005 and 2015.[38] When the 2015 research concluded, a number of recommendations were made to the Government to address the issue – but to date not a single one of those recommendations has been implemented. As I am writing these words, on a blisteringly hot August day in 2020, 271,869 mothers have been forced out of their jobs since that report was published, while the Government has stood idly back and done naff-all to protect them.[39] The thing is, it makes absolutely no economic sense. Based on the established 'middle earner' salary of £28,000, if each of these women remained out of the workforce for just a year, that's a direct loss to the exchequer (through income tax and employee NI contributions only) of approximately £1.6 billion.[40] Why do we continue to see complete inertia from the Government on this issue? Is it because we value male employment more than female employment? Do we inherently believe that if a woman loses her job then it's okay because her husband will look after her, even though this isn't the reality for many mothers? When will we realise that mothers are dedicated, committed and highly skilled workers and their employment is just as valuable as anyone else's? All we are asking for is respect and a system that works for us.

6

Isn't That Illegal?

'I was working for a huge construction company and, while I was still on maternity leave, I had submitted a flexible-working request, but I heard nothing back. A week before I was due back to work, I was called and asked to attend a meeting the following day.

A list of mundane roles were discussed as if I had somehow given birth to my own competence. I had been in charge of winning new business – £8 million contracts – and had been reporting into the CEO, but now I could return and do some photocopying.

I was in the very fortunate position that my friend is an employment solicitor, so she guided me through the legal process, all broken ego and vagina. We were about to go to tribunal, but I just couldn't afford the fees, the test of character and the heartbreak – a decision that haunts me to this day. I settled for less than I was worth, for less than I deserved, but to face a Goliath that was filled with men who had once told me 'to learn to keep my legs shut', I was no David.

My friend explained to me that the process is brutal: you're scrutinised, your character is unpicked and accusations thrown. With all of this in mind, I felt like the biggest barrier was perhaps in being robust enough to deal with this. Especially after you've already torn yourself apart wondering if you're getting parenting nailed down.

I remember reading a letter from the other side and they laid out the financial risk to me if I lost. It was intimidating, threatening and condescending – who was I to stand up to that? I wish I'd had the bravery I would have now.'

I always believed I was a scrapper. If there was even a sniff of injustice in the air, I would be at the front of the queue to call it out – nostrils flared, ready to beat my chest and lead an invisible army of injustice warriors until the wrongdoing was rectified and normality resumed. At least that was my inflated perception of myself. The spirit-crushing experience of pregnancy discrimination threw that perception into turmoil. I was sacked by an employer I knew and trusted when I was at my most fragile, and I allowed them to get away with it. With hindsight, I can see that I had no choice.

You know the tale by now: I was broke, and I watched helplessly as my solicitor withdrew the last £250 I had in my bank account. I was then informed I was having a high-risk pregnancy and medical professionals made it very clear that any serious stress could kill my unborn child. Getting myself into horrendous debt was one thing; potentially being responsible for the death of the human life that was swelling inside me was another. I gave up. I had to. I retreated to lick my wounds. Whatever justice might look like, it wasn't worth it.

Mine is by no means the only story of a pregnant woman or new mum who was screwed over by her employer and then found it absolutely impossible to pursue justice. If you've been paying attention, you will know that only 1 per cent of women who experience pregnancy or maternity discrimination raise a tribunal claim.[1] The law may be pretty clear that discrimination is illegal, but if you try to access any form of justice you will soon discover that the system is stacked against you at every turn.

Firstly, the costs can quickly mount at a time when you're likely skint, and the potential gains are small. Legal aid for employment cases was abolished in 2013, leaving you with a big bill if you instruct a solicitor. If you've just left your job and have no idea where your next pay cheque will be coming from, the idea of spending thousands of pounds and potentially losing the case is utterly terrifying.

'I was made redundant when I was around four months pregnant with my first child. When they told me, it came so out of the blue I had a panic attack and couldn't breath. I contacted a solicitor for advice and they said I definitely had a case, but it would have cost thousands. I don't have that sort of money.'

'I started my case against my previous employer – the bill racked up to £3,000 in the blink of an eye. That was every penny I had, and it was the money I had been saving to see me through maternity leave. I considered taking out a loan, but sense prevailed – I could have lost my house.'

Solicitor firms are now required to publish an overview of their costs on their company website. Using the scientifically proven method of 'a quick google', the first ten firms that specialise in employment law all say that the average cost for a solicitor to support you through a basic case is £5,000–10,000; complex cases can be upwards of £30,000. Compare this with the average amount awarded in sex discrimination cases in 2018–19, which was £8,774, you would be excused for wondering what on earth the point is.[2] In fact, in 2017–18, there were only thirty-nine cases of sex discrimination that were awarded any kind of financial compensation whatsoever.[3]

Shelly was working freelance for a local council when she announced her pregnancy. They sacked her and Shelly took legal action against them. 'I ended up with what could be considered a fair and possibly generous settlement – some people told me it was a bonus amount – not something I was counting on (I was counting on my wages, thanks); like a lottery win! Lucky me, right? This, however, doesn't take into consideration the fact that I had lost a large amount of money when they pulled my contract, and then I had to pay legal fees and court costs, which due to the other party dragging their feet (nice tactic, guys) meant my costs rocketed at the end. Although we settled the day before we went to court, I had to pay for everyone to be court-ready. All I wanted was my contract value – I wanted to be paid the money that I had planned for, the money that was unfairly taken away from me. My final legal costs were in the region of £9,000; the settlement I received was less than this. I'm too nervous to say how much it was because I've been gagged by an NDA, but it didn't cover my legal costs. I could have refused their offer but there was no guarantee that, if I had gone to court, my settlement would have been higher; it could have been less, or I could have lost.' Shelly was right to be cautious about potentially losing her case; your chances of success if you make it to tribunal are perversely slim, which is complete insanity considering no one in their right mind would go through the pain and expense of taking an employer to court unless they felt that this was their only option for justice. In 2013–14, only half of employment tribunals were awarded in favour of the claimant.[4]

Cases such as that of Jagruti Rajput, a senior compliance officer for Commerzbank AG who was awarded £185,720 for gender and maternity discrimination, are incredibly rare and unfortunately give people false hope of larger financial awards.[5] Jagruti is yet to see a single penny of the money she was awarded, despite the incident taking place in September 2016. After the first tribunal finished, her employer contested the judgment and was given the opportunity for a retrial on one element of the case. Because of the retrial, the case is still ongoing, making it very difficult for Jagruti (who was still employed by the bank until they made her redundant in 2020) to get on with her life, particularly as her legal costs now far outweigh any money she has theoretically been awarded. Her astonishing levels of courage and tenacity after years of fighting a financial giant have, so far, left her very much out of pocket. 'I just have to keep fighting,' she told me. 'I need to get justice, not just for me but for every woman who has had to go through this.'

If you're staring into the abyss of an empty bank account, you may decide that your only option is to take a case to tribunal without any legal support. In July 2017, the Supreme Court ruled that the £1,200 fee to raise a tribunal claim, which had been in place since 2013, was unlawful (though in June 2020, officials asked the Law Commission to set out proposals on how a fee regime might work in the future – so watch this space). Therefore, theoretically, there should be no direct financial cost if you represent yourself. But, of course, it's not all that simple. Learning employment law isn't easy when you have three years to study and a tutor. Imagine trying to teach yourself employment law without those luxuries, throw a newborn into the mix, and you've got an overwhelming cacophony of chaos. Employment tribunals are complex and full of terminology that feels like a different language – a language only accessible to anyone privileged enough to have gone to law school.

Helen Larkin won her tribunal against beauty brand Liz Earle in January 2020 after they made her redundant when she was eight months pregnant.[6] With astounding pluck and determination, she took on the beauty behemoth (owned by Walgreens Boots Alliance), without a solicitor, and she represented herself at tribunal. She said that not having the stress of spiralling costs hanging over her head meant she could throw herself into the case without this added pressure. When reflecting on what had happened, she admitted she had been somewhat naive, though: 'I didn't realise how much of an undertaking it would be. I learnt to knuckle down and break it into pieces so that it didn't feel so daunting. Every time I received a letter from the tribunal or respondent, I would feel sick with worry; but the hardest part by far was the tribunal itself. I was totally out of my comfort zone and felt enormously intimidated – but you know what? You will be capable of far more than you realise.' Helen says she doesn't regret going it alone and felt that taking on this battle was the only way she could recover from such a traumatic experience – but the process is absolutely not for the faint-hearted, notwithstanding that any effective justice system should ensure vulnerable women who face discrimination receive the legal advice and support they need.

In February 2019, the country's top judge admitted that sexism in court is 'a significant feature which needs investigating'.[7] In 2018, Lady Hale, who was the president of the Supreme Court at the time, said that our white and male judiciary can seem like 'beings from another planet'.[8] Also in 2018, anonymous complaints emerged of unnamed judges making lewd, sexist and derogatory comments to female law professionals, including one allegation that a circuit judge had asked a trainee barrister what her favourite sex position was.[9] A string of complaints lodged with the Criminal Bar Association from female lawyers regarding the sexist behaviour of male judges led Chris Henley QC, then chair of the Criminal Bar Association, to say that talented women were leaving the profession, resulting in 'a crisis'. Joanna Hardy, a barrister at Red Lion Chambers in London, took to social media to say that male colleagues behaved as though they were on a 'stag do' when working with women lawyers.[10] With all this in mind, it will be of no surprise that Pregnant Then Screwed have also received a number of complaints from vulnerable women who felt victimised and undermined by the judge ruling on their case. Imagine taking a case to tribunal with no legal support because you've lost your job and have no money, while trying to teach yourself employment law as a new mum, then going to a hearing and being shouted at by the judge because everything isn't quite in the order they'd like it to be:

> 'I made a one-word error in my statement and the judge treated me as if I was a pariah. In fact, the judge treated me like an outsider all throughout the hearing, having little in-jokes with the respondent's solicitor.'

Even with the support of a barrister, I have received complaints from women who say the judge seemed entirely disinterested in their case and had little empathy:

'The preliminary hearing was shocking, honestly. My barrister was running late (no fault of her own) and we made it in with minutes to spare, which made us ever so slightly flustered. However, the judge was vile. Honestly, I couldn't have wished for a more textbook, sexist, Masonic butthead if I'd tried. He proceeded to wave my case papers around while spouting, "So, Mr Johnson, I believe I'm just as confused as you? So ... what? She's upset she has to reapply?" Mr Johnson was the employer's representative, who the judge couldn't help but backslap all the way through, even going as far as to, mid-hearing, ask him what his plans were for the afternoon! He consistently referred to me as "she" throughout, while waving his privileged old sausage-finger in my direction. Myself and my barrister were literally lost for words. Which is just as well because she could barely get a word in anyway. I spent most of my route home listening to Morrissey and inventing scenarios in my head of what would happen one day if I met that judge on an equal playing field.'

The whole legal process neglects to consider the chronic exhaustion that pregnant women and new mums often experience, and the impact this could be having on a mother and her baby. We know that stress can be damaging for an unborn child. A recent study published in the *British Journal of Psychiatry* said the children of women who experience severe stress when pregnant are seven times more likely to develop a personality disorder by age of 30. Even moderate prolonged stress may have an impact on child development, and there are few experiences more stressful than a legal battle with an employer who has every resource at their fingertips.[11]

'I was so certain I wanted to do something about the discrimination I had faced. I was doing it for other women,
for my daughter. The stress was out of this world. I was
crying every day and barely eating, even though I was
seven months pregnant by this point. I started getting
pains, and then there was bleeding. I knew it was affecting my health and the health of my baby, so I gave up. I
felt like a failure, like I had let other people down. My
baby was born with lots of health issues and none of the
doctors could tell me why. There was no discernible
reason and the doctors investigated all aspects of my
labour and birth. In the end, they said it was due to stress.'

In my case, the final nail in my justice coffin was the three-
month time limit. You have three months (less one day) to
submit a tribunal claim from the point that discrimination
occurs. This rule meant that I couldn't wait until my baby
was born, make sure he was healthy and then start tribunal
proceedings, because by then it would have been at least six
months since that fateful voicemail message. That said, a
tribunal does have the power to accept your submission after
the time limit has passed, but only if it is considered 'just and
equitable' to do so – basically a fancy way of saying 'if they
feel like it'. You also have to show that it wasn't reasonably
practicable to submit your claim earlier, which can be really
difficult to do, particularly if the issue was related to your
mental health. Pregnancy hormones can, at points, make
you feel completely bonkers – well, that was definitely my
experience. Tom, my partner, likes to remind me of the time
I fell out with him because he ate the last slice of his own
birthday cake. I was so livid that he had apparently not considered the hunger of his growing unborn child that I threw

all the cutlery off the counter in a hot rage and then sobbed on the cold tiled bathroom floor for the rest of the day. If you were to look through my Google search history during that phase of pregnancy, you would see regular searches for a local psychotherapist, explorations into whether I could start taking antidepressants while pregnant and panicked research as to why I didn't have morning sickness when every other pregnant woman seemed to have it (with two websites claiming that this meant I was going to give birth to a stupid child!). Four out of five women who responded to a 2017 survey by the Royal College of Obstetricians and Gynaecologists experienced at least one mental health issue during or after their pregnancy.[12] Low mood was experienced by over two-thirds of these women, anxiety by around half and depression by just over a third. We are putting women in the position of having to take on highly stressful tribunals when they are mentally and physically unable to. There is already a precedent in employment law for six months to raise a claim for equal pay or redundancy payment, while other areas of litigation have limitation periods of up to six years. Why does our judicial system place this unnecessary stress and burden on pregnant women and new mums? Could it be that they know it inhibits access to justice and they want to reduce the number of claims?

'I was working as a patient services manager with five years' experience of NHS strategic management. One of the consultant surgeons spotted my engagement ring and told me that I was not to have a baby. I found out I was pregnant a few years later. During advanced pregnancy, I found myself in the position of having to reapply for my own job and was unsuccessful. As a consequence of the stress, I became ill soon after the birth of my child and could not face the prospect of fighting my case. Once I started to feel mentally and physically well again, it was too late. I have never worked in the NHS since.'

Research conducted by Gorvins Solicitors has shown that 14 per cent of women who didn't raise a claim said that the time limit prevented them from doing so, but the response from the Government when Pregnant Then Screwed have repeatedly campaigned for an extension is that there is no proof that the three-month time limit is a barrier.[13] I mean, really. Either they think we're stupid or they've given fewer than eight seconds' thought to what it must be like for a mother of a brand-new baby to take legal action against a corporation.

In response to the Women and Equalities Select Committee's investigation into pregnancy and maternity discrimination, the then Minister for Small Business, Consumers and Corporate Responsibility, Margot James MP, said: 'The legal framework in place to protect pregnant women and new mothers from discrimination is strong. If women are discriminated against because they are pregnant or take time away to care for their baby, they have a legal means of redress.'[1] Sure, the 'legal means' exists, but not everyone has equal access to those means. Cillian Murphy exists but sadly that doesn't mean I get the same access to him as Yvonne McGuinness does. The justice system doesn't work for women, particularly women who are pregnant or have recently given birth, and the poorer you are, the further down the chain you sit and the less chance you have of ever accessing the justice you deserve.

I realise for women reading this who are currently experiencing discrimination it will feel like a lost cause – but it isn't. There are organisations out there working tirelessly to support women just like you, so don't give up yet. Here is what some women had to say who had been forced to take their employer to tribunal:

> 'In my opinion, win or lose, it is always worth holding a company accountable for their abysmal prejudice against working mums. It is brutal, but it's a small chapter in a moment of time.'

> 'It's a truly horrid process, but, if you win, or you agree a settlement and good reference, at least you can pick up your career again and have the confidence that you were right and they were wrong and they had to pay for it (quite literally). That does amazing things for you as a person and gives you the strength and confidence to jump back into your career.'

> 'It is impossible to articulate the unbelievable relief you feel when a judge rules in your favour. When you hear them say that you have been wronged, that your company should not have treated you that way. You are finally vindicated. You are finally free.'

Practical tips for judges

If you are a tribunal judge and you have bothered to read this book so you can get a better understanding of what it's like for women who face pregnancy or maternity discrimination, then drop me a note so I can buy you a pint. I wish there were more like you. Just in case it wasn't clear, these are the types of behaviours all judges should try to emulate:

1. Try to address the claimant by her name, rather than referring to her as 'she' as if she isn't in the room and only needs identifying by her gender.
2. Remember that, if someone represents themselves, it doesn't mean that they somehow have a miraculous understanding of employment law. The justice system is meant to work both for those who can afford a lawyer and those who can't. Be kind.
3. Don't attempt a humorous exchange of 'banter' with any of the lawyers, or anyone else in the room for that matter. You're not Judge Judy and this is not funny.

Practical tips for the Government

Stop pretending that just because the justice system exists everything is hunky dory. It is not.

Practical tips for you

If you are still in your job, are an employee (rather than a worker) and face some form of really shitty behaviour, then you should raise a formal grievance if it cannot be resolved informally. This sounds very fancy and intimidating but essentially it just involves a letter to your employer and HR setting out what has happened with enough detail to ensure they can investigate it properly. This should be followed up with a meeting and the company will decide if your grievance is upheld. The problem with the grievance system is that the people you are complaining to are employed by the company and their job is to protect the company from problems, so in some companies there is more chance of hell freezing over than your grievance being upheld. However, you need to go through this process to demonstrate to the company (and potentially a judge) that you are serious and that you tried your best to come to a formal agreement. Alongside this, register your complaint with the Advisory, Conciliation and Arbitration Service (ACAS). They are an independent public body, funded by the Government, that provides free and impartial advice to employers and employees on employment rights and tries to resolve workplace disputes. You may think there's no chance of resolving your dispute, but all claims should still go through ACAS before the legal process can properly start. Also, call the Pregnant Then Screwed legal advice line to make sure you are getting a second opinion. Keep your eye on the clock at all times – remember you only have three months, less one day, to raise a tribunal claim from the point that discrimination occurs. The formal grievance process does not stop the clock.

Taking a case to tribunal without legal support is tough – instead the best form of representation is a highly qualified, specialist employment lawyer (make sure you check out their credentials before instructing them), but it's a catch-22 because proper legal support can be very expensive, and the likelihood is you don't have bags of money to chuck around. A little-known trick is to check all your insurance documents (home insurance, car, mobile phone etc.) as you might find that your legal fees are completely covered – hallelujah! So, if you have insurance and you're facing a potential legal battle, get your paperwork out immediately and read the small print. If you're yet to get home insurance, then make sure you choose cover that includes your legal costs – it could literally save your sanity and your bank account. If you don't have insurance, then there are a few organisations that may be able to provide full tribunal support, including: Free Representation Unit, Advocate (weareadvocate.org.uk) and Citizens Advice Bureau. If you're lucky, you will live somewhere that has a law centre. Some law centres will offer tribunal support and/or support with preparing documents – go to lawcentres.org.uk to find one local to you. The Employment Tribunal Litigant in Person Support Scheme (ELIPS) has a bunch of volunteer barristers who can offer free help on the day of a hearing. Be aware that everything is massively oversubscribed, though.

You may be registered with a trade union. Unions exist to advance the interests of workers in the workplace. Research clearly shows that if you work for a company that recognises unions you are far less likely to be pushed out, made redundant or encounter negative treatment when pregnant, on maternity leave or when returning to work.[2] This is because those workplaces tend to be more likely to consider the statutory rights of pregnant women and new mums to be reasonable, but they will also be aware that you have representation should you require it. Having spent the past six years speaking to women who have faced pregnancy and maternity discrimination, I have to tell you honestly that the experience of union members is mixed. For some it is absolutely invaluable – they are able to address issues with their employer swiftly and professionally, with dedicated support, and they don't have to pay out fistfuls of cash. Others say they were given bum advice, told that they didn't have a legal case when they did, or encouraged to settle when they didn't want to. If you are a member of a trade union, then my suggestion would be to get a second opinion if you have any reservations about the information you are told. In any case, there are plenty of other benefits to joining a union, including better pay and better workplace rights. Unions are also brilliant at organising workers to fight for specific changes in their workplace.

If none of the above options work, or even if they do and you need some additional support, we run a tribunal mentor service at Pregnant Then Screwed. You can use the service whether you have legal representation or not. Our mentors are a bunch of brilliant humans who have each previously taken legal action against an employer due to pregnancy or maternity discrimination and they want to be there to support women going through the same ordeal. They will offer you a big, bosomy cuddle when you need it most, and they will be able to guide you through the various stages of your case.

Most maternity discrimination cases are based on 'injury to feelings', which has a minimum payout of £1,000 and a maximum payout of £42,000 (unless the circumstances are exceptional). There is a low, medium and high scale within this. You're likely to get a payout of £900–9,000 for cases such as the employer saying you can't attend your antenatal appointment or unfairly refusing a flexible-working request; you're likely to get a payout of £9,000–27,000 if you lost your job because of discrimination; and you're likely to get £27,000–47,000 where there has been a brutal and lengthy campaign of discrimination and harassment. In addition to injury to feelings, the tribunal will take into account any lost income if you have been sacked or made redundant, or if you missed out on a promotion. Most 'no win, no fee' solicitors will take 35 per cent (plus VAT) of whatever you secure at tribunal or from a settlement agreement.

During the process, the defendant, and their solicitors, can become quite aggressive. I've heard countless testimonies from women who were told they would have to pay the defendant's 'unlimited costs' for bringing the claim, should they lose – but rest assured that this is very uncommon. If you've got a good case and have followed the process properly, it is unlikely a judge would rule that you had to pay costs unless you have clearly lied, not cooperated or misled the tribunal. It's an intimidation tactic to put you off.

7

Gagged

'I was made redundant just seven weeks after our son was tragically stillborn. I was the only person to be made redundant from the all-male leadership team and a department of over 1,500 colleagues. I had worked there for over ten years. My boss said that he was under pressure to cost-save, particularly among the leadership team, but why did they choose me? Why was I the only one to go? Still in the midst of desperate grief and being quite unwell, I signed a non-disclosure agreement and took the money, something that I will regret for the rest of my life.'

I doubt many people had heard of a non-disclosure agreement (NDA) until Harvey Weinstein's big beastly face filled every TV channel. A preposterously powerful man had been using these legal weapons with impunity to gag and silence the women he sexually assaulted. It had been going on for decades, leaving women's lives and careers in tatters. Once the first, clandestine clasp had been unlocked, it was like a domino effect as survivor after survivor came forward to share their traumatic experience of alleged assault at the hands of this vile and arrogant human. During the court case, in which he was convicted, he said, 'I'm totally confused,' and obviously he would be.[3] Non-disclosure agreements are meant to silence the victim while ensuring those with power and money have full exemption.

This wasn't just a problem in the States, though – something many British women were very much aware of. Our laws give the rich and the powerful the authority to blackmail people into silence. Behind the closed doors of corporations, universities, local councils and the British Government, non-disclosure agreements or confidentiality clauses are used with impunity to facilitate appalling behaviour and ensure the protection of those with prestige and privilege.

An NDA forms part of a settlement agreement between employer and employee. It is a legal contract intended to protect trade secrets and intellectual property but is now commonly used to hide wrongdoing. If an employee encounters discrimination and then kicks up a stink, it is likely they will be offered a settlement agreement – a lump of cash to shut them up and make them go away. This agreement will contain a confidentiality clause, preventing the employee from talking to others about what has happened to them, ensuring the company and those involved are never exposed. It sweeps their abhorrent behaviour under the rug, hiding it from the press, customers and colleagues. These agreements can be so all-encompassing that they prevent you from speaking about what has happened to anyone besides your lawyer, your spouse and your therapist.

The employer chalks it up as a business expense, a type of insurance they have to pay so they can continue to behave in any way they see fit without the morality police breathing down their neck. If the employee breaks this legally binding agreement, they may be prosecuted and forced to pay back every penny, plus more. Once the agreement is signed, the employer makes a quick BACS transfer and carries on as before – while the employee tries to weather the mental and financial repercussions of discrimination and of being forced out of a career they have likely spent years developing. They live with this dirty secret, one that obligates them to lie to friends and future employers about what really happened behind those closed doors.

'Signing an NDA took away my voice. I had to leave a job I had been in for ten years, and all because I had a baby. I felt like I was the one to blame. Previous colleagues would ask me why I left – I couldn't tell them, even though they were aware of the discrimination (it was very blatant). Friends and family ask me what happened, and I can't tell them a thing. I feel completely disempowered. I was a victim of discrimination and the NDA made me feel like it was my fault. My employer walked away with no repercussions and yet my life changed for ever.'

We don't know how commonly NDAs are used because, by their very nature, they're not disclosed to anyone. What we do know is that they are used in politics, with figures revealing that the House of Commons has spent more than £2.4 million forcing people to keep their mouths shut over the past five years.[4] They are also used regularly in UK universities, with the BBC obtaining figures that show approximately £87 million was spent on payoffs attached to NDAs between January 2017 and April 2019,[5] including some 300 students who signed an NDA after they complained about everything from sexual assault to bullying.[6] We also know that some charities aren't averse to using a non-disclosure agreement to hide whatever it is that's going on in their place of work. *The Guardian* discovered that the Alzheimer's Society had spent a whopping £750,000 on NDAs, and whistle-blowers accused the charity of allowing a culture of bullying within the charity to persist.[7]

As mentioned in Chapter 5, 1,814 tribunal claims were brought against employers due to pregnancy, parental rights and maternity issues between 1 February 2019 and 3 November 2021. The names of the company and claimant are listed on the Government website.[8] The majority of these cases are suddenly dropped before they receive a court ruling. According to *The Times*, more than 60 per cent of work discrimination claims are dropped before a judge can rule on them.[9] It could be that the victim ran out of funds or the stress became too much, or maybe they decided they didn't have a case for discrimination, but the likelihood is that most of those listed cases disappear due to pressure to settle the claim, and, when you settle, you usually sign away your right to speak. The companies listed as having claims brought against them that were subsequently dropped by the claimant before they reached tribunal include: Asda, West Yorkshire Police, Barclays, HSS Hire Service Group, Arcadia Group, Wagamama, the Home Office, HM Revenue & Customs (HMRC), British Gas, Marks & Spencer, Tesco, Holland & Barrett, Adecco, David Lloyd Clubs, the DVLA, Goldman Sachs, Sainsbury's, Amazon, John Lewis, Santander, Kurt Geiger, Bupa Global, Pret A Manger, Brewdog, HBOS, the Ministry of Defence, IBM, Small Wonders Nursery Ltd (which is by no means the only nursery listed), Sports Direct, William Hill, HSBC, Estée Lauder, Unilever UK,

Morrisons, Vodafone, Lord of the Pies and Carlsberg (because if Carlsberg did maternity discrimination . . .).

These are the cases that almost made it to tribunal. The majority of discrimination cases don't get that far, so no record of them exists. I know of well-known companies, household brands that win awards for their dedication to gender equality, that behind closed doors kick women out of their job as soon as a pregnancy is announced, and while she is confused and vulnerable they say, 'Here's some cash and a good reference as long as you sign this agreement. If you don't sign now, you'll get nothing.' No one knows how frequently this happens because there's no central record of it anywhere. The person signing the NDA won't know whether they're the only victim of this callous treatment by their employer or if there's a procession of other victims that have passed before them.

Danielle Ayres, a senior employment lawyer at Gorvins Solicitors, deals with thousands of NDAs. She says: 'Some companies who face a serious claim that could trigger reputational damage will do their utmost to ensure a settlement is reached before any tribunal claim is submitted. In these situations, they simply want the problem to go away, so they think a settlement agreement with a confidentiality clause is the only way to protect their business.' This fierce drive to settle the case so it doesn't hit the headlines can mean some employers play dirty:

> 'I felt bullied, victimised and harassed. I was backed into a corner when I was vulnerable. I cried a lot and felt like a failure because I wasn't strong enough to argue – and I work in human resources, so I understood my legal rights.'

'I was made to agree to things I didn't agree with. Things were said about me in that NDA that weren't true. Prior to signing the agreement, I was made to feel like I wasn't pulling my weight or doing my job properly, even though I had been successfully running a department for many years. To this day, I can't bring myself to read that NDA again.'

'I felt I was given no choice, no other option, no recourse. I couldn't talk to other colleagues in the same situation – we were all bound and gagged by the same NDA and the fear that if we didn't follow their orders we might lose the small pittance we had to pay our mortgage that month.'

Some women describe signing an NDA as feeling as though you're trapped, cornered by your employer and legal professionals; there's no escape. They wear you down with bullying tactics, suggesting that if you don't sign then they won't give you a good reference, so you'll never get another job. In December 2018, we ran a survey to better understand what's happening to the women who sign NDAs after experiencing pregnancy or maternity discrimination, as no other research on this topic existed. The results from 260 women showed that more than 90 per cent felt signing an NDA was their only option. A shocking 70 per cent of respondents said they felt signing the NDA had a negative impact on their mental health.[1]

'When I told my boss I was pregnant, he suggested I have an abortion. He said having a baby would ruin my career. He took clients away from me and made vile comments about my weight gain and my ability now that I had "baby brain". He started giving elements of my job to a more junior, male employee. It was clear what was going on. In the end, he said that I wouldn't be welcome back after maternity and offered six months' pay and a good reference if I signed an NDA. I was heavily pregnant and being legally blackmailed. I signed the NDA and left quietly. It has been over a year and there isn't a day that goes by when I don't feel angry and hurt. Who knows if I will ever get my career back on track, but at the moment it feels impossible.'

The real issue for these women is that they sign an NDA to make it all go away; they are desperate for the anguish to end so that they can fully immerse themselves in the life-changing experience of new motherhood. But many come to realise that signing an NDA doesn't make it all go away – on the contrary, it can mean that they're never able to deal with it. The trauma of the discrimination hangs over them like a dark cloud, affecting their relationships, their career and their confidence. It's a secret they're forced to keep, as if they should be ashamed, and that can play havoc with your mental health. In the words of Zelda Perkins, who was forced to sign an NDA by Harvey Weinstein: 'You can't own your own trauma.'

The constant worry that you might slip up and say the wrong thing to the wrong person can be overwhelming. The terms of an NDA can be so aggressive that women live with the almost constant fear that the employer will be coming after them if they slip up, dragging them through another brutal court process and forcing them to pay enormous sums of money due to breach of contract. Many feel tormented that they have let other women down because they didn't fight, thereby allowing the employer to cover their tracks. This was echoed by the Women and Equalities Select Committee, which conducted a consultation into the use of NDAs. The committee reported: 'We were struck by the fear, anger and raw emotion that witnesses expressed and still felt about their experience years – even decades – after signing an NDA.'[2]

The problem is that you can't get rid of non-disclosure agreements. You'd think the solution would be pretty straightforward: let people settle out of court, sure, but make gagging clauses illegal. However, if you abolish gagging clauses you leave women even more vulnerable – firstly, because many of the women actually *want* anonymity to ensure the issue doesn't affect their future job prospects; secondly, because, without gagging clauses, fewer companies would settle out of court. Why would they bother? A settlement agreement ensures they can avoid public scrutiny. The gagging clause is the gnarly carrot; without it, there is nothing to prevent the claimant from exposing them, so they may as well go to tribunal and hope they get a sympathetic judge who lets them off. The NDA silences the woman while protecting the company. It's a process of buying the victim's silence. In return, the woman receives some money so that she can pay her rent and put food on the table while she licks her wounds. Without NDAs, the only option available to women is an employment tribunal, and we all know what a really shitty option that is.

That's not to say that more can't be done, and indeed should be. Companies should be held accountable if they use NDAs regularly to mask discriminatory behaviour, and we need a way to break the silence if we are to improve the outlook for future generations of women in work. If we allow this cloak of silence to continue, then nothing will change. You can't fix a culture of discrimination if you don't know the extent of the problem. We also need a way to identify patterns of abhorrent behaviour. If there is one bad apple within a company (such as Harvey Weinstein) who is using their power and authority to intimidate, harass and crush the careers of others, then we need to know about it. This is why I believe it is imperative that an independent body is established to whom the use of NDAs can be reported to by the employee. After a number of complaints, the independent body should have the power to investigate and implement sanctions should the behaviour continue.

Gagging clauses may be the weapon of choice for some employers, but in reality there is little evidence that if you break an NDA anything will happen to you. From my research, I cannot find a single case where an employer has taken someone to court for breaking a non-disclosure agreement if it had been used to cover up wrongdoing. If you decide you want to tell the press what happened and know that the story will receive good coverage in the media, the likelihood of the employer making the problem worse for themselves by dragging you through court due to breach of contract is slim. I'm certainly not encouraging you to drop everything and call the tabloids immediately. I'm just saying that the fear they purposefully instil in you shouldn't weigh on your shoulders as heavily as it probably does. On a particularly wistful day, I like to daydream of the moment when every mother who has signed a gagging clause decides to break it at exactly the same time. It would be like #MeToo on speed.

In the wake of the whistle being blown on Harvey

Weinstein, the #MeToo movement exploded across the world. It was bittersweet for so many women as the silence was shattered around workplace sexual harassment and bullying. We were reminded of the discomfort, the feelings of guilt, our own vulnerability, but we were also emboldened to speak about our experiences in the hope that future generations would not be subjected to similar vile behaviour. For a short while there was hope that it would all come crashing down, that gagging clauses would cease to exist, that a new wave of transparency and morality would dominate, but those hopes eventually fizzled away. The #MeToo movement can only do so much if it constantly butts up against gagging clauses. These legalised weapons are of ultimate importance to the rich and the powerful – they will not relinquish control of them easily.

Change is triggered by stories. They are the root of a revolution. We don't know how many mothers have been silenced by these legal agreements, but we do know that this silence prevents change from happening while protecting the powerful. The women who face pregnancy or maternity discrimination deserve the dignity of being able to tell their story. They deserve the dignity of being heard.

What to do if you're offered a settlement agreement

A settlement agreement is only binding if you have received independent legal advice, so it's worth asking your employer to pay your legal costs for the agreement to be looked over. The standard cost for this is around £350. The lawyer you instruct should be able to explain to you exactly what the settlement means; who you can, and who you cannot, talk to about your experience; how much cash you will get; whether your employer has agreed to give you a reference; and what the terms are and whether it's a good deal – taking into consideration your claim, or claims, and what rights you are being asked to waive.

You may wonder whether they're offering you enough cash: your lawyer should be able to advise what your case is worth based on a mixture of factors including injury to feelings and, if you are no longer employed, how long you have been employed and how much you have ended up out of pocket. You also need to decide if what the employer is offering is enough to keep you going for the duration of time you are likely to be unemployed (if you're not still working for the company). Generally, the first £30,000 of compensation is not subject to tax or an employee's National Insurance contributions, while payments made over £30,000 are subject to tax.

Remember that a settlement agreement is negotiable, and you may not want to sign it at all. If you do, these are the things you might want to negotiate:

- A clause that stipulates that you will receive a good reference for future employment.
- An agreement as to what the announcement will be to staff and clients about your departure.
- Assurance that all your payments and benefits will be covered by the company – e.g. car allowance, private health cover, accrued holidays, pension etc. You may want to consider asking for an extension to your private health cover or company car as part of the settlement agreement.

- You may want to include additional people you can tell the truth to. You may also want to agree how you communicate what happened with a future employer.

8

Cheer Up, It Might Never Happen

Okay, enough of the depressing stuff. All of this sounds like we're doomed, right? As I'm writing this, I'm imaging pregnant women weeping into their non-alcoholic beers, feeling like there's no hope. The good news is that there is hope. There are some absolutely cracking employers out there who really get why it's important to look after their staff and go out of their way to do so. Here are just a few of the wonderful stories I've heard over the years:

> 'My work has been so supportive and my manager (male) is extremely happy for me and my growing family. I've been incredibly sick over the past seven weeks and I've barely worked as a result, but it hasn't been a problem. I was told to take as much time as I needed to get better.'

> 'I was scared to tell my boss I was pregnant with baby number three as I had only been back at work for four months after having baby number two. I told her I was

worried about my career and she said, "Why? You can have a family and a career, you know."'

'My boss and HR team have been incredibly supportive through both of my pregnancies. My boss was always getting me a glass of water or a cup of tea, making sure I was sitting down (I do events), and he was always available to discuss things. I left him in the lurch the weekend before a big and important event as I felt so unwell and exhausted, and he just said, "Don't worry. Take a week off, speak soon and stay off emails."'

'I was eight weeks pregnant and had hyperemesis when I started a new job on a fixed-term contract. My husband begged me not to tell them I was pregnant and to leave it as long as possible, but I wanted to be honest, so I told them on my first day. They couldn't have been nicer. I worked for six months before I went on maternity leave, had my contract extended while on maternity leave, and chose what days and how many hours I wanted to do when I returned.'

'I returned from maternity leave and one week later my boss offered me a pay rise and a promotion, which I gladly accepted. He said he wanted to show me how much he values me and my work.'

Then there are the high-profile good-news stories, like when Jess Brammar was promoted to the top job at *HuffPost* while seven months pregnant; or there's always Jacinda Ardern, who was prime minister of New Zealand when she gave birth, and, though she encountered many who took issue with a woman becoming a mother while holding the most important position in the country, her global popularity was clear for all to see. She is the only world leader to have dealt with a terrorist attack, a deadly volcanic eruption and a global pandemic all while parenting an under two-year-old. Never one to sugarcoat parenting, she openly discussed the challenges of potty training while simultaneously dealing with a pandemic, shared a picture of herself with nappy cream on her blazer just before she attended an important meeting with world leaders, and has been honest and frank about wrestling with mum guilt.

What employers are yet to cotton on to is how maternity leave is a breeding ground for learning and development. If you were to place a manual of all the skills a good manager needs to have next to all the skills a person develops while they parent, you would see there are some very striking similarities.

Valeria Leonardi is an adviser at Life Based Value, a company that specialises in transforming life experiences into business skills. After she gave birth to her two children, Valeria became acutely aware of the skills she was developing while parenting and how useful this expertise would be to her professionally. She did an MBA and entitled her dissertation 'Parenting skills and their impact on business leadership development', and discovered that parenting was an incredibly effective training programme for the development of the following:

1. **Personal attributes:**
- Efficiency
- Emotional intelligence
- Tolerance
- Patience
- Learning-agility
- Intuitiveness

2. Communication
- Giving individual attention
- Giving and receiving feedback
- Reading non-verbal cues

3. Developmental
- Mentoring
- Enabling others to become independent in their work
- Motivating others

4. Organisation/management
- Prioritisation
- Increased productivity
- Effective delegation
- Switching off from work-related tasks, thereby recharging

Funnily enough, this sounds like the sort of training course a business would spend an absolute fortune on to upskill their staff so that they have the necessary attributes for good leadership. Listen up, employers: why not save your cash and just start making your workplace the best it can be for working parents?

But don't just take Valeria's word for it, because researchers have also found that mothers make exceptional employees. A recent study from the Federal Reserve Bank of St Louis found that, over the course of a thirty-year career, mothers outperformed women without children at almost every stage of the game. In fact, mothers with at least two kids were the most productive of all.[3] Researchers from Clark University and the Center for Creative Leadership in Greensboro found that parents – at least, those committed to family life – perform better in the office. Research director Marian N. Ruderman said the reason is that 'Parents learn to multitask, handle stress and negotiate.'[4]

Then Microsoft did some research on their employees and found that almost two-thirds of working mothers believe they've become better at doing more than one thing at a time at work since having kids.[5] Of course they have. If you've ever had to repeatedly deter an energetic toddler from kamikazeing off the top of a climbing frame while breastfeeding a baby and simultaneously working out what you're all going to have for dinner (I have), then you know how gifted we are at multitasking (while remaining serenely calm – well, mostly).

A study published in the *Journal of Social Issues* found that both mothers and fathers were perceived as warmer than their childless counterparts – a rather useful characteristic in any form of work that involves customers, building relationships or working in a team (*racks brain for any job that doesn't fit this description*).[6] To be fair, it's probably because they're so relieved to be at work, mixing with other actual adults, and anything feels easy when you've spent your days caring for a precocious and, let's face it, often savage, toddler.

I asked working mums what skills they felt motherhood has taught them, and here are just some of the responses:

'I no longer procrastinate and leave things to the last minute, because in that last minute a child will get sick or there'll be a snow day, or you'll lose half the night looking for medium-sized dog (my son's favourite toy). I'm now that person who is the most organised in our department and hits deadlines days before they're due.'

'I keep seeing all of these young, trendy businesses talking about "pivoting". Honey, until you've performed the seventeen distraction techniques needed to get a toddler fed, dressed and out of the house, don't even *think* of telling me you can pivot.'

'I can smile the world's biggest smile when I feel like I want to cry inside. I can function perfectly well on almost no sleep, something *Business Insider* seems to insist entrepreneurs must do to be successful. I have tenacity the likes of which you will not see anywhere else, as demonstrated by my 16-year-old having attended 100 per cent of his final school year despite not getting out of bed voluntarily on a SINGLE BASTARD DAY.'

'I think what it has given me is an allergic reaction to time-wasting. Motherhood demands an efficient mindset.'

'Negotiation skills and patience: I spend so much time persuading my toddler to come around to my opinion, work is easy in comparison!'

'I can pack a bag in my head for an event that's not happening for another 12 hours. I can manage programmes that cover every eventuality including, but not limited to, everyone and everything being caked in poo. I can grate cheese one-handed. I can exercise patience and understanding on astronomical levels (which I demonstrated when my lovely husband told me he was "knackered" immediately after I'd pushed out a 10lb baby). I can detect hazards on the minutest scale. Finally – and, for me, most importantly – I know my limits. I recognise early signs of stress or tiredness and know the importance of acting on them before it effects my flow; I am more in tune with my instincts and know exactly when to trust them.'

'Ultra-efficient! Every day that I go to work is 10–12 hours away from my son. I wanted to be a mother so that I could nurture, care, love and contribute an amazing and compassionate little human to the world, but working full-time means that for 40 hours a week someone else is doing that job. So, I'll make damn sure that for those 40 hours I'm on fire. I maximise each ten-hour day because otherwise the sacrifice of time away from him would not be worth it. I have an inner force that seems to make even the impossible tasks somehow possible as I'm doing it for this little person.'

If employers and the Government want women to be employed – and I am sure they do, with income tax from women's employment contributing 47.6 billion to the UK economy in 2016–17 – then they need to figure out how we can make our workplaces work for women.[7] We hear a lot about how maternity leave inconveniences employers, and I am not unsympathetic to some of the challenges posed by replacing someone on a temporary basis, but pregnancy is a normal condition of employment, just like illness or family obligations, and it must be treated as such. Pregnant women and mothers are not an expensive, distracted, uncommitted burden to business; we are talented, dedicated, multitasking ninjas. With a bit of thoughtfulness and care, you might be lucky enough to retain our freshly refined skill and expertise within your company.

Making it work

If you're on PAYE, here is some information about your rights that should help you during pregnancy and new motherhood at work. (If you're self-employed, there's more detail on your rights in Chapter 13.) Note: this was correct at the time of writing in 2020, but things change, and, given that I am writing these words while in lockdown due to a global pandemic, I expect there will be quite a few changes on the horizon, so please do double check the government or Pregnant Then Screwed websites for updates.

1. **Automatic year off**
   Your employer should assume you'll be taking 52 weeks' leave, unless you tell them you'd like to take less. But don't worry: if you planned to take a full year but miss work so much that you need to go back earlier, all you need to do is give eight weeks' notice of when you want to return.

2. **Time off for your antenatal appointments**
   If you need to go to an antenatal appointment during work time, you have the legal right to do so without loss of pay – and you don't need to book time off or use annual leave, no matter how much your boss face-aches about it. The time you're allowed should include the time needed to travel to the clinic or GP. And don't forget, you don't always have to attend the appointments alone – fathers and partners are also entitled to unpaid time off for up to two antenatal appointments.

3. **If you're made redundant while on maternity leave**

   Maternity leave, those glorious months when you're trying to figure out how to keep a new human alive on no sleep while picking bits of poo out of your hair, is possibly the worst time to be dealing with work problems, so if you are made redundant during this period it can be completely overwhelming. You do have options, however, even if it feels like you don't. If a suitable alternative vacancy exists, your employer has to offer it to you before they offer it to any other employee. You do not have to go into your workplace for an interview or assessment procedures for any suitable vacancy if you are on maternity leave. These protections also apply if you are on adoption leave or Shared Parental Leave. Speak to HR and be clear on your rights, and that you expect them to be upheld. If they mess you about, you may have a legal case for discrimination so call the Pregnant Then Screwed free advice line.

4. **You're still an employee, the whole time you are on maternity leave**

   Although your colleagues may do that annoying thing of making out like maternity leave is a holiday, or, worse, suggesting that they won't see you again now that you've had a baby, you are still an employee and your company must treat you as such. That means that they mustn't discriminate against you by failing to consider you for opportunities such as a promotion or a pay rise while on maternity leave. Additionally, you still have a right to your holiday allowance. Everyone with a full-time job on PAYE has a legal right to 28 days' paid annual leave, whether they're on maternity leave or not. You will accrue this holiday entitlement while on maternity leave, and you can use it as you wish. Some tag it onto the end of their maternity leave and others use the days to help stagger their return to work.

5. **You can do up to ten 'keeping in touch' days**
These can be an absolute lifesaver for those who feel like they've lost an arm when they first head off on maternity leave. 'Keeping in touch' days are a chance for you to stay in the loop at work and to have regular catch-ups with your manager. On the flip side, you may not want to think about work at all when you're off, never mind step into the office, and that's absolutely fine, too – it's your decision; you're not legally obliged to attend these days and your employer isn't legally obliged to offer them. If you and your employer decide that 'keeping in touch' days are the way to go, you can request to be paid for them (by law your employer must pay at least minimum wage, but you should expect to receive your usual rate of pay).

6. **Telling your boss the big news**
When to tell your boss is a question I am regularly asked, and the truth is that there is no right or wrong answer to this. What I usually say is that if you have even the slightest inkling that it will impact your job, then wait as long as you can. For example, if you're up for a promotion I probably wouldn't tell them until the promotion is in the bag. I also wouldn't mention it at interview stage. Pregnancy shouldn't factor into their

decision, and telling them could cloud their judgement. The way I see it, not telling them is the fairest thing to do for everyone concerned. Apart from that: you should tell your boss the good news when you feel it is right for you. Saying the words out loud can feel very weird, and naturally you might be anxious about the implications on your career. Don't put it off for *too* long, though: legally you should tell your employer that you are pregnant by the fifteenth week before your baby is due. Hopefully they won't be a total dick and say something like: 'Well, I *thought* you'd put on weight.' If they do say that, send me a message and I'll pop a dog poo through their letterbox.

7. All employers should carry out a workplace risk assessment

A risk assessment is good for the employer and employee. As a pregnant employee or a returning mum, you're not an inconvenience and your workplace must be a safe place for you and your baby. Your employer has a legal obligation to keep you safe and a risk assessment helps them to do that. If you reasonably believe that your workplace is not a safe place for you and your baby, then you can refuse to go into work until your employer has rectified the problem while you continue to be paid as normal – this is Section 44 of the Employment Rights Act 1996 (look it up). If you are returning to work and you are breastfeeding, then you should write to your employer to let them know before your first day back. It can feel weird talking about boobs to your boss, but don't be embarrassed about breastfeeding and needing to express – you're doing it so you can keep a human alive. Make sure you are listened to and provided a suitable place to do it – note to employers: that is not the toilet.

8. **You are protected from discrimination from day one**
You can claim discrimination and unfair dismissal on the grounds of pregnancy and maternity leave from day one of your employment. Don't believe the hype that you have to have worked somewhere for two years to have any rights – it just isn't the case. You can even claim for discrimination before employment: if you go for an interview and some douchebag asks you if you want children, or if you are married, or asks whether you are pregnant they have broken the law and you may have a case for discrimination. If you feel you have been sacked, made redundant, bullied, harassed, demoted or overlooked for promotion or other opportunities because of your pregnancy, or because you will be taking, or have taken, maternity leave, then you may have a legal case. Don't feel like you're on your own and don't think this is your fault. It is not. Thousands of women have, unfortunately, been in your shoes.

9. **Returning to your job**
Leaving your job to go on maternity leave can feel very strange. All kinds of thoughts will probably be running through your head about your return. So, here's what you need to know: if you return to work within 26 weeks, you have the legal right to return to *exactly* the same job, contractual terms and salary as before. If you

return to work after 26 weeks but before the maximum 52 weeks of your maternity leave, then you are entitled to return to exactly the same job, contractual terms and salary, unless your employer can prove that it is not practicable to give you your job back. In this scenario, your employer must offer you a suitable alternative on the same salary and contractual terms as before. If you are placed in a different job or you are offered different shift patterns, you should get legal advice straight away no matter how long your maternity leave was.

10. **When sickness gets in the way**

With all the will in the world, when it comes to your return date, life can simply get in the way, and if your kids are at a nursery it is likely they will hoover up every single illness known to man and kindly dish it out to the whole family. If you are ill and unable to go into work when you had agreed to, don't panic and don't feel guilty – it's not your fault and people get sick. Any illness after maternity leave should now follow your employer's normal sickness reporting procedures. If your child is sick, then you have a right to take emergency leave for dependants. This may be unpaid, depending on your employer's policy. If your manager refuses to allow you the time off or they try to discipline you for taking it, then call the Pregnant Then Screwed help line.

11. **Funding your maternity leave**

Finances can get pretty tight during maternity leave. Statutory Maternity Pay is paid for 39 weeks of your leave to women who qualify for it and earn at least

£120 a week. To be eligible for SMP you must have worked for your employer continuously for at least six months by the time you are 25 weeks pregnant (or, more specifically, for at least 26 weeks in the fifteenth week before your baby is due). Your employer pays it to you and then claims most or all of it back from HM Revenue & Customs (HMRC). You can get it even if you do not plan to go back to work or you are dismissed or made redundant after the twenty-sixth week of pregnancy, and you do not have to pay any SMP back if you do not return to work. If you get enhanced maternity pay from your employer, then the likelihood is they will have slipped something in to your contract that says if you don't return to work for six months, or maybe more, then you will be expected to repay the money that is over and above SMP. Just be sure you really do have every intention of returning before you spend that extra cash, or you could get yourself in a right old pickle.

How much is SMP?

For the first six weeks, you get 90 per cent of your average pay. After that, you're paid £151.97 per week (this will increase in April 2022), or 90 per cent of your average earnings if this is lower, for 33 weeks.

Maternity Allowance

If you are not entitled to SMP, then you may be entitled to Maternity Allowance (MA) – for example, if you are self-employed, or you are employed and are earning less than £120 a week, or started a new job while pregnant – which you can claim if you have been employed or self-employed for at least 26 of the 66 weeks before the expected week of childbirth and you can find 13 weeks (not necessarily in a row) in which you earned more than £30 per week, on average. If you qualify, then the highest rate MA is paid at is £151.97 per week (as with SMP, this will increase in April 2022), or 90 per cent of your average pay if this is lower, for 39 weeks.

Discrimination

If you feel you are currently experiencing pregnancy or maternity discrimination, then I suggest you do the following:

- Firstly, if you feel able to, I would suggest you confront it head on. Say to your employer why you feel that you are being treated unfairly – sometimes open dialogue can nip it in the bud. The majority of employers don't necessarily mean to discriminate; they just let their unconscious bias run wild or they panic, and, rather than asking the pregnant employee what she wants or needs, they avoid her and quite quickly the communication between employee and employer deteriorates. Addressing the issue in an open and collaborative way, telling them what it is you need, can break the ice, but it also very clearly says: don't fuck with me.
- Document absolutely everything – make detailed notes of exactly what was said, at what time, on what date and by whom. Where you can, get the

information in writing; ask people to confirm what they have said by email. Take people into meetings with you if that's an option.

• Call the Pregnant Then Screwed legal helpline and we'll talk you through what to do next.

9

Childcare Is Infrastructure

I arranged to meet Rachel for a mug of hot tea in a hipster café in Manchester one Wednesday afternoon. She had long curly auburn hair, sparkling bright-blue eyes and a fidgety toddler attached to her calf. Rachel had messaged me after I'd been ranting on social media about the many challenges our childcare system poses for families. I do this a lot. We hugged our mugs of tea while her daughter gobbled down a sticky chocolate brownie, and I asked Rachel to tell me the story of how our childcare system had ruined her career.

Rachel had been working as a production manager for five years. She was responsible for the technical management and control of various industrial production processes; a job that sounded so complex and specialised that I honestly had no idea what she was talking about when she tried to explain it to me, so I just nodded politely. She had developed an enviable level of knowledge and skill in the industry and she was highly respected by her colleagues, who were predominantly male. After she had her daughter and returned to work, she was told that flexible working wasn't an option. This meant she had to secure childcare for her daughter from 7 a.m. until 6 p.m. each day, thereby increasing the already extortionate childcare fees as she had to pay extra for an early start. After childcare costs, Rachel's take-home pay was £25 per month. TWENTY-FIVE POUNDS a month for working 52 hours a week. She was exhausted, she missed her daughter dreadfully, and she was flat broke.

With tears in her eyes, she handed in her letter of resignation after six months of trying to make it work, waving goodbye to the five years she had invested in her career. She now has a part-time job in a Wetherspoon's. She works half the hours but can organise the time so that she and her husband rely much less on childcare and her take-home pay is now £200 a month. When I asked her if she thought she had made the right decision, she looked me dead in the eye and said: 'What would you do if you had the option to work fewer hours, see your daughter much more and bring home more money?' I thought about her question for all of two seconds: 'I would do exactly what you did,' I replied.

Childcare is infrastructure. It's as important as roads and hospitals and power supplies. Without access to good-quality, affordable childcare, we are left with two potential outcomes: either we stop parents from working or we stop humans from procreating. I'm going to say something totally radical and suggest that neither is helpful. If we make it impossible for parents to work, then our economy goes down the swanny, and, as I am writing this, mid-pandemic, when our economy has just shrunk by 20 per cent[1] and the Organisation for Economic Co-operation and Development (OECD) has said that the UK economy will likely take the world's biggest hit, I think we're probably going to need all hands on deck if we have any hope of a relatively swift recovery.

Meanwhile, if we stop procreating, we're creating a huge problem for the future; there will be no one to keep our economy ticking over when we're old and infirm. Everything will descend into total chaos, pensions will cease to exist, and there will be thousands of unwiped wrinkly bottoms. Try not to think about that too much.

Whenever I talk about childcare, some clever clogs will inevitably say, 'Why should my taxes pay for your lifestyle choice?' – as if having a baby is the ultimate act of narcissism and self-indulgence, like a day trip to a fancy spa, rather than it being the reproduction of the human race. Ensuring our children are well cared-for in those early years has positive benefits for everyone. It has an immediate benefit because it means that parents can go to work, improving our economy, decreasing poverty and reducing our reliance on benefits; and it has a long-term benefit because good-quality, accessible childcare reduces the inequality gap. Really high-quality early years provision has a profound effect on child development and school readiness, particularly for children in areas of deprivation.[2] Affordable, good-quality childcare is an investment in our future, and studies show that there is a positive return on that investment, both economically and socially.[3]

The trouble is that the current system in the UK is not fit for purpose. It is extortionately expensive, and the quality is rapidly deteriorating.[4] That's not because those who work in childcare don't care about children and have a penchant for bleeding parents dry, it's because, unlike other countries, our childcare system is privatised and grotesquely underfunded. Providers struggle to maintain a decent standard of care with the money available. Schemes dubbed as 'free childcare', such as the Government's 30 hours free from the age of three, are not free at all, and the subsidy provided by the Government doesn't cover the provider's costs. This forces the childcare facilities to decrease their overheads, while increasing the cost for younger children to attend, and to find other ways to make up the shortfall, such as charging for 'extras' like food and nappies.

In 2018 The Early Years Alliance filed a Freedom of Information request to the Department of Education asking for the Government's calculations when they implemented the 30 hours 'free' scheme. After a two-and-a-half-year battle, those calculations were finally released in June 2021. It revealed that the Government was knowingly underfunding the scheme by £2.60 per child per hour. Not only that but the Government knew that the proposed funding levels for the 30 hours 'free' scheme would lead to increased costs for parents of younger children.[5] In December 2020, ministers further cut funding to the childcare sector right in the middle of a pandemic.[6] Between 1 January 2021 and 31 July 2021 the Government's own figures showed a net loss of almost 3,000 childcare providers.[7]

Katherine Wright owns a nursery in Kirkley. She told me that she gets paid more money cleaning toilets than she does caring for children; despite it being her own business, she has a second job to ensure she can survive financially. Her nursery is in an area of high deprivation, and many of the parents and their children are facing particular challenges such as homelessness and drug addiction. Some of the children are also on the child-protection list. This means that Katherine is weighed down with reports to complete and meetings she has to attend, none of which are funded. 'I'm very worried about what the future holds,' she sighed, 'but I need my nursery to stay open for the sake of the children.' And this was before the pandemic hit, creating further economic challenges for childcare providers.

Childminders are finding it almost impossible to continue under the current funding regime. They offer fewer places than nurseries, so have less opportunity to make up the shortfall from parent fees. Ofsted statistics show that there were 9,500 fewer childminders in November 2019 than there were in 2015.[8] The way the Government subsidy works benefits much larger conglomerates, working on a large scale, while penalising the independent and individual operators.[9] Busy Bees, the biggest nursery chain in the country with 360 sites across the UK, was bought by a Canadian company for £220 million in 2013 and has now expanded into Europe and beyond.[10] All is fair in love and capitalism, right? But what happens if the company goes bust? It's a prospect that isn't beyond the realms of possibility and recently happened to the largest nursery chain in Australia, ABC. Provision in the UK is already low. The Childcare Survey 2020 revealed that only 60 per cent of local authorities have enough childcare across all their areas for children under two, while only 32 per cent of local authorities had enough after-school-club care for 5–11-year-olds.[11] If a big nursery chain were to go bust, this would leave thousands of parents, and their employers, in a right old mess.

Due to the limited supply of childcare, parents in certain areas across the UK are forced to register their child for a place in a nursery before they are even pregnant. Waiting lists can be so out-of-control that, alongside mapping your menstrual cycle, you have to stump up the cash to reserve a place with your preferred nursery. (As if planning a family were that easy.) One parent told me she had to pay a £300 non-refundable deposit to a nursery when she was six weeks pregnant to secure a place. That included telling them exactly what days and times her unborn child would be attending.

When her baby very sadly died, the £300 was swallowed up, never to be seen again.

It's not just hard for nursery owners to stay afloat; parents also really struggle to pay the extortionate daily rates, which isn't really surprising when you consider that we have the second most expensive childcare system in the world (with the Slovak Republic being the most expensive).[12]

As for what happened to Rachel, it's most certainly not unusual. Parents are regularly forced out of their jobs, or have to work far fewer hours, to cope with the rising cost of childcare. Research by Save the Children in 2018 found that there are 870,000 stay-at-home mums in England who wanted to work but couldn't because of childcare cost and availability.[13] That's half of all out-of-work mums at the time.

According to the Child Poverty Action Group, childcare in the UK forms the majority of the overall cost of raising a child for working couples, having risen from 41 per cent of the total in 2012 to 56 per cent in 2020; and for lone parents, this percentage has risen from 38 to 46 per cent.[14] As a percentage of earnings, childcare in the UK is double that of other countries, on average, sitting at 30 per cent of a couple's income.[15] In a third of households (rising to 47 per cent for Black Asian or Minority Ethnic parents), childcare costs families more than their housing.[16]

At the time of writing, the average cost of full-time childcare across the UK is a wallet-punching £263.81 per week. For all you maths fans, that's more than £1,000 per month.[17] Childcare in London cost an average of £8.60 per hour in 2018;[18] that's more than minimum wage during the same period.[19] In September 2021, Pregnant Then Screwed surveyed over 20,000 parents and discovered that half described childcare as completely unaffordable, while one in three parents with a household income of less than £20,000 had to cut back on essential food or housing as a direct result of childcare bills.

Good-quality, affordable and flexible childcare is a means of freedom for women. It's why free, 24-hour nurseries were one of the four demands of the Women's Liberation Movement in the 1970s. They were wise enough to understand that, if women were working night shifts, it wasn't because they had a deep desire to graft in a factory until late at night – it was because they desperately needed the dosh, so charging extortionate rates for childcare would make escaping from poverty impossible.

Having no access to childcare keeps women firmly in their place. It acts as a form of oppression. Caring for children is a full-time job; it leaves limited time for anything else. You can barely go to the toilet on your own, let alone start a revolution. Forcing women back into their homes and keeping them there due to childcare responsibilities means they'll have little financial or social independence. I'm sure you're thinking, *But what about the dads?* And it's a perfectly reasonable question; I mean, they do exist, but the truth is that in the majority of cases the childcare automatically falls to the mother. We saw this during lockdown: while fathers could do three hours of uninterrupted work, mothers could only manage one hour,[20] and it was mothers who were more likely to be furloughed than fathers.[21] In fact, research by the Fawcett Society found that one in three working mothers had lost work or hours due to a lack of childcare during the pandemic. Before the pandemic, mothers were doing more than double the childcare of fathers.[22] A lack of childcare is a problem for all parents, sure, but, when push comes to shove, it's the mothers who scoop up the vast majority of the unpaid work.

The quality of the childcare setting is important to children's outcomes. If you've been on a nursery pilgrimage, visiting all the local settings, you'll have no doubt stumbled across some pretty grotty scenes. Though it's not so much that the building and facilities need to be fancy (perhaps best to avoid the nursery that stinks of marijuana because the building next door is full of stoned students), it's more about the staff. In 2019, the National Day Nurseries Association found that 26 per cent of the childcare workforce was made up of unqualified assistants. Speaking anonymously in the report published by the association, one worker said: 'We need help. This sector is collapsing.'[23] Charlotte, the owner of Welton Free Rangers, a Forest School nursery in Somerset, told me that nurseries in areas of high deprivation with vulnerable children are closing because they can't recruit staff and are struggling to stay financially sustainable. 'Can you blame the childcare professionals for leaving?' she said. 'All with qualifications they have paid for and committed to. They get paid less than a dog-sitter (£10 an hour is the going rate for a walk around the block). It's a bloody joke and a ruddy mess.'

Meanwhile, a report by Ceeda in 2019 stated that 'Progress in narrowing the gap between the average performance of all children and the 20 per cent lowest attaining children has gone into reverse.'[24]

The appalling pay of childcare workers should be a cause for alarm. The average wage in the sector is £7.42 per hour, in part due to the fact that one in eight childcare workers earns less than £5 an hour.[25] The average wage of a refuse collector is £8.66 per hour. A customer assistant in Morrisons earns an average wage of £9.50 per hour (according to indeed.com). I am in no way suggesting that these jobs don't deserve decent pay, I am merely questioning whether caring for the next generation should be classed as less valuable than these roles. The awful pay and long hours mean that the industry is haemorrhaging staff and is struggling to recruit skilled professionals.

In 2019, almost half (44 per cent) of childcare workers had to claim state benefits and tax credits,[26] and research by Nursery World found that one in ten childcare workers is officially living in poverty.[27] This matters for two reasons: firstly, because it's all part of a system that undervalues care and the work of women; and, secondly, because research into childcare quality shows a direct link between workers' conditions,[28] their pay and the quality of the service.[29] It's completely obvious when you think about it; the more qualified and better paid the childcare professionals are, the better the educational and care experience for the children. When my eldest was in nursery, he was cared for by a confident, kind and excitable teenager who spent ten hours a day cuddling, cleaning, rocking and soothing multiple snotty, screaming babies. I personally can't think of a harder but more important job. Her daily pay was £39. She left to become a palliative-care nurse, and who could blame her? While she was training she became our regular babysitter (this makes me sound like I have a very active social life, which isn't at all accurate) and would get paid almost the same amount of money for watching four hours of trashy TV as she had received for doing ten hours of insanely pressurised child management.

Laurinda worked in childcare for eleven years. She had various childcare diplomas, a degree in early childhood and business management, she specialised in SEN (Special Educational Needs) and has medical training to help children with epilepsy – but despite all this training she says her pay never increased, as the nurseries just didn't have the money to pay her more. Her take-home pay was £60 a day. When she had her own child, her take-home pay was the same as her nursery fees so she was forced to quit and now works in Aldi.

Childcare workers and parents are quite literally the architects of a child's brain. Data compiled by the Rauch Foundation found that 85 per cent of the brain develops by the time a child is five years old.[30] Government publications have waxed lyrical about the first 1,000 days of life being the most critical phase of a child's development. Yet, in 2019, less than 5 per cent of the education budget was spent on early years education and care.[31] In 2015, OECD data showed that only 0.1 per cent of UK GDP was spent on childcare; the average across the OECD countries is more than double this.[32] In 2019, a report conducted by PwC found that, in Australia, for every dollar spent on pre-school, two dollars will be returned to the economy.[33] A 2013 paper by the Foundation for Child Development that explored a variety of studies on childcare concluded that the return on investment ranges from 3:1 to 5:1.[34] Childcare is an investment, not a cost.

Childcare offers us a magnificent opportunity to give each child a more equal start in life, no matter what their background. With the right investment, the UK could be using childcare as a vehicle to develop creativity and language skills. Without sounding too much like a Whitney Houston song, these children quite literally are our future, but instead of investing in them, our Government has repeatedly underfunded the facilities that provide their early education and care, despite the research showing that this makes no economic sense whatsoever.

The challenge is that, according to the 2018 British Social Attitudes survey, one in three Brits thinks mothers of under-fives should stay at home so they are blatantly not going to support their taxes being spent on childcare.[35] In 2021 a single mum reported to ITV News that she had contacted the Department of Work and Pensions to explain that, due to childcare costs, she couldn't afford to return to work. The DWP advisor told her that, as a new mum, she shouldn't be working.[36]

Those who feel uncomfortable with kids being placed in childcare often cite John Bowlby's attachment theory. Bowlby believed that attachment is an important survival instinct with which babies are pre-programmed. If they don't form attachments, then they may encounter mental health issues or behavioural problems in later life. Although Bowlby does make allowances for other primary attachments, he supposes that the child's relationship with the mother is somehow different altogether from other relationships; and, according to Bowlby, any maternal separation will adversely affect a child to some degree.[37] As if just by possessing a vagina we have this mythical hold over small people, and if we ever dared to leave them it would undoubtedly sabotage their chances of becoming a well-functioning adult.

Since Bowlby's bold statements in 1953, other psychologists have tested his theory and agreed that attachment is important. However, they identified some key differences. Namely that children show attachment for all sorts of people, and even objects and pets. They also concluded that temporary separation from the mother has no adverse impact on the child.[38] In 1990, Schaffer said there is evidence that children develop better with a mother who is happy in her work than with a mother who is frustrated by staying at home.[39] Say it louder for those at the back! Indeed, in later life Bowlby abandoned his original insistence on the irreversible consequences of maternal separation.[40]

One thing is for certain: any discussions about childcare can quickly become explosive, something that is pretty inevitable when we are discussing the care and protection of the most vulnerable people in our society. No parent wants to be told that they're putting their children somewhere that is harmful for them, and those who believe a mother's role should be at home caring for her offspring find childcare an abhorrent concept, particularly if it is to be paid for out of the public purse. What's interesting is that these types of discussions and debates don't take place in other countries. In Sweden, the childcare model is based on access and affordability for all children, so the cost is never more than 3 per cent of a parent's earnings. This means that 84 per cent of pre-school children (age 1–5) go to a formal childcare setting every day,[41] compared with 53 per cent of pre-school children in the UK.[42] Susanne Garvis, a professor of child and youth studies at the University of Gothenburg, says that, in Sweden, childcare is based on the principle that early years education acts as a form of poverty prevention; children are not responsible for their life situation, so pre-school is an opportunity to give all children a good and equal start in life – and that makes sense, right? Surely the UK could learn a thing or two from that, particularly when the gap between the rich and the poor in the UK keeps on growing.[43] And while Sweden ranks in the top 10 best countries for children's mental well-being, the UK ranks 27th, according to a 2020 report by Unicef.

Childcare workers are very highly regarded by the Swedes. Susanne Garvis says that working in early years education is seen as a very respectable job, with childcare workers being held in high esteem. She also points out that those working in childcare in Sweden get paid very well. In fact, the lowest-ranking person in a Swedish childcare setting is paid 68,800 SEK per month,[44] which works out at about £5,600.[45] You may think, *Well, those Swedes get paid a fortune whatever they do,* but the average monthly salary in Sweden is 45,100 SEK (£4,000 per month).[46] So, Swedish childcare workers are paid way above the national average salary; in the UK, meanwhile, we pay our childcare workers less than half the national average hourly rate of pay.[47]

In 2016, the Women's Budget Group (WBG) calculated the costs of free universal childcare from the age of six months until primary school age for kids in the UK. Their calculations were based on what is good for children and parents, with key factors including staff who are paid fairly for their skill and time (paid at the same rate as primary school teachers), highly qualified childcare workers, and childcare being available for 40 hours a week, 48 weeks of the year. If this were to be implemented, they estimated that the cost would be £55 billion, about 3 per cent of GDP. However, most of this cost could be recouped through an increase of employment, which would in turn trigger new spending in the economy. It would also reduce benefit costs, as there would be less reliance on Universal Credit and Child Tax Credit. When you plug all these numbers in, the Women's Budget Group found that 75 per cent of the cost could be recouped. The other 25 per cent could be found either through parental fees or other taxation. It is also worth noting that this type of investment by the Government creates jobs. Lots and lots of jobs. The Women's Budget Group estimates that 1.8 million full-time, well-paid jobs would be generated both directly and indirectly by such a policy.[48] The long-term benefits for parents and children would be enormous. Not only would the standard of childcare improve, but families would be wealthier. Yet the benefits shouldn't be focused just on money and the economy. As the author of the WBG report stated, a properly functioning care system would 'improve well-being, quality of life and long-term social mobility and cohesion'.

While the Government continues to ignore the desperate need for investment in suitable, cost-effective, good-quality early years provision, there is an opportunity for companies to step in and save the day. Patagonia, an American apparel company, were the first organisation to build on-site childcare facilities within their headquarters, which are now full to the brim with the chirpy children of delighted staff. They recently opened up their accounts to show other companies what brilliant financial sense this makes. The turnover of staff who use their childcare facilities is 25 per cent lower than among their overall workforce and 100 per cent of their female workforce who have a baby return to work at the company.[49] 'Having children at the workplace creates a kind of richness to the experience of being at work. It lightens the place, it makes people feel closer to their community. This is the kind of world we need to live in,' said Rose Marcario, Patagonia's president and CEO.[50]

Building on-site childcare isn't a solution for all businesses, but I do wonder why more companies aren't lobbying the Government for better investment in our childcare system. Releasing hundreds of thousands of talented and skilled women from their caring responsibilities if they want to work is good for business as it improves the recruitment pool. There's a skills shortage in the UK costing us billions in lost revenue; meanwhile there are 1.7 million women who are prevented from taking on more hours of paid work due to childcare issues, and 870,000 stay-at-home mums who want to work but can't because of childcare costs.[51] All this money sloshing down the drain because the infrastructure isn't there to allow mothers to access the labour market. Where is the sense in that?

Such childcare will close the poverty gap, the gender pay gap, and children's attainment gap. A failing childcare system fails us all.

Childcare tips

Don't calculate childcare costs against one salary if you live in a dual-earning household. Childcare is a joint cost and it should be viewed that way. What some folk forget is that returning to work and paying for childcare may look like a bum deal for now, but by staying in work you are more likely to progress through the ranks quicker. You might accrue pay rises and promotions, as well as contributing to a pension pot. Think about your future, and do some sums based on projections, before you walk away.

If you're a freelancer and you need some ad-hoc childcare for a few hours to meet a deadline, or if you need weekend or evening childcare, there are a few babysitting apps available that can come in handy, such as Bubble and Baby Sittor.

If you and your partner (if you have one) are both working, earning at least the minimum wage for 16 hours a week, or you're on parental leave, sick leave or annual leave, then you should be able to access tax-free childcare. This will reduce your childcare bill by 20 per cent. You have to use the Government's incredibly clunky system to apply – you might want to smash your computer on the floor while trying to access it and you will question whether the Government has made it purposefully galling just to put you off – but persevere because, if you are eligible, it can save you loads of cash.

If you get Universal Credit, the stupid and nonsensical system makes you pay for childcare upfront and then you reclaim the money. Obviously, that can mean a pretty hefty bill. Thankfully, a bevy of brilliant women calling themselves Mums on a Mission is taking the Government to court over this, so hopefully it will change, but, if it doesn't change, try contacting the charity Turn2us, which may be able to support with a loan. If you are newly starting at work, you may be entitled to the Flexible Support Fund, which is a discretionary grant administered by Jobcentre Plus. There is also a Budgeting Loan, which is interest free, available through various Government benefit schemes, and a Budgeting Advance is available for those on Universal Credit, though the eligibility criteria is pretty strict and it can take up to two months before you receive your loan. Check if you are eligible online.

The 30-hours-a-week 'free' childcare scheme for working parents kicks in after your child turns three – but not immediately: once they hit their third birthday you have to wait for one of the three key dates before you're eligible (1 January, 1 April and 1 September). Also, if you live with a partner, you both have to be working to be eligible to receive 30 hours, though you can still access 15 hours' free childcare per week if only one of you works. You have to apply online (and, yes, it's another frustrating online Government system). Remember that the 'free' childcare only applies during term time and that you may also be charged for food, nappies and trips.

10

The Domestic Load

'I am the person who notices we are running out of toilet paper,' wrote Ellen Seidman in a blog that perfectly encapsulates the domestic load. 'I am the person who notices that veggies in the produce drawer and fruit in the basket are rotting. I am the person who spots the squished raisins under the kitchen table, the dustballs under the dresser, the mound of lint in the dryer filter and the mystery substance on the sofa. I am the person who foresees needing gifts for the birthday party, graduation party, anniversary party, every party ... I am the person who notices the throw in the living room hasn't been washed in approximately eleven years. But at least I finally noticed.' She goes on to talk about all the information she retains in her brain: 'My family's clothing and shoe sizes. When library books are due. School permission slips and medical forms that need signing. When prescriptions need to be refilled. Which of the kids' friends has nut/sesame allergies ...' The list ends with a serious sentence: 'It doesn't take a village – it takes *me*.'[1]

The 'domestic load' is the work that is done in the home; the unpaid labour that keeps a household ticking along and ensures your children aren't taken in by social services.

Essentially, it's skilled and agile project management. When you're a mum, it's highly skilled project management that has to be conducted on about 46 minutes' sleep a night. When you're a working mum, it is highly skilled project management that has to be done on 46 minutes' sleep a night while also being utterly dedicated to all of your paid work. It can be a full-time job on top of a full-time job, so it's pretty fortunate that you're only getting 46 minutes' sleep a night.

As luck would have it, the Office for National Statistics (ONS) have been measuring domestic and unpaid labour and they have kindly broken down their data by sex. The results clearly show that women do 60 per cent more domestic and unpaid labour than men. On average, men do 16 hours per week of the cleaning, cooking and caring for children or elderly relatives, and women do 26 hours per week. According to the ONS, the average man would earn an extra £167 a week if his unpaid work were paid and a woman would earn an extra £260, so women are doing almost £100 extra unpaid work a week.[2] If those figures aren't enough to retrigger your sleep-deprived eye twitch, then maybe the annual sum is: that's around £5,000 per year that women are missing out on because we bothered to do the majority of the laundry and clean the bog. Or perhaps you might be more frustrated to learn that men have much more time to relax than women – in fact, men in the UK have five hours' more leisure time than women per week.[3] That's enough time to learn how to change a tyre or become a lifesaving first aider, it's almost enough time to watch the whole second series of *Fleabag* and it's definitely enough time to have a five-hour lie-in – imagine that! Then there's the research from the University of Michigan that shows that husbands create seven extra hours of housework per week, and it's the women who do it.[4] If your eye twitch has gone into overdrive, I would encourage you to take a long, leisurely nap – you deserve it. In every country that collects statistics for paid and unpaid labour, women work more hours per day than men when you combine the two, and the fact that women are doing way more of the unpaid care work inevitably means they are unable to do as much of the paid work, thereby affecting their careers, their earnings and their pensions.[5]

But unpaid work is essential for keeping our society going. Without the unpaid labour, the paid labour couldn't happen. I don't know a single person who gets any pleasure from putting on a wash or changing a nappy; we do it because it has to be done or the house descends into chaos, everyone starts to smell and there is literally shit everywhere. This work has a value to society. ONS figures for 2014 show that total unpaid work had a value of £1.01 trillion, and that's because, if it weren't being done for free, then it would need to be either paid for by the state (think elderly care) or privately subcontracted (think cleaner). The value of unpaid work is equivalent to approximately 56 per cent of GDP.[6] However, GDP fails to include unpaid labour. British economists James Meade and Richard Stone invented GDP in the 1940s and they recruited a 23-year-old woman named Phyllis Deane to apply their method in a few British colonies. Phyllis told Stone and Meade that it made no sense to exclude unpaid labour from the calculations, but she was ignored by the two men in charge.[7] I mean, what would a woman know about the intrinsic value of unpaid labour to a country's economy? The notion that caring and domestic labour have no value is sewn into the fabric of our system. There's an old saying in economics that if a man marries his housekeeper then Gross Domestic Product goes down. Why would that be? Well, it's because housekeepers get paid for all the labour they do in the home when wives do not.

The fight for caring and housework to be recognised has a rich and eventful history. Mother's Day was created in the US by Anna Jarvis in 1908. Anna Jarvis's mother – Ann Maria Reeves Jarvis – was a socialist and feminist in the 1800s who organised mothers' groups, but, instead of sitting around singing 'Row, Row, Row Your Boat', these meetings existed to advocate for women's labour rights. She wanted mothers to be properly paid for the work they undertook. Anna Jarvis took on this mantle when her mother died and campaigned for a day where the hard work of women was respected and valued.

In 1914, Mother's Day became a national holiday in the US, but, rather than it serving as a 'fuck you, pay me' movement for mothers, it quickly became the ultimate exercise in sentimentality and commercialisation, and not at all what Anna Jarvis or Ann Maria Reeves Jarvis had had in mind. For instance, one day Anna Jarvis was dining in a Philadelphia tea room when she spotted a 'Mother's Day salad' on the menu. In a fit of rage, she ordered the salad and, when it was served, she stood up, dumped the salad on the floor, and then marched out. She referred to the florists, greetings-card manufacturers and confectionery industry that profited from Mother's Day as 'charlatans, bandits, pirates, racketeers, kidnappers, and termites that would undermine with their greed one of the finest, noblest, and truest movements and celebrations'.[8] Anna Jarvis then spent the rest of her life trying to remove Mother's Day from the national calendar but with no success, and she died furious about it.[9]

The Wages for Housework campaign in the 1970s proposed that the state would value domestic work if it had to pay for it, the central argument to this and other campaigns being that domestic labour is essential to production, not least in the role it plays in reproducing the labour force. If women weren't looking after the children and doing the thousands of other tasks required to keep a home running and everyone nourished and healthy, men would be unable to work. In short, both women and men were working, but only the men were materially benefiting, and only men's work was valued.

The Labour government under Blair chastised 'workless' mothers when Blair said they can't stay 'on the dole' as if caring for children 24/7, without any access to holidays or sick pay, and doing the cooking, washing, shopping and cleaning is completely worthless work. Our current government also makes it very clear how little they value stay-at-home mums by simply labelling them as 'economically inactive'.

While women's participation in paid work has increased considerably, men's share of the unpaid labour has largely remained stagnant since the 1980s.[10] Well, it had, until Covid-19 exploded, in spring 2020. During lockdown, women were doing 31 hours per week more housework than before the pandemic, many while still holding down paid jobs. The good news was that men's share of the housework also increased; with men firmly trapped in the house, they were scooping up more of the home schooling, cooking and cleaning, but mothers were still doing 12 hours more per week than fathers.[11] Clearly, there are only so many hours in the day, and the more unpaid work someone is doing the less time they can spend on paid work. This had a devastating and immediate impact on mothers, who were 50 per cent more likely than fathers to have quit their jobs or have been pushed out by May 2020 (only two months into lockdown).[12] In fact, the only households where childcare and housework were being shared equally were those in which fathers had been furloughed while mothers continued to do their paid jobs.[13]

Even when we are not wading through the shitstorm that is a global pandemic, the disproportionate burden of domestic labour can prevent mothers from earning a decent crust. Many opt for part-time work as they need more time to fulfil the domestic duties, thereby slamming the breaks on any potential career progression. Plus, we don't have the time to hang around the office to show our boss how unbearably dedicated we are and we can't go for those after-work drinks where all the corporate secrets get spilled and friendships are sealed. No, instead we are spending any 'spare time' we have staring at the crusty, congealed bean juice that has gathered in the crevices of our kitchen floor, wondering when we might have the energy to remove it.

Sensibly, you would expect that couples would monitor and segment their time to ensure maximum efficiency for the family and to try to prevent either parent from self-combusting due to exhaustion, but unfortunately the research doesn't seem to back this up. In fact, it does quite the opposite. The more paid work a woman does, the more unpaid work she also does. Yes, you heard me right. It seems that we're all so brainwashed by deeply entrenched gender stereotypes as to who should really be doing the cooking and cleaning and caring, and who should really be out winning all of the bread, that this extreme switch of gender roles somehow creates a need to compensate. As women in heterosexual relationships become the primary breadwinners they do more of the domestic tasks to reinforce traditional gender identities.[14] After all, we wouldn't want men to feel emasculated, now, would we?

When I posted online about the imbalance of domestic duties, I was soon drowning in messages from frazzled and frustrated mums. I picked up the phone and called Patricia, a mum to a 16-month-old son who is profoundly deaf. She is the head of a recruitment team for a large tech business. Her working week is between 45 and 50 hours, plus a daily 90-minute commute, and she earns about four times what her husband earns. Yet she does the majority of the housework. She told me that she is exhausted, and the pressure places an enormous strain on her relationship. I asked her whether she ever discusses her frustrations with her partner. 'We have these discussions, and I think we're getting somewhere and for a short while it will feel like things have changed, but then after a week or so I realise we're back to square one. I can't keep bringing it up. There's no joy in feeling like you constantly have to ask people to do things, so I just do it myself. I'm too tired to keep arguing.'

Next I called Jane. She has two young sons and works full-time for the Civil Service, commuting regularly from Newcastle to London for work. Her partner is a part-time mechanic, a job that she says is physically demanding but, unlike Jane, he never brings his work home with him. Her salary is double what his is. 'I do 97 per cent of the house-work,' she told me. 'He believes he does about 70 per cent of it because he spends a day a week with our kids. I don't get to do that because I work full-time. If I had a day with the kids, I would spend half of it doing household chores while trying to entertain them, but he doesn't think like that. Some days he even forgets to feed them. I will ask him what they had for their lunch so that I don't make them the same thing for their dinner, and, as he ponders the question, it will dawn on him that he forgot to feed them. I mean, how the actual fuck does he forget to feed our children? To make sure certain tasks are complete, I set a reminder on Alexa so he can't forget. He has absolutely no idea about the bills or the mortgage. It's basically like having three kids and a dog.'

I asked her why she doesn't do something about this situation. 'I have tried,' she said. 'I was going to just stop doing everything, just go on strike, but then the house will turn into a shithole and no one will eat and he won't care. We have arguments about it, usually when I'm stressed and harassed, and I explode on him, so in a fit of rage I end up listing the tasks that he hasn't done, and his response is to list the tasks that he *has* done, sometimes going back months. He just can't see it and I don't know how to make him understand.'

We also know that when men are asked how much housework they do, they tend to overestimate.[15] During lockdown, research from data intelligence company Morning Consult showed that nearly half of men said that they were doing most of the home schooling but only 3 per cent of women agreed with that claim.[16] Plenty of women will attest to discussing the housework imbalance with their partner, only to be met with a full and exhaustive list of all the household chores that their partner has done:

'My husband messages me when I'm at work and he is working from home to tell me he has brought in the washing when it rains or washed a few of the dishes.'

'I got so frustrated with my partner wanting to be praised for the smallest task, I bought a medal from the pound shop and presented it to him.'

But what I hear time and time again is women saying that the most rage-inducing response they get from their partner when they broach the issue is: 'Why didn't you just ask me to do it?' Which sounds pretty sensible; helpful, even. But it perfectly demonstrates the unconscious expectation men have that their female partner will project-manage the running of the house. The household is seen as the domain of women – we manage it and we distribute the work, but the distribution of work takes a toll on our mental well-being and ability. It is emotionally draining to be the one who sets the standards and ensures everyone else lives up to them, even if you aren't actually placing the new loo roll on the loo roll holder yourself.

'Cognitive labour' is a term coined by Harvard sociologist Allison Daminger to summarise the 'labour of the mind' that tends to be done predominantly by women. Allison interviewed college-educated couples with children and found that women were disproportionately likely to take the lead in anticipating upcoming needs (such as my child will have grown out of that car seat in a month or so) and monitoring outcomes (now I've got a new car seat, is it working as it should be?), whereas identification work (such as selecting the car seat) was more often split or shared and decision-making work (buying the car seat) was overwhelmingly a collaborative activity. Allison suggests that this is because men enjoy the power associated with decision-making; they also received the credit of being involved without doing the mental legwork.[17] This 'cognitive' or mental labour is invisible. It can't be tracked or quantified, so, when the OECD said that women do 60 per cent more of the unpaid labour than men, that doesn't include this type of work.

Many of my mum-friends often mention how incredibly forgetful they've become since having kids. I have two children and constantly forget their names. I once called my son 'Willow', which is the name of our dead cat. We apologise for our forgetfulness and worry that our brains are deteriorating, but medical research has shown that, when our brains are dealing with information overload, we become forgetful and our ability to process information becomes inhibited. My friend told me a story in the pub a few years ago about Barack Obama. I have no idea how true this is but, apparently, he had a member of staff who would choose all of his meals for him and would dress him each day – the theory being that your brain has a threshold for decision-making, so any decisions that could be removed from the president without triggering potentially negative consequences for the United States would be taken away. I see all mums as being a bit like Barack Obama. We're making thousands of decisions every day and are overwhelmed with information. Most of us could probably do with someone to choose our daily outfits and plan our dinner. But it's not just the mental labour of tasks and chores that's more likely to be done by mothers; we're also more likely to monitor our child's well-being and emotional states, and research has shown that this combination of cognitive, emotional and invisible labour has 'strong, unique links' with women's distress.[18]

When scooping up the majority of the domestic and mental labour is clearly harming our career, our mental health and our relationships, why the hell do we do it? Research has shown what we mothers already know – that we will be judged negatively if the house is a chaotic mess and the children are running feral, but, if we have a male partner, he won't be judged in the same way. We know this pressure has an impact on how women behave, even if they have progressive views about gendered roles.[19] Of course, pregnancy itself also plays a role. As the baby grows, you inevitably take on more of the responsibilities for planning for its arrival, because you can physically feel it kicking and punching its way into existence. When you go for hospital appointments, the midwives and doctors address the mother with all the questions and information; her partner is relegated to the role of sperm donor – he's done his job, the rest is up to mum. People offer you, the expectant mother, their advice on what to read, what to buy, what position the baby should sleep in or when to wean them, while your partner is invited out to wet the baby's head, is warned that if he looks down during the delivery he will never want to look at another vulva again, and is directed to the toolbox to ensure he builds the cot in time.

Then comes maternity leave, and, as we still don't have legislation that encourages men to take time out to care for their children (more on this in Chapter 11), it is left to the mum to work out all of the complexities involved in caring for and connecting with their new baby. Dad comes home and his job is to ask you what you need, because by that point he is firmly in the position of secondary carer. In the main, it happens entirely unconsciously; it just makes sense for the dad to take a back seat and to act as the scaffolding, supporting the mother with what she needs, while she becomes chief feeder, burper and shusher. Once these roles have been cemented into place – due to a mixture of gender stereotypes, societal pressure and skewed legislation – it's pretty tricky to change them, not least because you are too exhausted to think beyond the next 20 minutes. Even when we try to address the imbalance through conversations or (more likely) huge arguments, the change is unlikely to last as these roles are so deeply embedded and men are given a free pass by society to believe that this isn't really their job, it's a woman's, and deep down we both know it. I am in no way blaming men here. There are plenty who have the best intentions, who really strive to be the best dads they can possibly be, but every interaction they have, every system and structure they encounter, pushes them onto the childcare reserve bench.

Before you have kids, the disproportionate levels of unpaid and emotional labour definitely exist but to nowhere near the same extent, mainly because, if you choose to concentrate only on yourself and your own cleanliness and nourishment, that's fine; it probably won't make for the happiest of relationships, but no one will die. Once you have kids, that isn't the case at all. This extreme shift in responsibility can make you feel dizzy with exhaustion. Trying to sustain your energy and resilience, alongside the pressure of managing a household and keeping a child alive, and the intense pressure to be the perfect mother and partner, can feel totally overwhelming; it's no wonder research has shown that single and childless women are the happiest and healthiest subgroup in the population. Speaking at the Hay Festival in 2019, Paul Dolan, Professor of Behavioural Science at the London School of Economics, said, 'If you're a man, you should probably get married; if you're a woman, don't bother.' Men benefited from marriage because they 'calmed down', he told them. 'You take fewer risks, you earn more money at work, and you live a little longer. She, on the other hand, dies sooner than if she never married.'[20]

Tonnes of research supports the notion that same-sex couples have a more egalitarian split of the domestic chores. Sensibly, gay and lesbian couples often shun the usual gendered roles, i.e. man is immediately responsible for fixing things and putting the bins out, while woman has ultimate responsibility for pretty much everything else. Lesbian couples base the domestic division of labour on skill and quality of the task.[21] If one of you is a better cook then it makes perfect sense for them to take the lead on knocking up a cordon bleu dinner while the other ploughs their way through the dirty laundry – and that's totally logical, right? But there's a catch, and it's a big one: more recent research has shown that, in both male and female same-sex relationships, there is an equal and non-gendered division of housework ... until they have children. Though the couples are still more equitable than heterosexual couples once they become parents, they tend to fall into more gendered roles, with one being the main breadwinner and the other taking on a greater portion of the household chores and childcare. A report on this in the *New York Times* supposed that 'roles are not just about gender: Work and much of society are still built for single-earner families.'[22]

And this is the crux of the issue: our structures and systems continue to reinforce gendered roles in the home through public policy, such as better-paid maternity leave than paternity leave, and through employers' behaviour, such as pregnancy discrimination that kicks women out of their jobs, but also because we constantly butt up against competing schedules such as school starting at 9 a.m. and finishing at 3.30 p.m. while most jobs expect you to be in the office 9 a.m.–5 p.m at minimum. Then, alongside this, a mother will usually earn less than the father (hello, gender pay gap) and there's all this work that needs doing in the home, so someone has to take a step back from the paid work to deal with it all. No matter how much we try to escape traditional gendered roles, and how 'enlightened' both parents may be, women are constantly being nudged back to the kitchen sink. But, for the love of God, it has got to be possible; we all need to know it is possible, right? Reducing the motherhood penalty, reducing our stress and anxiety, female emancipation – it's all dependent on roles in the home not being predetermined by our gender. We will never have equality in the workplace until we have equality in the home. There is a clear and strong link between the number of hours of unpaid work that women do and their participation in the paid labour force. The more hours of unpaid work, the fewer hours of paid work.[23] That's in part because the continued unequal distribution of unpaid care work encourages stereotypes and therefore increases discriminatory behaviour from employers towards women, but also because, as my mum used to say with obscene regularity, 'There are only so many hours in't day' (she's from Yorkshire). A report by McKinsey in 2016 stated that the 'disparity in unpaid care work is higher in the United Kingdom than in many developed-nation peers' and also that 'a decrease from five to three hours of unpaid care work a day has been found to correlate with a ten-percentage-point increase in the female labour-force participation rate'.[24] We will only reduce the motherhood penalty if we find ways for women to reduce their unpaid caring and domestic duties, and we do this through affordable childcare, ring-fenced and properly paid paternity leave, flexible working for all and leadership from the Government to show that unpaid domestic labour is valuable.

Thankfully, some other countries are showing us that there is a glimmer of light at the end of a very unkempt tunnel. In Sweden, educated men are doing more of the childcare than they did previously, and way more than men in the UK, because caring for children is seen as 'high status', while Swedish women who earn more than their partners no longer 'compensate' by doing more housework.[25] In Sweden, 74 per cent of women do housework or cook for at least one hour every day, compared with 56 per cent of men. The European average is 79 per cent[26] compared with 34 per cent.[27] Sweden has shown us that, if you implement policy with gender equality in mind, real change may take time, but it is possible.

The thing is, we have to deal with it because, if we don't, we're allowing the problem to persist. Our children watch and copy our actions. If they spend their time in a house where the mother is the carer, the comforter, the cook, the cleaner, the project manager, the administrator and the CEO of the house, then it's likely they'll imitate the same. Sons will come to expect that domestic duties are the responsibility of women, and so it goes on. We may stick our head in the sand because we want an easy life without arguments, without having to sound like a nagging fishwife, but we need to remember that this comes at a cost. We don't want the same for our daughters, and in a few years' time I want to look into the eyes of my son's partner and know I did my best to make him understand that housework and childcare are as much his responsibility as they are hers (or his). Which is why I encouraged my six-year-old to clean the loo the other week. His little hands sheathed in bright-yellow Marigolds, he apparently took great delight in scrubbing the skid marks off the porcelain while I barked instructions at him. I'm not convinced that his gleeful participation was related to the satisfaction of making our toilet sparkle, but more the fact that I agreed to pay him £1, which probably made the attempted lesson one that wasn't really worth learning. Strangely enough, he hasn't offered to do it again. Either way, I am determined that my boys will do their fair share of the domestic duties both now and in the future.

Research shows that, as parents, we play a defining role in how domestic labour is viewed by our kids. Boys aged 15–19 do half an hour of housework per day, compared with girls of the same age, who do 45 minutes a day.[28] None of this is easy, and I hate to add more tasks to your already-overloaded plate, but if we want change then we have to model it ourselves. As more and more men proudly proclaim that they are feminists who care deeply about gender equality, we need to make sure they know they have an active role to play in making equality a reality. In the words of journalist Helen Lewis: 'There is one great contribution men can make to feminism: pick up a mop.'[29]

Until we can either fix the gendered division of the unpaid domestic and mental labour, or we can create a system where this work is recognised as just that – work – then the motherhood penalty will remain. As we've seen, despite women vastly increasing the number of hours they spend in paid work over the past few decades, men's contribution to unpaid work has barely changed since the 1980s. The workplace isn't structured around a person who is responsible for the school drop-offs and pick-ups, the doctor's appointments, the sports days, the impromptu tantrums and the emotional availability required to parent. It's built around someone being at home to do all of that, while the unencumbered other parent dedicates their whole self to their job. In the words of Amy Westervelt, author of *Forget Having It All: How America Messed Up Motherhood – And How to Fix It*, 'We expect women to work as if they don't have children and raise children as if they don't work.'

Without Government policy that puts gender equality at its heart, this problem will endure, and, as the Government is dominated by white men, equality of any kind is unlikely to be a key focus. In the absence of a Government that is committed to equality, employers, men and women all have a role to play in striving for a more egalitarian split of the unpaid domestic labour. So, let's get to work, shall we?

Here are a few ideas to try to make a change in your house:

Do it for the kids

It's really important that you don't expect to have a chat with your partner about the division of domestic labour and the distribution to immediately change – and then, when it doesn't, you chastise him or her. Just as women have been told all their lives that this is their domain, men have been told all their lives that it isn't theirs. From the conversations I've had with women who feel they've made it work, after struggling for years with the imbalance, it was a change in language that did the trick. Rather than focusing on what their partner *hasn't* done or what they've done incorrectly (which inevitably leads to a tit for tat – well, I did this and I did that), it's much more effective if you talk about modelling the type of behaviour you want your children to see. We know that daughters and sons benefit enormously from seeing parents share the domestic load equally, so keep reminding your partner of that: this is about the kids and them being able to have positive future relationships.

If all else fails, get an app

A friend recommended the app Our Home, which I found unbelievably useful because it allows you to list all the regular and irregular chores you need to get done around the house and assign points to each task. It's the gamification of domestic labour so it's perfect for my partner as it appeals to his unbelievably competitive nature. You agree between the two of you what the tasks are that need to be done and how many points each task is worth, and then the person who completes a task wins the points. We set ours based on time, so the points are the same as the approximate number of minutes it takes to complete a particular task. Obviously, you get extra points if you take the kids swimming because no one in their right mind enjoys freezing their tits off in an underheated swimming pool, followed by the unsheathing of two soggy infants in a cubicle the size of a postage stamp.

Not only does the app help with the mental load, as the tasks are there for all to see, but it means your partner can't pretend that they do 75 per cent of the housework, because if they did then they'd be winning most of the points. Rather than nagging him about the laundry, you can just swipe open the app and regularly proclaim yourself the *victrix ludorum*.

Be at one with your inner Girl Guide

My very organised friend who has four children and runs her own business swears by a rostering system. She and her husband sit down every Sunday night and map out everything that needs to be done that week, then cross-reference it with their own work and social diaries as well as the kids' social events. They assign the tasks for the week, do the shopping list and plan the meals they'll eat together each day that week, and, *apparently,* they manage to do it without a single argument or passive-aggressive remark. Imagine that.

Go on strike

Another friend told me that, after months and months of resentment towards her husband for doing naff-all to support her in the house, she decided to go on strike. She didn't tell him about her plan; instead she silently colluded to not lift a finger for 48 hours to see what would happen. She woke up that morning and the kids were screaming 'MUMMY!' repeatedly from their beds. She would usually stagger through and carry them both downstairs for their breakfast while her husband snoozed for a while longer or took his time in the shower. Not today, though. The screaming became more and more hysterical and her husband became more and more bewildered. As he looked at her, hoping for some clarification as to why usual procedure was not under way, she simply gave him a wry smile and turned over. She found the next 48 hours difficult – the impulse in her to tidy, organise, nurture, feed, clean and discipline was great – but she forced herself to stop so that her husband was forced to step in. When the 48 hours were complete, she explained what had happened and asked him how he felt. 'Bloody knackered,' he said. 'Well, now you know what it feels like, don't you?' she replied.

It's certainly not the first time women have had to strike to ensure the work they do is valued. On 24 October 1975, Icelandic women went on a national strike. It was a demonstration of women's contribution to Iceland's economy and society, and a demand for equal pay and equal representation. Male news anchors read the news while bouncing a baby on one knee. Shops, schools and institutions were forced to close their doors, and the country ran out of sausages – the favourite ready meal of the time in Iceland. To this day, the men of Iceland refer to it as 'The Long Friday'. This strike paved the way for the world's first democratically elected female president, Vigdís Finnbogadóttir, who then implemented many changes to Iceland's legislation to trigger a much more gender-equal nation.

It seems that striking works. You don't have to nag and all you're doing is having a day off; but, by doing nothing, it's painfully apparent just how much you actually do.

Lower your standards

I'm probably not the right person to write about this because, honestly, my standards are pretty low already, but I have many friends who seriously stress out about mess and I really think we should all stop worrying so much. No one is judging you; in fact, I think most people are just relieved that it means they can relax a bit more when you go to their house. I host regular playdates and the kids who have incredibly tidy, clean and organised houses make some hilarious comments: 'Joeli, have you seen all the spider webs on your ceiling?' 'Joeli did you know that not a single toy in that toy box actually works?' 'Joeli, we just found a really old banana skin next to your TV.'

Sure, I would love my house to be tidier, but I'm not going to sacrifice my mental health to live in a show home. The personal-care brand Dove conducted research that revealed that nine out of ten mothers feel the pressure to be perfect, but, ladies, it's never going to happen – you will never be perfect, so you're heading for a life of disappointment.[30] The proliferation of the self-proclaimed 'tidy gurus' or 'cleanfluencers' doesn't exactly help. When Marie Kondo politely entered my TV screen talking about the joys of organisation, it didn't spark any joy in me; in fact, I felt pretty furious. The last thing women need is more tips to ensure you have no excuse for mess. By aiming these tips at women, we are reaffirming that unpaid labour is our responsibility. Surely it's time we had some men in Marigolds explaining to a predominantly male audience what the mental load is and how being a good partner involves so much more than doing what you are told to do by your exhausted and harassed wife.

If you're still feeling totally hopeless about ever attaining parity in the home, then you could always hold out for Mark Zuckerberg to develop an artificially intelligent butler, something he has apparently been working on since 2016, though I must admit to a sense of indignation that men might get to skip the bit where they take on the burden of responsibility that women have had to bear for hundreds of years, and instead hand it all to robots.

11

What about Dad?

'Here's a weird thing: when you're a man on your own, some people assume that you can't possibly be in charge of a baby or toddler. Twice now someone's had a go at me for parking in parent/child spaces when I've actually got Charlie in the back seat. They see a man pull in and assume that I am just another childless dickhead taking advantage of the space.

I was in Asda car park just last month when, upon arrival, a woman knocked on my window before I could even turn the engine off.

"Excuse me! You know these spaces are for people with children?" she demanded.

I literally had to point my thumb in to the back of the car and say: "What's that? A fucking cat?"'

Matt Coyne, *Man vs Toddler*

Fatherhood is seen as dispensable. People freely and frequently undermine a dad's role in child-rearing by asking if he is 'babysitting' or by suggesting that he is such a great dad because he spent ten minutes rocking his own child to sleep.

What a hero – doing something that he shouldn't have to do because, if we're all honest, it's a mum's job.

Stories of fathers in the media tend to focus on their absence. Until relatively recently, fathers were either missing, played a very specific and distant role of breadwinner, or were hapless idiots incapable of using a washing machine. We're programmed to believe that fathers don't possess the 'nurturing gene' and that this should be the sole responsibility of the mother. The thing is, this is bullshit. Like mothers, fathers have been shaped by evolution to be biologically, psychologically and behaviourally primed to parent. The hormonal and brain changes seen in new mothers are mirrored in fathers. Their ability to parent is not based on biology; it is based on how much time they spend with their children.[1]

Nonetheless, no matter how hard couples try to rebalance the caring duties, we continue to bang our heads against a gendered wall. When my son was in nursery, his dad dropped him off and collected him every day. It was Tom who said hello to the staff and kept them up to date with everything, from our son's nap arrangements or medical needs to how often he had pooed himself that weekend (our son, not Tom). Yet, when notes got sent home, they would be addressed to 'mum'. When Tom took our son to a hospital appointment, the doctor asked him why I wasn't present and said that I must attend next time. When I went to the hospital without Tom, no one even blinked. When I was pregnant with our second child, Tom and I discussed him taking three months' paternity leave so that I could return to work, but Tom had left his job and gone self-employed so he had no legal right to time with his new son whatsoever. Instead, the early childcare conundrum rested solely on my shoulders.

'Our heads – and the heads of everyone around us – are filled with nonsense by advertisers and the media who love nothing more than creating a "gender war" out of everything. So, even though it's 2021 and science is telling us the complete opposite, the narrative remains that women are better and more "natural" carers, that they're the only ones who can multi-task, men don't really care about children – and are dangerous around them – and so on.

All of this can be hard to dismantle when you realise that the only way you can make ends meet is for the mother to stay off work or go down to part-time when the baby arrives, and for the dad to stay full-time with a killer commute.

And of course it's true that some of us end up internalising all of this and start to believe that our place really is on the 7.15 to Waterloo or half-way up an electricity pylon, rather than elbow-deep in projectile diarrhoea or sat singing 'Wheels on the Bus' on a splintery church hall floor. Some dads really do have very little confidence at the hands-on stuff – maybe that's not so surprising when you see how little support we get.'

Dr Jeremy Davies, Fatherhood Institute

When men become fathers, their testosterone reduces and they are rewarded with dopamine whenever they interact with their child. Their brain changes: the regions linked to affection, nurturing and threat-detection see increases in grey and white matter. Both parents are wired to understand their child's practical and emotional needs. What's really striking is that, because it hates any sort of duplication, natural selection ensures that men and women play different and complementary roles in a child's raising and development. From analysing the brain activity of parents while they were watching videos of their child, researchers could see that mums are more likely to engage the parts of the brain associated with risk–detection and affection, while dads are more likely to engage the parts of the brain associated with planning, problem-solving and social conditioning. That's not to say that same-sex couples or single mums are unable to offer their child a rounded development environment; the brain has a degree of plasticity, so it adapts and ensures that both dads and mums are using all parts of the brain when caring for their child.

The relationship between a father and his child is based on affection, yes, but it is also based on challenge. Dads interact with a child in a way that supports an understanding of the world outside of the home. According to the anthropologist Anna Machin, 'It is fathers who aid the development of appropriate social behaviour, and build a child's sense of worth.'[2]

A study by the University of Newcastle, which looked at 11,000 British men and women born in 1958, found that the more time fathers spent with their kids, the higher the children's IQs and the more socially mobile the children were. The differences were still detectable at the age of 42.[3]

For the mothers reading this who are heroically raising their children alone, none of this is meant to undermine the incredible work you are doing, or to act as any kind of judgement. Nor does this research mean that your child will never be as clever or as socially mobile as his/her peers who have two parents. We know how hard you work to bridge that gap and ensure your child has everything. The selfless devotion of one parent is worth a gazillion times that of two parents who have better things to do than parent. In countless families, one parent barely sees their child due to the enormous pressures placed upon them by the workplace. Research shows that when fathers are present but do not take an active role in child-rearing, they have no impact on a child's IQ. Our current system and structures do not support men to actively care for their children, and our obsession with focusing entirely on the mother can ultimately lead to many men feeling like their contribution is surplus to requirements. It's yet another way that pernicious gender stereotypes have woven their way into our minds and our societal structures to the detriment of everyone in their wake.

Just as women who raise their children on their own find ways of compensating, men who raise children without the involvement of women do the same:

> 'When fathers engage in active day-to-day care of children – particularly when fathers assume the traditional maternal primary carer role and raise their babies with no maternal involvement – they become as attuned and sensitive to the baby's cues as mothers do. They show greater activation in the "emotional network" of their brains like mothers do, something that does not happen unless they are continually involved.'[4]

> Eyal Abraham

The argument that mothers are the natural caregivers is completely unfounded by scientific research. Women do the hard graft of growing the baby and giving birth, and some women breastfeed, but beyond that both sexes are just as capable of caring for babies and children.

I regularly hear from mothers who tell me that their partner is desperate to spend more time with their kids but they can't make it work due to insanely pressurised work schedules and outdated legislation that favours a mother taking parental leave over the father. My partner, Tom, works away regularly, and whenever he leaves us his bristly beard quivers a little; you see, unlike me – who would be skipping around at the thought of spending a week in a hotel – he is devastated when he can't see the kids every day. Tom is the breadwinner, the one who makes sure we can keep a roof over our heads and our cupboards full of peanut butter. When our first baby was born, he was heartbroken that after only two weeks he had to return to the office, pining for more time to gaze in wonder at his new son. But, because he has a penis, the significant transformation that had taken place within our family and within his heart was ignored. And he's not the only one – dads all over the country are pining to spend more time with their kids:

> 'It's like watching your wife, the love of your life, free-falling without a parachute. You are terrified but unable to help or stop it. Some days she begs me not to go, and I smile and walk out of the door – she thinks I'm horrible and that's the hardest part, because I would give anything to be there and the smile is to stop me from crying. My boss complains when I leave my job on time to go home, my friends laugh when I say I want to be home at a good hour to see them both. I'm a daddy but it means nothing, it seems, apart from to me. Two weeks' paternity leave is no time at all.'

It's no exaggeration to say that giving dads more time to bond with their babies, and to build confidence as a new parent, has lifesaving and lifelong benefits for children, and families. A study of 5,000 young people, published in the official journal of the American Academy of Pediatrics, found that a father's absence damages a child's telomeres – vital pieces of DNA that protect cells. Having an absent father shortened telomeres by about 14 per cent. Shortened telomeres have been linked to premature ageing and cancer.[5]

It's pretty bloody obvious that if dads were given the opportunity to be around more in the early days of parenthood, this would also enormously benefit the mother. I vividly remember the first time I was left alone with two children. As my one-week-old son screamed hysterically while I changed his nappy, full to the brim with milky yellow poo, my two-year-old managed to lock himself in the bathroom, popped the plug in the sink and ran the tap until the water gushed onto the bathroom floor. He didn't stop there, though, squirting shower gel into the sink to make sure it frothed up into a perfect frenzy of white, foaming bubbles. As I attempted to knock down the door, placing my still-screaming baby on the corridor carpet, my damaged pelvic floor gave way and I pissed myself. I would love to say I found this moment as funny as I do today, now that I am recalling it, but I didn't. Instead, once the two-year-old had been retrieved from the bathroom and the tap turned off, I sobbed uncontrollably, convinced I was an awful, awful mother and petrified at the thought of nine more months of doing this on my own. Things pretty much deteriorated from that point onwards; with a baby that woke every 45 minutes until he was 13 months old (this is no exaggeration) and a toddler that sprang out of bed at 5 a.m., I was exhausted to the point that I was literally hearing voices and seeing things that weren't there. When I fell down the stairs – and thankfully landed with only a bruised coccyx and ego – I scooped up my children, made a beeline for the local A&E

and refused to leave until a doctor did something to save my sanity. There was nothing they could do – apparently this did not constitute an emergency – and I was asked to leave. Thankfully, I muddled through and I'm here to tell the tale, but others aren't so fortunate. If Tom had been supported to take time out of work to help me through those early days, things would have been very different.

In 2012, Sweden remodelled their parental leave so that the other partner had the flexibility to take up to 30 days, as required, off work in the first year of a child's life. Researchers were therefore able to do a direct comparison of the outcomes for new mothers prior to 2012 and after 2012. They discovered that mothers, after 2012, were 14 per cent less likely to be hospitalised for childbirth-related complications. They were also 11 per cent less likely to require antibiotic prescriptions and 26 per cent less likely to need anti-anxiety medication.[6] The results of this research are also reflected in other studies. Analysing data from an English national maternity survey, Maggie Redshaw and Jane Henderson found that in couples where the other partner had taken no parental leave, the mother was more likely to report feeling unwell and she was more likely to experience post-natal depression.[7]

Creating opportunities for the dads (or the other parent) to be there to physically and emotionally support their new family in those early days could literally save the life and/or mind of a new mother – just think about all the money the Government spaffs up the wall dealing with the symptoms rather than the cause. In 2021, Birthrights commissioned research which found that perinatal anxiety and depression could cost society an additional £17.5 billion.[8] In 2014, the London School of Economics found that perinatal mental health problems cost £8 billion a year.[9] Many of these problems could be prevented if mothers had support systems in place to help them cope, and that would include properly paid leave for the other parent. As a Brucie Bonus, the outcomes for the whole family would be improved.

We know that this is also something dads are hankering for. The 'State of the World's Fathers' survey found that 85 per cent of dads would do anything to be home with their baby.[10] Yet, if we look at how much time dads are taking off to care for their children, we see a very different picture. A 2020 study by EMW Law analysed HMRC data and found that roughly a third of eligible fathers took some sort of paternity leave in the previous year.[11] The number of men taking paternity leave has fallen year on year since 2015, while the number of women taking time out to care for children is increasing.[12] There's clearly a rather enormous disconnect between the number of dads who want to be there for their kids and the number that actually take the time off; but there's also the rather worrying evidence that the gender care gap is widening, rather than shrinking. This care gap will inevitably be influenced by the fact that not all fathers who are employed are eligible for the two weeks' measly paternity pay. According to the TUC, a quarter of dads were not eligible for any paid paternity leave whatsoever in 2018 either because they were classed as self-employed or because they hadn't been with their employer for long enough.[13] This care gap has an impact on a mother's lifelong earning potential. According to a study in Sweden, a woman's earnings rose by 7 per cent for every month of leave taken by her husband.[14]

Things get worse when we start to scratch at the surface of Shared Parental Leave, used by about 2 per cent of dads.[15] Pushed through by the coalition government in 2015, Shared Parental Leave was hailed as the new way to balance the care conundrum and ensure greater equality in the home – parents can share up to 50 weeks of leave, 37 weeks of which is paid. The mother has to use the first two weeks but the rest can be divvied up as a couple sees fit – well, sort of; the thing is it is so darn complicated that many employment lawyers I've spoken to don't understand how it works, so how on earth Barry from Stockport is meant to wrap his head around it I will never know. This isn't the only problem with the way Shared Parental Leave has been set up – oh no – there are plenty of other issues to choose from; one of the key ones being that it actually isn't shared 'parental' leave at all. Instead, it is shared *maternity* leave – the mother has to give the other parent a portion of her leave. Of course, many are reluctant to do that. Then there's the issue that, overall, families may get less money if they use Shared Parental Leave than if they just use maternity leave alongside the traditional two weeks' paternity leave. Women are far more likely to have access to enhanced maternity pay from their employer, while enhanced paternity pay is incredibly rare, again encouraging women to take the leave rather than men, and ultimately discouraging the use of Shared Parental Leave.

Then there's the problem that not everyone is eligible:

'To take shared leave, one parent must have been an employee with at least 26 weeks of service with the same employer by the end of the fifteenth week before the baby is due, or when matched with an adopted child. The other must have worked for at least 26 weeks in the 66 weeks leading up to the due date and have earned at least £30 a week in 13 of the 66 weeks.'

Kevin Peachy, BBC News
personal finance reporter[16]

Still with me? I doubt it. I'm barely with myself – that's why I used a BBC quote to explain it. But basically, if you're self-employed or haven't worked for the same employer for very long, then you're likely scuppered.

The cultural barriers that men have to contend with if they want to take time out to care for a child are completely ignored by Shared Parental Leave. Men tend to face pure bewilderment and sometimes quite extreme discrimination when they request flexibility or some time off to do the parenting.

'My boss said, "You're not going to do any of that ridiculous Shared Parental Leave nonsense, are you?!"'

'My husband was up for a promotion, but they said his promotion wouldn't go through unless he changed his request for Shared Parental Leave.'

'One of the directors said to me, "Oh, right, so you're going to be playing mum for three months, are you? Shall I buy you a dress while you're at it?"'

'My husband and I are doing Shared Parental Leave. He sent an email to work while he was off and his boss replied, starting the email, "Hello nanny".'

Shared Parental Leave does not account for the fact that, in most couples, the man is likely to earn more than the woman, so, when you're bracing yourself to reduce your income to £151 per week, it makes much more sense for the woman to take the financial hit, as overall the family loses less money.

The only possible way of dealing with all of these challenges is by scrapping the current system and starting again.

Firstly, it is crucial that paternity leave is ring-fenced, meaning it belongs to the dad (or the second parent) and cannot be transferred to anyone else. If they don't use it then the whole family loses it. This is the model established in countries including Sweden, Luxembourg, Belgium, Norway, Portugal, Canada (specifically in Quebec) and Iceland. In other countries, including Austria, Finland, Germany and Italy, they don't ring-fence the leave; the entire parental leave period can be used by either or both parents, but additional, bonus weeks of paid leave are offered if the father claims some of the leave. Both models are far more effective than what we have in the UK.

Additionally, it is imperative both parents receive a percentage of their salary to make the leave financially viable. Currently, in the UK, mothers can access six weeks' maternity leave at 90 per cent of their salary if they are an employee (and fulfil some other criteria), but fathers have access to no such thing unless their employer offers this. In 2006, Quebec changed its parental leave system so that dads received a 'Daddy quota' – five weeks' leave that could not be transferred to the other parent. They also offered dads 70–75 per cent of their salary when they used the leave. The impact was immediate: take-up rates among eligible fathers jumped 250 per cent. Now, 86 per cent of Quebec parents share their leave. In comparison, in the rest of Canada, where no such scheme exists, only 15 per cent of dads take parental leave.[17]

If you want to tackle deeply entrenched gender stereotypes head-on, then it takes a bold pledge. You can't just say, 'Oh look, men, fancy a slice of your partner's leave?' and expect everything to be okay; then, when you realise hardly anyone is using it, spend £1.5 million on marketing the policy, thinking this will solve the problem (this is what the UK government actually did with their 'Share the joy' campaign).[18] It's the very definition of polishing a turd.

Giving dads ring-fenced, properly paid paternity leave sounds horribly expensive and a pretty radical step for our government to take, but, when we compare our position with other member countries in the OECD (Organisation for Economic Co-operation and Development), we are lagging way behind. Slovenia and Lithuania do better than us.[19] In fact, the average length of paid, father-specific leave across the OECD countries was 8.6 weeks in 2016; in the UK, it is two weeks. In 2015, the OECD published a comparison of public expenditure on maternity and paternity leaves across thirty-four member states. The UK came very close to the bottom in terms of investment, ranking twenty-sixth.[20]

In addition to the challenges dads face when wanting to take parental leave, they also face huge challenges when trying to reduce or change their hours so that they can pop their dad-jacket on and do more of the childcare. According to a study co-authored by accounting organisation Deloitte and parenting website for dads DaddiLife, nearly 40 per cent of dads have asked for their hours to be changed to better fit around their newborn, but 44 per cent of those who asked said they were not given permission.[21] Compare this with research by the TUC, which showed that in 2019 one in three flexible-working requests was turned down by employers, and it suggests that men struggle to secure flexible working more than women.[22]

'I put in a flexible-working request after my second son was born. I wanted to work four days a week so I could spend a day with my children before they started school. I was called in to a meeting room with only five minutes' notice. My boss and the HR manager read my letter out loud, chuckled to themselves and said: "Let's face it, you didn't write this, your wife did, didn't she?" Before I could say that I had written it and my wife had nothing to do with it, my boss said, "Your request has been rejected. I don't want to hear any more about this nonsense."'

There are some benefits to the gender stereotypes that employers exhibit, however. Well, there are for dads. Once a man has sown his seed and reproduced, the implicit belief that his only responsibility is to financially support his family plays out in new dads receiving pay rises and promotions. In fact, dads working full-time earn 21 per cent more than men without children, and the more children you have, the better, with dads who have two kids earning 9 per cent more than dads with only one. If we compare this with what happens to women when they become mums, it's a pretty stark contrast. Women who become mothers before the age of 33 typically suffer a 15 per cent pay penalty.[23] As we know, mothers are likely to work fewer hours in paid work than fathers, and obviously that will be a contributor to this difference, but it doesn't account for such a large gap. Fathers tend to work about half an hour longer per week than men without children – is that really worth a 21 per cent pay increase?[24] Mothers tend to work about an hour less per week than women without children – again, a 15 per cent pay decrease seems pretty extreme. There's clearly bias at play with both and, as we've discussed in earlier chapters, as soon as women procreate, they are seen as less competent and less committed to their jobs. The opposite is true for men: now that they have a family to financially provide for, surely their career will be even more important to them?

It's not just at work where we're surrounded by subtle and

not-so-subtle messages that parenting is a mum's job. When Steven took Shared Parental Leave and tried to take his son to baby classes, he was regularly greeted with well-meaning people who would say, 'Aah, is mum having a well-earned break?' Then there are the dads who chuck the changing bag under one arm and the child covered in shit under the other and head to the bogs, only to be greeted by a sign showing a silhouette of a woman changing a baby's bottom. Why do baby-changing tables get automatically placed in women's toilets, but not men's? It certainly doesn't help when Piers Morgan describes Daniel Craig as an 'emasculated Bond' because he carried his own child around in a carrier.[25]

There are huge potential benefits for everyone if we can close the gender care gap. A study of 13,000 heterosexual couples found a direct correlation between involved fatherhood and long-term relationship stability, regardless of other variables such as ethnicity or wealth. The study reported that fathers who spend more time caring for their babies alone are less likely to separate from their partners than those who are less hands-on, and that fathers who took sole charge of babies before they turned one were as much as 40 per cent less likely to subsequently break up with their partners.[26] Isn't that insane? It perfectly mirrors my own upbringing. My parents fulfilled traditional roles: my dad was the hard-working bread-winner, never changing a nappy, with barely a single sighting of him before 8 p.m. at night and, even then, he was either on the phone or had his face glued to the sports channel; my mum was omnipresent, never missing a trick, so much so that she could actually read my mind, which became somewhat bothersome during my teenage years. (The first time I had sex she knew immediately, without me saying a word. Weird.) My upbringing was undoubtedly one of the drivers for me setting up Pregnant Then Screwed. My parents lived entirely different lives, neither understood the other, and, while both adequately fulfilled the roles handed down to them by years of cultural conditioning, neither was happy, and ultimately it ended in misery and divorce. Sharing the load of both caregiving and breadwinning between couples makes a partnership one of equals. If men don't spend time with their children, they will find it impossible to understand how challenging it can be for women and it will inevitably impact the bond they have with their kids, making a family's affection all feel rather lopsided.

Other research has shown a positive correlation between dads who take paternity leave and the amount of caring they do for their babies and children after they return to work. This paternal involvement, if established during the early weeks, can last through to toddlerhood and beyond. One UK study found that fathers who took formal leave were 19 per cent more likely to feed their 8–12-month-old babies and to get up with them in the night. It also showed that these dads were 25 per cent more likely to change nappies.[27] Perhaps it's something that Conservative MP Jacob Rees-Mogg should have been encouraged to do after the birth of one of his six children, considering he bragged during an LBC interview in 2019 that he had never changed a nappy in his life.[28] What a dreamboat.

Loads of men jump ship once they become a father to ensure they can play an active role in their child's life. According to research from DaddiLife and Deloitte, a third of dads have changed jobs to try to strike the best work–life balance since becoming a parent.[29] The cost of replacing an employee is high, totalling between 90 and 200 per cent of their annual salary.[30] It therefore makes perfect financial sense for companies to implement policies that will work to retain an employee once they become a parent; otherwise it's going to cost them a whole lot more than a few extra weeks' paternity pay. Companies such as alcoholic-drinks business Diageo, insurance and saving plans company Aviva, the comparison website Go Compare known best for its moustachioed opera singer, and finance company Investec all seem to understand the value of paid paternity leave and flexible working options for their staff. But, while some companies are doing what they can to help their workforce strike a really good work–life balance, many more expect their staff to always prioritise their job over their children. Four out of five employees are reluctant to discuss maternity and paternity leave policies with the company they work for, with many dads scared that if they take the full two weeks it would affect their prospect of promotion.[31]

'My little girl was born in July 2018 and I only took three days off. I was in car sales at the time, working for a well-respected family company. My daughter was born on the Wednesday; I was back in on the Monday. I wasn't entitled to any paternity pay as I hadn't been with the company long enough and my manager informed me it would be frowned upon if I didn't come back ASAP as we were a small sales team. At the time, I didn't really give it too much thought. I was excited – my little girl had just arrived – but then I knew I needed to get back to selling to help support my new family. Now, when I look back on it, I can't believe how they treated me. That they denied me the most important two weeks with my daughter. I'll never forgive them for it.'

'I didn't take paternity leave when my first two children were born. At the time, I was working in a very competitive sales environment. Other people in the company wanted my job and they could be really sneaky. I knew that if I had taken the two weeks I was legally entitled to that my job might not have been there when I returned. The third time, when the twins came along, I was working for a different company and my boss asked me whether I was going to take paternity leave. I said that I wouldn't because I thought it might jeopardise my job. He laughed and demanded that I take two weeks off, full pay.'

The big challenge is that many employers come from a generation where paternity leave and being an active father just wasn't a thing. There is a lack of empathy from those in senior positions, a lack of understanding and indeed a lack of language to discuss the issues at hand. Families are changing the way they manage their time and responsibilities, but companies are struggling to move away from the alpha-male role model.

'Aside from the process and policy improvement needed, one of the main challenges exists between the "boardroom dad" and the "modern dad", with a previous generation of men who are now senior, and in positions of leadership, failing to be fully empathetic with the new desires of more hands-on fathers. From the dads I've spoken to, there's this blasé attitude they get of, "Well, that's not what I did, so why should you?"'

Han-Son Lee, founder of DaddiLife

The dads want the leave, the mums and the kids want the dads to have the leave and the research shows that if dads take time out to care for their kids it's good for the mental and physical health of the whole family. Without dads taking time out to care for their children, workplace equality for mums is impossible. We will never have equality in the home until we change legislation to deal with the structural and cultural issues that disproportionately favour women taking time out to care for the kids. Most modern-day dads wipe almost as many bottoms as the women do, and they are keen to wipe more – who wouldn't be? Let's give the men a system that allows them to do that.

Now, for the practical stuff ...

It's good to talk

According to Han-Son Lee, founder of DaddiLife, what makes the biggest difference is when couples discuss in advance how they're going to work as a partnership once the baby is born. If both parents agree that they'll have equal involvement in their child's life from the outset, and that they'll make it work regardless of outdated legislation and cultural barriers, then equal parenting is possible. Han-Son says that many men feel nervous about approaching the conversation of sharing the leave as they believe women deserve to spend more time nurturing and caring for their new baby; after all, they were the ones who did all the hard work of pregnancy and labour. If you're a mum and you want to instil equal care from the outset, then broach the topic as soon as you can with your partner.

Paternity – what's the law?

If you're a dad (or second parent) with a baby on the way, because you've sown your seed, adopted or are the partner of an expectant mother, then you may be entitled to two weeks off, paid at £151 a week (this will increase in April 2021). To access this, you have to be an employee, not a 'worker' or self-employed (you can check what your employment status is at gov.uk/employment-status), and have to have been employed for at least 26 continuous weeks by the end of the fifteenth week before the baby's due date or by the time you're matched with a child for adoption. You also have to keep working for your employer up until the baby is born, no matter how much of a douche-canoe they are, and you need to be earning at least £120 per week (this may increase in 2021). You must complete the leave within 56 days of the birth or adoption.

You'll need to give your employer notice that you want to take paternity leave, otherwise they can veto it. You should do this by the end of the fifteenth week before your baby's due date or within seven days of being matched with a child for adoption. You do not have to give a precise date when you want to start your leave (for example, 1 February) because that would be actually impossible. Instead, you can give a general time, such as 'the day of the birth' or 'one week after the birth'.

As an employee, you're entitled to take unpaid leave to accompany a pregnant woman to two antenatal appointments. Clearly, two appointments are nowhere near enough if there are complications, but hopefully you'll have a cordial employer who realises there's little point in tying you to your desk while your pregnant partner deals with the emotional battle of a difficult pregnancy. You're allowed to take up to six and a half hours for each appointment – I'd like to say that's enough time to take your partner for a romantic cheese-and-onion pasty once the appointment has finished, but, from my own experience, it probably isn't.

What is the law with Shared Parental Leave (SPL)?

Takes a deep breath

This is the information in its most basic form, so it doesn't cover all potential situations – make sure you go to gov.uk/shared-parental-leave-and-pay for a more detailed explanation. If I were to write it all out here, there would be little room for the rest of the book.

In total you can share up to 50 weeks of SPL, and access up to 37 weeks of pay, between you. The total leave time is 52 weeks, but the mother has to take the first two weeks, as apparently that is the length of time it takes a mother to recover from birth (ha!). The really good thing about SPL is you can take it in blocks (up to three blocks in a year), you can take time off at the same time, or you can literally split it so one of you has a number of weeks off then you hand the baton over to your partner. So, for example, while the mum is on maternity leave, her partner can take four weeks SPL (in addition to the two weeks' statutory paternity leave) to hang out with his (or her) new family, mum included – though this would reduce the birth mother's overall maternity time. Or the birth mother could take 20 weeks' maternity leave (plus the two weeks' recovery period), then return to work for six weeks while the other parent takes SPL to care for the baby. Then mum could take the last 24 weeks of SPL. BUT …

this has to all happen within the first year of when your baby arrives. Are you with me so far? Good.

To be eligible, if you are the birth parents – this includes same-sex couples (it's different if you're adoptive parents, just to add that extra layer of complexity – see below) – you or your partner must be an employee who has been employed continuously by the same (i.e. your current) employer for at least 26 weeks by the end of the fifteenth week before your baby's due date (an easier way of calculating it is if you have been employed for at least 12 weeks by the time you go for your 12-week scan then you should be eligible). Once you've worked that out, then be sure that each of you earns at least £120 a week over an eight-week period (again, check the Government website, as this figure tends to increase each year). You must also stay with the same employer while you take SPL.

If the mother is self-employed, then she is not entitled to take Shared Parental Leave but her partner may still be eligible if he or she is employed. So, the self-employed mother could take maternity leave and claim maternity allowance (this is different to SMP) up to a specific date, and then the partner could take SPL. But it's worth noting that, once you stop your maternity allowance, then you can't start it again. Self-employed dads or partners are not eligible for Shared Parental Leave and pay, or for paternity leave.

If it's just the partner who wants to take SPL, then the mother must have earned at least £390 in total across any 13 of the 66 weeks before the baby is due.

To start Shared Parental Leave and Shared Parental Pay, the baby must have arrived and the mother must have given what's known as 'binding notice' to her employer of when she will return to work and eight weeks' notice of when she wants to stop receiving maternity pay.

The Government has an online parental leave calculator so you can work out what maternity, paternity or SPL pay you may be entitled to.

For those adopting a child, the 'primary' adopter and their partner can take Shared Parental Leave if they fulfil certain earnings and employment requirements. For starters, you must both have responsibility for the care of the child at the date of placement. To qualify, the 'primary' adopter must have been continuously employed by the same employer for at least six months before they were matched with a child. Your partner must have been employed or self-employed for at least 26 weeks (not necessarily continuously) in the period of 66 weeks immediately before the week the adopter was notified of being matched for adoption and must have earned at least £30 a week, on average, in 13 of those weeks. Essentially, if you qualify for Statutory Adoption Pay and Statutory Paternity Pay, you will definitely qualify for Shared Parental Pay.

12

Don't Be a Schmuck, Flex It Up

I vividly remember the day I returned to work after eight months of maternity leave. The night before, I dragged my weary body out of bed three times to shush and soothe my insomnious son. I kept the lights low and my eyes only partially peeled, hoping for a quick breastfeed followed by a satisfied nestle back to sleep for both of us. Unfortunately, my son had recently ripened his first pair of front teeth and he was keen to make good use of them. Every few sucks were bookended by his jaw clamping down on my gristly nipple so tight that it made my eyes water and my face flush red, jolting me out of my soporific state. He woke for the final time at 5.55 a.m., filling the house with his high-pitched screams until I scooped him out of his cot and his tense body softened in my arms. I carried him to my bed, clinging to the entirely unrealistic hope that he might lie there peacefully, allowing us a 20-minute doze. Instead, he yanked my hair and shoved his plump little fingers into my mouth, screeching with a mixture of frustration and delight.

Eventually we slumped on the sofa together and stared

gormlessly at the TV. When I next looked at the clock it was 7.30 a.m.; 95 minutes had vanished in a blur of Mr Tumble and the Twirlywoos. Panic set in – I was going to be late for my first day back at work. I quickly showered and then pulled on the only clothes I could find that weren't encrusted with some kind of bodily fluid (the baby's, not mine). I popped him in his high chair and briskly fed him porridge, changed his nappy, dressed him, shoved some vaguely useful items into his nursery bag while simultaneously breastfeeding, mopped up the chunks of porridge that had been callously thrown overboard, brushed his two teeth, brushed my teeth, put some blusher on in an attempt to look vaguely alive – and we set off for his first day at nursery.

I'm not going to pretend that it doesn't feel extraordinarily odd to leave your baby with a bunch of veritable strangers so you can head back to work as if the life-changing process of procreation – followed by the intensity of maternity leave – never happened. *'There you go: just plonk that new human down there – you know, the one who has turned your world upside down and your heart inside out – yep, just leave him there, and off you go back to the world as it was before they existed.'* But I was extremely lucky, for two reasons: I had a really supportive employer and a couple of colleagues who understood the mental and emotional gymnastics of early parenthood; and I had a baby who wasn't clingy. Of course, my unforgiving brain told me that this was because he didn't actually like me, but, on the plus side, he waved me goodbye without anyone having to prise him away. Now that I think about it, he actually looked quite pleased with the situation. I'll try not to dwell on that too much.

Despite these positives, the return was painfully difficult. I cried in the toilets every single day for two months. Going to work felt like an out-of-body experience; people were using words I couldn't compute. I felt like an interloper, an undercover agent thrown into a peculiar scenario without the necessary detailed briefing. The only way to survive was to mimic their actions and clone their terminology. It seemed to work – well, at least no one directly questioned whether I really belonged there.

When my boss (a man without children) said I mustn't put pressure on myself, that he knew it would take a little while for me to settle back in, I sobbed ferociously. His words were such a relief, like a therapeutic warm hug. I had returned for three days a week and that was more than enough. I was exhausted, an emotional wreck, constantly unwell.

Slowly it all started to slot into place. I found a routine that worked, I stopped crying every day, my son became slightly less ill slightly less often, the clouds started to clear. I became efficient and productive. If my son was sick, I left work to look after him – no questions were asked. If I arrived at the office late in a morning, nobody even blinked. I worked hard because I loved my job. Being a mum made me better at my job, and having a job made me a better mum. After seven months I increased my hours. I was given a pay rise and a promotion. I was on a roll.

I cannot imagine what it would have been like to work in an environment where I was tutted at for leaving on time to collect my son; where I was expected to work more days or hours than I felt able to; where I was pressured to hit the ground running without any compassion for my feelings; where I wasn't trusted to do my job whether I was in the office or not. I know I wouldn't have coped. My mental health would have unravelled. I would have been crap at my job and crap at being a mum. I would have believed that I was crap.

Few returning mothers have an experience like mine. The EHRC found that one in four mothers did not feel that her needs were supported willingly, rising to more than one in three for single mums.[1] Even when a flexible-working request was approved, 86 per cent of mothers said they experienced unfavourable treatment as a result.[2]

Let's quickly untangle the sticky, perplexing mess that can be the term 'flexible working' – it does not mean zero-hours contracts. This is the type of one-sided flexibility that, in the main, only benefits the employer. For an employee, a zero-hours contract usually offers inflexibility of the worst kind, with few legal rights. The MP Frank Field goes further, calling them 'a form of modern slavery'.[3] Legitimate flexible working comes in a variety of guises, including working part-time, working from home, concentrated hours (working your weekly contracted hours in fewer than five days), job shares (two people do one job and split the hours) and flexitime (you have a contracted number of hours but you decide when you work those hours).

Two-thirds of working mums make a flexible-working request but 38 per cent don't request the type of flexibility they want because they expect it to be rejected or they think it will reflect badly on them.[4] Whether you request what you actually want or not can be a moot point; in 2019 the TUC found that one in three flexible-working requests was turned down by employers.[5]

Of course, there's got to be a balance. The type of flexibility requested has to work for the business and the employee – a shop needs to have enough sales assistants to serve the customers, the mail needs to be delivered every day – but there are very few jobs that can't be done without some form of flexibility, unless you're posted on an oil rig or you're due to be hopping onto a spaceship to make an exploratory trip around the solar system. If an employer is prepared to be flexible, particularly in those early days, it can make a world of difference for a returning mum. Going from spending 24/7 with your baby to placing them in full-time childcare sits really uncomfortably with many mothers. It's an extreme change for everyone, and, when you've got a clinger and you're forking out bucketloads of cash for someone else to look after your child, it's not surprising that many quit their job if flexible working isn't on the table and finances allow. It's not that they want to do that – many still want to work – but, when faced with the stark choice of being a stay-at-home mum or barely seeing your small and vulnerable new baby, many feel they have no option but to give it all up and focus entirely on their child.

Without flexible working, mothers can face some very real logistical challenges. Most nurseries have fixed operating hours of 8 a.m. until 6 p.m., five days a week; mix that with the type of job where you're expected to be in at 8 a.m. and can't leave before 6 p.m. and you're bashing your head against a procedural brick wall. Unless we all think a baby would be fine left on a doorstep for an hour or so with a blanket and a packet of beef-flavoured Hula Hoops. Sometimes parents need a bit of leeway so they can ensure work fits with the other structures they are forced to interact with. It's a situation perfectly articulated by eminent flexible-working campaigner Anna Whitehouse, who was ten minutes late to collect her daughter from nursery because someone got their suitcase stuck in the Tube doors. After a full telling-off from the nursery staff, she asked her employer if she could possibly leave 15 minutes earlier each day, but her request was denied, leaving her with little choice but to quit. When your child starts school, that headache can turn into a migraine, with very few jobs working around the school run, not to mention the plays, sports days and random invitations to come and watch your child do something pretty innocuous – but, if you don't attend, well, you're clearly one of *those* mums who is more dedicated to her job than to her child; and, if you do attend, then you're one of *those* mums who is more dedicated to her child than her job.

This isn't just a problem when your child is young. Caring for a teenager can be incredibly time-consuming and mentally exhausting – I am quite certain that my own mum would attest to that. Being wholly present can be critical as your teenager wrestles with raging hormones and new experiences that can create an emotional roller coaster, such as relationship break-ups or bullying, or you may need to support them with their education. Not being there because you have yet another meeting that's drifted on into the evening can make some mums feel as though they are sacrificing their child's well-being for their job.

Then, of course, there's the domestic labour issue, with many mothers who are doing a full-time paid job trotting back home to another full-time job of cooking and cleaning and caring and organising, only this one is unpaid. We're all going to lose our bloody marbles if we're expected to carry out those two full-time jobs without any respite. It's another reason many mothers will ask for flexible working and will end up leaving their paid work if their request is denied; we are keen to keep our marbles very much intact.

Thankfully, there have been some great flexible-working strides in the past ten years, particularly since the pandemic, which had few positives but a big one was a revolution in the way we view home working. But, even before the pandemic, the UK HR associations said that job sharing was becoming more common, particularly among the higher earners,[6] and, at the beginning of 2020, 40 per cent of employed women in the UK worked part-time,[7] compared with a third of women in Europe (and 13 per cent of men in the UK).[8]

It's little wonder companies are jumping aboard the flexible-working Vengabus when studies clearly show that it's where the party's at. If implemented correctly, the benefits of flexible working, from an employer's perspective, are abundant. They include improved staff retention, increased staff well-being, better productivity and, ultimately, a more profitable businesses.

A survey of 8,000 global employers conducted by Vodafone found that 61 per cent think flexible working increased their company's profits rather than reduced them. A further 83 per cent reported that productivity was boosted by flexible hours.[9]

Morgan Stanley found that companies that do not offer flexible working underperformed in the MSCI World Index, the common benchmark for world stock funds.[10]

Research by YouGov (the public opinion and data company) on behalf of Family Friendly Working Scotland found that almost nine out of ten employers in Scotland believe flexible working has had a positive impact on their business.[11] Research by HSBC found that flexible and remote working motivates staff more than financial incentives, and there's a direct correlation between UK regions with the highest levels of productivity and UK regions where businesses are most likely to offer their staff flexible working.[12]

This is not just a perk for the mums – I wouldn't be so bold as to suggest every company reworks the way they manage their workforce just to include the 40 per cent of the population who have children and a vagina. Most employees want some form of flexibility in where and when they work. 'The Future of Work' report published by the UK Commission for Employment and Skills in 2014 contained the startling statistic that '92 per cent of Gen Y participants identify flexibility as a top priority when selecting a workplace'.[13] According to Deloitte, millennials will make up 75 per cent of the global workforce by 2025 so, if companies want to recruit the best people, then they'll be forced to implement flexible working policies that work for everyone or be left limping along with their 1970s attitude to work weighing heavily on the back of their failing businesses.[14]

But, while new mothers celebrate their freshly agreed flexible-working arrangement, pleased that they can now earn some cash and still see their child, this agreement may well mask other, unforeseen challenges. Working part-time has a number of drawbacks that directly contribute to the motherhood penalty. Part-time working can mean that any chance you had of being promoted grinds to a stubborn standstill. Parents working part-time have a 21 per cent chance of being promoted, while their full-time counterparts have a 45 per cent chance.[15] Your employer may stop viewing you as ambitious and committed, thereby mentally removing you from the career track, no matter how brilliantly you do your job. Meanwhile, part-time work is paid on average £5 less per hour than full-time work.[16] Even if you control for job, sector, experience and qualification, there is still a 29 pence-per-hour pay penalty for part-time work compared with full-time work.[17] If you are forced out of your job and need to find a new job on a part-time basis, it's highly likely you will end up in a role that is well below your skill and pay level – in 2021, only 10 per cent of jobs were advertised as part-time, according to analysis by Timewise.[18] If you want to be earning a salary that reflects your worth, with a chance of progressing up the ladder, then, as much as it pains me to say it, you need to be working full-time.

> 'A lot of women spend time in part-time work, and you seem to get almost no benefit from that in terms of increased pay later on. The value of part-time work in terms of increasing your pay further down the line is almost as low as the value of not going to work at all.'
>
> Paul Johnson, director of the Institute for
> Fiscal Studies[19]

In 2017, only 25 per cent of mothers with children aged 3–4 years old were working full-time compared with 83 per cent of men with children of the same age.[20] Mothers are pushed onto what is sometimes termed the 'mummy track' – low-paid, part-time work with little chance of progression – because companies don't value part-time workers and they aren't adapting their workplaces to ensure their employees can have a fulfilling career and be hands-on parents.

Many mothers I have spoken with accept that their career will stagnate if they work part-time; some even accept that they'll be demoted. They feel this is a sacrifice worth making so that they can see their child and earn some cash. Many resign themselves to there being no other option, and for many mums that's true. You're caught between a rock and a hard place. You need the job to be part-time so you can cope with the domestic work and the care work and to reduce the number of hours your child is placed in the extortionately priced childcare, but part-time work reduces your income and it can leave you languishing in a lake of career stagnation.

This is despite the fact that you are just as talented and just as skilled as you were before you had children – in fact, I would argue that you are more so – and, as with many new mums, your ambition hasn't decreased. You just have fewer hours to warm the office chair.

The additional problem is that, for many women who remain in the same job but agree to work a reduced number of days, thereby going from full-time to part-time, their employer doesn't implement it properly. They give very little thought as to how they will reduce your workload if you're working fewer days. I've heard from countless women who end up doing exactly the same job they were doing five days a week but trying to shoehorn it into four days, which means taking work home with them and a constant overwhelming feeling of panic – yet they are being paid less for the privilege and are far less likely to ever progress.

Susie, who works in marketing and research for a large national company, encountered this exact issue. She returned to her job after her first son was born and requested to work three days a week. After much toing and froing, causing her a great deal of anxiety, the request was declined, but her boss agreed to her working four days a week instead. She told me that she was initially very happy with this option. It gave her a full day to spend some quality time with her son, and she began plotting their social calendar to ensure they got out of the house and made the most of their time together. But, when she went back to work, it was a million miles away from the managed, calm utopia she had envisaged. 'I had the same number of clients and exactly the same objectives as before. They made absolutely no adjustments for the fact that I would be working fewer days.' Her 'day off' with her son turned into a chaotic juggling act. She would be manically trying to get through some of her emails so she could cope with her workload the following week, then there was the laundry and the hoovering, and the birthday present for the three-year-old's party and a dash to the supermarket to get the big shop. That all had to be done on the day she was meant to be spending quality time with her son. Instead of the blissful baking and singing sessions she had envisaged, she was restraining a writhing baby in a car seat so she could complete her seemingly never-ending list of domestic tasks or plonking him in front of the TV while she did her work. Her work started to slip and she wasn't achieving her targets. The emails and reports were piling up. She was missing important meetings that were scheduled for the day she had with her son, so she was playing constant catch-up. She felt guilty because she wasn't spending the time with her son that she'd imagined they'd have, and she felt guilty because she was failing at her job. When she raised this with her boss, he just replied: 'There should be no reason you can't do that job in four days' – completely ignoring the fact that the job had been designed to be done in five days, not four. It became obvious that she had two options: either quit or go back to full-time. After six months of working four days a week, she asked to go back to full-time hours. 'It was the best decision I could have made,' Susie said. 'The stress reduced and the standard of my work improved. The extra bonus was that I got paid more. Working one day less a week really had made a dent in my earnings, and my sanity.' She has since moved departments, into a role she much prefers, something she said would have been impossible had she continued working part-time because, simply by dropping one day of work, promotion opportunities were off the table.

These frustrations are clearly felt by a number of workers in the UK. A survey ran by CIPD, the professional body for human resources, showed that only 59 per cent of those who have access to flexible working used those opportunities.[21]

Susie isn't the only one who found part-time working more stressful:

'I had my flexible-working request approved when I came back to work from maternity leave recently, and, while I haven't yet quit, I am mainly miserable at work. I am often given a full-time workload and made to feel that I should be grateful for my one day a week where I am not working, and I mustn't dare moan about anything else. I've found it all really frustrating. My employer has also been clear that I won't be considered for any promotions, so I feel really unmotivated.'

'I initially went back three days a week after giving birth to my little girl nine months prior. I've actually got a pretty supportive boss; however, after a few months I started to work on my days off, using precious nap time to jump on calls (without being paid, of course). Part of this was my fault as I felt I needed to say yes to calls with senior staff so that I am not seen as a 'part-timer'. From January I have upped my hours to work every other Friday as I can't cope working three days a week. I'm still trying to cram a full-time job into 24 hours. Working in a pretty much 95 per cent male industry does make things tough.'

'I was offered to return three days a week after my maternity leave, which sounded perfect. However, it soon became clear that I was just expected to do the same job in three days, working nights, weekends and my days off

> to make up the time. After a year I couldn't take it any more and so I quit, and I am now in a full-time job where I work the same, if not fewer, hours, but I actually get paid for it! I really miss my days off with my daughter but the hours I was doing were unsustainable.'

Good and bad experiences of part-time and flexible working can very much depend on what job you do. Implementing flexible working is relatively straightforward for some professions, but not for others. If the job is based in a specific location, dealing with a multitude of transient patients or customers, such as for doctors, dentists, nurses, hairdressers, or in retail and hospitality, then it boils down to a rostering conundrum. With the right software (or someone who is shit-hot at Excel) and enough skilled staff, you can solve that particular puzzle. But, if you work in the service industries and your job is client-focused, things can be somewhat more complicated. Clients can be terribly demanding, and they expect you to be available when they need you, otherwise you run the risk of losing them as a client. In many of these sectors (such as law, the stock market, advertising, accountancy and so on), the hours you work are driven just as much by the client as they are by the employer. Some of these companies will also work internationally, meaning no hour of the day is sacrosanct. Flexibility may be offered as a favour or a perk, but it is expected that in return you will work outside your fixed hours to ensure your clients remain happy. This feels like a win–win for everyone, but there's trouble at t' mill. Now that we're starting to move away from the traditional 9–5, we are blurring the boundaries of what constitutes work time and personal time, and that can pose real dangers as employers may be happy to take advantage and many parents find themselves unable to be fully present in their personal lives, leading to burn-out. Ultimately, it can result in longer hours of work for less money and less chance of promotion.

Veronica is a mum of two who was working at a marketing agency and managing a small team. She would deal directly with the clients and then enlist her team to deliver elements of the work. 'My office hours were 8 a.m.–4.30 p.m. so that I could do the nursery pick-up while Jake (my husband) did the morning drop-offs, but I found it so draining to leave the office early so I could collect my kids and to then have to pick up work again in the evening. It's particularly hard if you manage a team – they need you around for feedback and to get things signed off. I also worked one day from home but found it really difficult to stick to the same day each week as client needs would change and I would have to work around them. Because my employers had reluctantly agreed to me leaving the office early each day, I felt as though I couldn't ever say no to them. I was constantly on my phone, responding to messages. I would be shovelling forkfuls of spaghetti hoops into my daughter's mouth with one hand while frantically typing out an email to my staff with the other. I remember my daughter once bashing her toy on my phone while I was mid-email to a really important client and the email accidentally sent, mid-sentence. I totally lost my shit. I was raging. But it obviously wasn't her fault. And then the guilt . . . It just consumed me. In the end, I decided that the only way I could escape this constant feeling of pressure and guilt was to go freelance. I reduced my days and worked normal hours. It genuinely saved my sanity.'

Those who work full-time but with some form of agreed flexibility, so they can do the nursery or school drop-off and pick-up, can find themselves doing the lion's share of the unpaid domestic labour – all the cleaning and cooking and homework and scraping-of-encrusted-porridge and bath times and bedtimes; then, when they should be lying in a horizontal position devouring deluxe chocolates and chuckling at *First Dates*, they switch their computer back on and spend another three hours writing reports and responding to urgent emails. And they are expected to feel grateful for the privilege – when the reality is they feel completely and utterly frazzled.

It's not that part-time working or 'flexitime' should be eradicated – on the contrary, it's absolutely necessary if we want to ensure those with caring responsibilities can work – but we have to be more ambitious than this. Encouraging employers to reluctantly agree to individual flexible-working requests isn't the solution. Currently, flexible working is dished out as a perk, a precious gift or generous favour granted to particular employees. But, unless everyone works flexibly, those in receipt of flexible working will be seen as less committed. What we really need to tackle is workplace culture. The UK has a long-hours culture, with employers awarding pay rises and promotions to those who keep the office chair warm. This notion is exemplified by 'presenteeism', the practice of working long hours when there's no real need to do so. In 2018, Research by CIPD showed that presenteeism has increased year on year, with 86 per cent of employees saying they had witnessed it, compared with just 26 per cent saying the same in 2010.[22]

By 2021, employees in the UK were working an extra two hours a day, an increase of 25 per cent on top of the already very long working week.[23] 'Leaveism', where people use their annual leave to work, is also a growing problem. More than two-thirds of respondents (69 per cent) reported that leaveism has occurred in their organisation in 2020.[24] There's little point in shoe-horning different types of flexibility into a structure that prioritises and values presenteeism and then think our work here is done. The individuals who are working flexibly will always lose in a culture that values long hours. A report from 2019 found that UK employees work an average of 6.3 hours per week without pay and that a fifth (22 per cent) work more than ten unpaid hours a week, more than twice the proportion of employees in other European countries.[25] Many UK employers now expect their employees to work long hours, unpaid.

It's not as if all this overtime is benefiting companies. UK productivity is worryingly low. The average UK worker produces 16 per cent less than their counterparts in the other seven leading economies. That is a statistic that should be keeping politicians and business owners awake at night.[26] The average French worker produces more by the end of Thursday than their UK counterpart can in a full week. Yet the average full-time working week is three hours shorter in France than it is in the UK.[27] In fact, according to the OECD, there is a direct link between the countries that work fewer hours and higher productivity.[28] In 2019, the UK received the rather unfortunate honour of being named the 'unpaid overtime capital of Europe'.[29] Way to go, team!

Presenteeism is killing our productivity and it is ensuring that those who work flexibly miss out on pay rises and promotions – and we know that mothers are more likely to work flexibly than other types of employees.[30] It's this we need to squash, and we need to squash it good. The only way we solve presenteeism is either through legislative reform, such as regulation to reduce the number of hours we are all working or ensure all jobs are part-time or flexible by default, or through imaginative leaders who are prepared to rugby-tackle the relentless culture of presenteeism to the ground.

PepsiCo CEO Robbert Rietbroek asks his executive team to 'leave loudly', the idea being to reduce presenteeism by showing all staff that it's okay to leave work early to get your kids. Robbert has kids of his own and is a passionate advocate for family-friendly working. He told News.com.au: 'What I've learned over 16 years as a father of two children is that it's very difficult to balance work and family commitments. We're supportive of fathers who want to participate more fully in family life. I say to my team, "I'd like you to be a hero at work, but I want you to be a hero at home. If you're only a hero at work, you're only doing half the job."' Through implementing flexible working and other policies, the company has managed to reduce its annual staff turnover from 12 per cent (the average for that industry) to 7 per cent.[31]

In 2016, France legislated for a 'right to disconnect'. The law gives some employees the right to ignore their smartphones. French legislator Benoit Hamon, speaking to the BBC, described the law as an answer to the travails of employees who 'leave the office, but they do not leave their work. They remain attached by a kind of electronic leash – like a dog.' In 2000, France also legislated for a 35-hour working week (it's 48 hours in the UK), though many companies have found ways to circumnavigate this restriction.[32]

Pursuit Marketing in Glasgow, which employs 120 people, reduced their working week to four days without cutting pay or holidays and saw a 29.5 per cent improvement in productivity in two years. According to a 2014 study for the Institute for Labor Economics, productivity drops after the thirty-fifth hour of weekly work, but productivity isn't just about hours, it's about well-being, fatigue levels and the overall health of a worker. Working for a company that gifts you an extra day to do the things that make you happy will inevitably refill a cup that was potentially on its last dregs, so it's no surprise that the move resulted in big increases in employee satisfaction and health. The key to Pursuit Marketing's success is that the whole company reduced their hours, rather than trying to shoehorn an individual's reduced working hours into an 'always on' culture. The company now expect to treble their revenue in one financial year as a direct result of their four-day working week.[33]

One form of flexible working popular among parents is home working, and, thanks to a global pandemic, it seems we have entered the era of a home-working revolution. When I got my first real job, in 2001, working for *The Crack* magazine in Newcastle, home working just wasn't a thing – everyone went to an office to do their job. But back then technology was still relatively new and nobody had a computer at home unless they were Bill Gates. Plus, the fanciest thing your mobile phone could do was to run the game 'Snake'. *The Crack* office had six computers between 11 staff, a well-used fax machine and a photocopier the size of a car. We each had a desk phone, and that's how you communicated with people outside of the office. I mean, we actually spoke to people in those days – can you imagine it? This meant I didn't spend hours dicking about on social media or doing domestic chores like sorting out house insurance or whatever. When I was at my desk, I worked. Yet, with the advancement of technology, if I was doing that job now, I could easily do it from home; there would be little need for me to be in an office apart from the odd meeting or to socialise, the power of which should never be underestimated, and socialising was definitely a core part of working at *The Crack* magazine (the stories from which are definitely not appropriate for this book).

Despite the advancement in technology, up until the pandemic very few people were permitted to work from home. People were still squeezing onto the morning Tube, sniffing each other's armpits and feeling the breath forced out of their lungs as everyone lurched forward before the doors closed. Of course, there are jobs that really can't be done from home. Medical operations can't be performed on your kitchen table, cleaning only works if you're in the home or an office block that needs a good scrub, and if you work for the fire service it would be particularly tricky for the fire engine to pick everyone up before putting out a fire. But there are plenty of jobs that are office-based with work being done via a computer or a phone, and now that we've all got more used to using Zoom and employers have realised that the world doesn't self-combust if employees aren't working from a specific office desk – well, let's just hope that there's no turning back. Almost half of all workers (49 per cent) were working from home at some point in June 2020, which was three months into lockdown;[34] before Covid-19, only 5 per cent of the country's 33-million workforce worked from home.[35]

As I am currently writing this during the pandemic, it's hard to say what the long-lasting impact of this home-working revolution will be. Certainly, some companies have already announced that their employees can work from home for ever after coronavirus forced them to trial it, including Twitter, Shopify and Nationwide. On the flip side, it's clear that some employers feel that, if they don't have their staff in their sight, there's a high likelihood they might just be watching *Jeremy Kyle* in their underpants instead of doing the weekly financial forecast. This was exemplified by a huge upsurge in sales of surveillance software that employers were installing on their employees' laptops so that they can monitor whether they were working or not. The company Sneek uses technology to take a photo of the employee, through their laptop, up to once a minute, and then uploads the photos for their colleagues to see. It's perfectly legal – the employee obviously has to know the software has been installed, but, unless they can prove the monitoring is not a 'proportionate' way to address a specific problem, then they have to like it or lump it. The company told the BBC that they had seen a five-fold increase in sales since lockdown had commenced.[36]

The thing is, since the pandemic thrust home working upon many of us, I have heard from plenty of parents who are craving a connection with their colleagues that video calling cannot satisfy, and a large proportion of employees and employers are now keen on a new model of hybrid working that offers the opportunity to network and socialise with colleagues while also spending less time doing that hellish commute. But hybrid working presents many challenges. Mothers, in particular, are hyper-aware of what being out of sight means when promotions and other opportunities are on the table. We've been pushed out, demoted and sidelined for taking maternity leave, and we've repeatedly bashed our heads against the promotional glass ceiling for working part-time or doing other types of flexible working. Sociologists call it 'proximity bias', others call it 'accidental favouritism', I call it 'bad management' or alternatively: 'ARGHHHHHH!' Ask anyone working part-time or flexibly if they feel they are judged less favourably by their employer for being less present in the office, and the majority will tell you they are. It's an unfortunate reality that if you work full-time in the office, you are much more likely to be offered that juicy promotion than if you produce the same quality and quantity of work but you do it from home. As mothers will likely be pushing for a larger slice of the home-working pie, it leaves us vulnerable. So, as I write this in November 2021, there is the worrying potential that unless employers are consciously trying to mitigate proximity bias, then hybrid working could cause a further rollback in gender equality at work. No doubt it will be women who are blamed for this because they dared to work from home, rather than us looking at employers and questioning their bias.

Flexible working is a way of squeezing women into a labour market that wasn't built for them. It can be the difference between a mother retaining some paid employment or leaving her career all together, but in many ways it's putting a plaster over a broken arm. In effect, it perpetuates the problem by keeping some women in low-paid work where they won't be promoted; or, worse, it increases their stress while decreasing their wage. If we want the labour market to work for parents, then we need everyone to work fewer hours and we need flexible working to be the rule rather than the exception. The concern now is that, due to the economic hit caused by the pandemic, companies will again revert to conventional ways of thinking and working as a method for recovery, expecting their employees to graft all hours of the day and night, believing that this is the way to rebuild their business and the economy. It's not.

The time is nigh for our government and employers to squash the culture of presenteeism for the sake of mothers, our economy and our mental health. We need to end the mentality that, the longer you sit at your desk, the more work you are producing, and we need to remember that the US Bureau of Labor says workers are only productive for two hours 53 minutes of an eight-hour working day. If you're sitting at your desk for a lot longer than that, then you're blatantly just dicking around on Facebook.

Some hot tips to help you or your partner secure the flexible working you need

* This is correct at the time of writing in November 2021, but as the Government is consulting on flexible working, it is highly likely that some of this information will soon change

1. If you've got a relatively chummy relationship with your boss, then it's worth running your request by them informally first. Maybe you could buy them a boozy drink in the pub and slip it in over a pint of Pinot? Or you could attempt the 'shit sandwich' method – say something really positive and then tell them what hours you want to work, followed by something else positive or complimentary. They may approve the request without you having to go down the formal route, which will save everyone a whole lot of time. Make sure it's all followed up in writing, though, as your contract will need to be amended.

2. If you're making a formal flexible-working request, it must be done in writing. Your employer has three months to respond so, if you're on maternity leave, you need to be doing this well before your return-to-work date.

3. When you're putting it in writing, ask for exactly what you want and need – don't dilly-dally. The law says that you can only make a flexible-working request every 12 months, no matter how many children you have, so nail it the first time around.

4. If applying for a job, then I would probably avoid

asking for flexible working in the interview. Wait until they offer you the job – that way they've decided they want you, so they're more likely to negotiate on terms. Currently, the law says that you must have been working for the same company for 26 weeks before you have a legal right to request flexible working. If you need flexibility, don't let this put you off if you haven't been with your employer this long – I would still try your luck and ask. They can only say no. After the 26-week mark, however, your employer has to give you a good business reason for rejecting your request. The challenge is that they can pick a reason from a pretty broad list, so it's relatively simple for your employer to fabricate an excuse if they're hell-bent on rejecting your request. By law, that excuse must be chosen from the following options:

- the burden of additional costs
- an inability to reorganise work among existing staff
- an inability to recruit additional staff
- a detrimental impact on quality
- a detrimental impact on performance
- a detrimental effect on ability to meet customer demand
- insufficient work for the periods the employee proposes to work
- planned structural changes to the business

Told you, eh? BROAD.

But, if your flexible-working request is rejected and you have been with the company for 26 weeks then there is a chance that you could have a legal case, so please do call the Pregnant Then Screwed free legal advice line.

5. Flexible working comes in a variety of guises. It can be like a delicious pick-and-mix – you don't have to choose a ready-made version. Think about what will work for you before you get your boss drunk, so that she agrees to it. As an idea, there's part-time, term-time only, working from home, job share, compressed hours/days, time off in the school holidays, and different hours in term time and the school holidays. You could offer to make up hours in the evening if you're a bit of a night owl/sadist, but really I would only ever do that if there wasn't any other option, because once those kids are asleep you really do deserve a rest.

6. If you're interested in doing a job share then get in touch with Pairents. They are as cool as a cucumber sandwich and offer a way of you meeting other parents with complementary skills.

7. If you're interested in finding a flexible job, there are some excellent flexible working agencies that work across the UK and place people in such roles. These agencies include 923 Jobs, MummyJobs, Daisy Chain, Working Mums, Mumsnet Talent, Ten2Two and Timewise. If you're a teacher then check out MTPT, Return to Teach and Flexible Teacher Talent.

8. Flex your flex around your job where possible – as in, think about what days your company run regular meetings, or times that are usually busier than others, or days when you have to complete reports, or times when other members of the team are already off, or whatever, and try to make sure you'll be in work at

those times. This gives your employer as few excuses as possible to say no.

9. It's the shit sandwich again: say something really positive, ask for the flexibility you really need and then sell the benefits. Go through this chapter and pull out all the stats on productivity and profit and staff retention and then think up any positives specific to your situation and business, e.g. could you cover the office out of hours for overseas clients, maybe?

10. If they say they don't think it will work, then say, 'Well, why don't we trial it for six months and if you still think it's not working then we can revert back to how it was before.' Appeal to their sense of innovation. You could maybe drop in a wanky Richard Branson quote if that sort of stuff is likely to float their boat.

11. Use a right to appeal if there is one – legally there is no right to appeal if your application is rejected; however, most companies do offer it. You don't get many rights when it comes to flexible working, so, if there is this right, then use it.

12. Oh, and did I mention Pregnant Then Screwed has a flexible-working helpline? It's staffed by incredible humans who will help you make an official flexible-working request and will talk you through your options if the flexible-working request is rejected. Have a look on our website for the number and opening times.

13. Do not feel guilty about asking for flexible working. You have nothing to feel guilty about. All you're trying to do is balance paid work with the work you have to do in the home to make sure your kids can

survive. It's the system that's broken, not you. Read the guilt chapter of this book again, eat some chocolate, hug your kids, pat yourself on the back and stick two fingers up at the patriarchy. You're doing splendidly.

13

No Ordinary Mother

It was 16 April 2020 when news broke that Mary Agyapong, a 28-year-old nurse, had died a few days after her daughter had been delivered by emergency caesarean section. Mary had contracted coronavirus. She left behind a two-year-old son, her husband Ernest, and a daughter she was never able to hold, who has since been named Mary in her mother's memory.

In the month leading up to Mary's death, Pregnant Then Screwed had been campaigning hard for pregnant women to be better protected during the pandemic. Research we had conducted between March and April 2020 had concluded that one in three pregnant NHS workers were still working with patients who could have Covid-19, despite pregnant women being listed as vulnerable. It was obvious that a disaster could unfold if these women were not better protected, so we had directed all our time and resources into a concerted effort to ensure pregnant women were suspended from front-line services. The news of Mary's death hit us hard – our worst fear had come true. It was a tragedy that could have been prevented.

When I posted about Mary online, someone pulled me up on the fact I had failed to mention that Mary was Black. At the time, there was data suggesting that more Black, Asian and Minority Ethnic people were dying from coronavirus than white people. I knew this, yet I had still failed to mention Mary's race in my post and I had failed to properly consider race when we first commenced our campaigning work to ask for better protections for working pregnant women during the pandemic. The comment on my post said: 'The lens for all pregnant women is not the same.'

When we conducted the survey again, we took a closer look at how Black, Asian and Minority Ethnic pregnant women were being treated at work during the pandemic and we found that they were more likely to be working in environments that were considered unsafe; and, if they were suspended for safety reasons, they were more likely to be suspended on incorrect terms, including no pay or sick pay, or told to use annual leave. Research published by Oxford University on 12 May, almost a month after Mary's death, found that Black pregnant women were eight times more likely to be hospitalised than white pregnant women when infected with Covid-19.[1] Despite the research study stating, 'It is concerning that more pregnant women from Black and minority ethnic groups are admitted [to hospital] with Covid-19 in pregnancy and this needs urgent investigation' more than three months after the report was published, no urgent investigation had commenced.[2] Mary was failed by a system created and designed by white people; a system that has racial bias sewn into its DNA. Indeed, the lens for all pregnant women is not the same.

Throughout history, motherhood has been portrayed through the eyes of white, middle-class, able-bodied women with perfectly healthy children, manicured nails and salon-styled hair. Those women definitely exist – I have seen them with my own fair eyes – but they don't truly represent motherhood in all its wonderful, glorious diversity. The stories and experiences of mothers with disabled children, Black mothers, Brown mothers, mothers in an interracial relationship, single mothers, gay mothers, physically disabled mothers, mentally disabled mothers, mothers whose children have not survived, young mothers, mothers of adopted children, working-class mothers and plus-sized mothers are often missing from the media portrayals of what a family looks like. Instead it's all OXO cubes and Lorraine Kelly. Their missing stories mean that policies are made and structures created that only work for one type of family, thereby triggering new types of inequality. Those with the power to make change happen are given a free pass to ignore the specific bias that these women encounter in everyday interaction.

You only have to look at some of the pay gap statistics to see the real-life impact of this bias. For instance, the difference between non-disabled women's pay and that of women with physical impairments ranges from 8 to 18 per cent, based on an hourly rate.[3] Employees from the Bangladeshi ethnic group earn, on average, 20.2 per cent less than white British employees.[4] In 2018, UK-born Black African employees were paid 7.7 per cent less than UK-born white British employees with similar occupations and education characteristics.[5] This isn't just about equality being morally and ethically fair; according to the Government's own estimations, equal participation and progression across ethnicities could be worth an additional £24 billion to the UK's economy per year,[6] while a 10 per cent rise in disability employment would raise an additional £12 billion for the UK economy by 2030.[7]

For women of colour, pregnancy and maternity discrimination is pretty far down the list of the types of discrimination they are forced to contend with on a daily basis, from micro-aggressions to full-on racism resulting in Black, Asian and Minority Ethnic workers being paid up to 37 per cent less, on average, according to an audit of public-sector pay in London carried out for the mayor, Sadiq Khan.[8] The Office for National Statistics also found that white households earned more than one-and-a-half times as much as their Black counterparts in 2020.[9]

What happened to Mary, and the statistics we saw during the pandemic relating to the number of Black and Asian pregnant women who were hospitalised, compared with white women, was frighteningly similar to a statistic released by MBRRACE-UK, a collaboration of researchers investigating maternal and infant mortality, in 2018. The statistic showed that four times as many Black women die in childbirth, or up to a year after childbirth, as white women. FOUR TIMES as many.[10] Black women are more likely to develop pre-eclampsia but there are many other complex reasons this might be happening. Dr Ria Clarke is working towards becoming a consultant in obstetrics and gynaecology. She attended one of Pregnant Then Screwed's live events to discuss this issue, where she said that Black and Asian women were more likely to be affected by social and economic problems. In other words, Black and Asian women are more likely to live in poverty or unsuitable housing and are more likely to work in unstable jobs, all of which affect health outcomes and therefore mortality rates. But both Dr Ria Clarke and Candice Brathwaite, author of *I Am Not Your Baby Mother* and founder of Make Motherhood Diverse, say that racial bias is at play.

Candice developed septicaemia after the birth of her first child. When she complained she wasn't feeling right after her C-section, she was told she was overthinking it. She returned to the hospital two hours later and was told they had to take her into the emergency ward or she might die. She says: 'Health trusts need to admit there is racial bias. There needs to be better training so people can say, "Am I responding to this person differently and why is that?"'[11] Unfortunately, the shocking disparity in mental and physical health between Black people and white people doesn't just end there – Black women are more likely to have a miscarriage,[12] they are less likely to receive fertility treatment[13] and Black babies are more likely to be stillborn[14] (although research in the US shows that a Black baby is three times more likely to survive if cared for by a Black doctor).[15]

Thanks to the Black feminist scholar Kimberlé Crenshaw, who coined the term 'intersectionality' in 1989, we know that race, class, gender and disability intersect with one another and overlap. We also see this play out in pregnancy and maternity discrimination. If you are a woman of colour, you are disproportionately more likely to experience disadvantages in the workplace because of motherhood.

'Ethnic minority mothers were more likely than white British mothers to report financial loss, a negative impact on opportunity, status or job security; or to have a negative experience related to breastfeeding.'

Equality and Human Rights Commission report, 2016[16]

Muslim mothers are often stereotyped as likely to have lots and lots of children and then to quit their job to focus on the home. According to the Women and Equalities Select Committee: 'Many Muslim women face a triple penalty impacting on their employment prospects: being women, being BME and being Muslim.'[17] Add to that motherhood, making it a quadruple penalty, and you can see that developing a career can be really challenging for a Muslim mum.

Research shows that Muslim women are much less likely to secure professional jobs in comparison with white women, even when they are well educated,[18] and there is strong evidence that Muslim women are more likely to be asked during an interview about their marital status and family life than white women are.[19] A recent report by the European Network Against Racism found that, 'In the UK, one in eight Pakistani women are asked about marriage and family aspirations in job interviews whereas only one in thirty white women are asked such a question.' There is also evidence that the outcomes of job applications are affected by name-based discrimination.[20] This type of discrimination is particularly problematic for women of colour who pursue justice when they have encountered discrimination in the workplace. Now that the Government is publishing data on tribunals, including the name of the claimant, women with less common names can be found via a Google search and that doesn't bode well if you're interviewing for a new job. All the interviewer has to do is type your name into Google and, hey presto, the case is available for anyone to read.

Mothers of disabled children are thrown headfirst into a world where their unpaid labour is disregarded and under-valued, while their paid labour is almost impossible to maintain. The structures and systems they are forced to inter-act with were not set up to accommodate the specific needs of mothers with disabled children:

'My son is living in one of the richest economies in the world as a vulnerable disabled child, with a system committed to preventing his educated single mum from working, forcing her to stay on benefits, ensuring she has dire mental health, expecting her to manage a 24-hour care plan, which puts both of our lives at risk. This could happen to anyone. I didn't ask for this. I didn't step forward and say, "I volunteer to be a parent of a child with disabilities." It just happened.'

Kaytee Jones

In the UK, there are 800,000 disabled children under the age of 16. That equates to one child in twenty.[21] Being the parent of a non-disabled child is itself a complex concoction of highs and lows – the highs can leave you feeling dizzy with happiness; the lows punch you in the face so hard you question your sanity. Many parents of disabled children say those feelings are so much more extreme, on both sides, and the system that doesn't work for mothers who don't have disabled children wholly fails mothers who do.

Penny Wincer is the single mum of two children. Her son has autism. She told me that one of the main challenges as a working mum to a disabled child is navigating the NHS. If a child has multiple problems, they will have multiple practitioners and multiple appointments, but there is no coordination between the departments to reduce the time burden on the parent. A friend of Penny's has a child with highly complex needs; the mum totalled the number of NHS appointments she attended with her son last year as 250. She was a teacher, and, despite her employer being incredibly supportive, bending over backwards to accommodate her as a parent of a disabled child, she felt forced to resign. She was working part-time to try to fit teaching around the appointments, but the days and times of those appointments changed

241

so frequently it became physically impossible for her to teach and care for her child.

Penny herself is a freelance writer and photographer. She says that owning her own business is what has made working and parenting a disabled child just about possible, as it means she can flex her schedule around her son. She receives Working Tax Credit to subsidise her son's additional childcare needs, but this in itself is fraught with challenges. To access Working Tax Credit, you must use a childcare setting that is Ofsted-registered, such as a nursery, but nurseries cannot cope with her son's additional needs, so Penny has no other option but to employ a nanny. She therefore becomes an employer, with all the responsibility that this entails, but nannies are rarely Ofsted registered and it can take months for an application to be accepted. In the meantime, Penny has to pay the nanny's wages out of her own income, which means her earnings are hugely depleted. Many of the nannies she has employed have been unreliable, calling in sick at the last minute or not showing up. One nanny lasted just two weeks before she resigned, telling Penny the job was too stressful and she was crying every night. Such childcare challenges create enormous professional difficulties, but they can also be really disruptive for her son. She told me that the difficulty of navigating such an intensely complex system, just to ensure your child is properly cared for, means that many parents give up and decide they have no choice but to stay at home and survive on the meagre benefits available.

The statistics speak for themselves. According to a report by the Papworth Trust in 2018, 84 per cent of mothers of disabled children were not working and only 3 per cent of mothers of disabled children were working full-time.[22]

And yet it costs the parents of a disabled child three times as much to raise them as it does to raise a non-disabled child.[23] Disability Rights UK estimates that 40 per cent of disabled children are living in poverty.[24] According to the 'Counting the Costs' survey in 2012, one in six families (17 per cent) with disabled children goes without food, one in five (21 per cent) goes without heating, one in four (26 per cent) goes without specialist equipment or adaptations, and 86 per cent go without leisure activities.[25]

Penny told me that life can feel really difficult. She is exhausted from the early rises, managing a business and giving her children the emotional and physical support they need. She is able to access respite funds from the Government, but she can't find a person or a facility that can effectively care for her son, so the money is gathering dust. It will eventually be clawed back as it hasn't been spent.

Despite the unrelenting pressure and sometimes debilitating exhaustion, Penny feels incredibly fortunate that she is able to work and care for her children. She is quick to point out that for many it is impossible. When I did a survey asking the parents of disabled children if they wanted to work, 100 per cent said they did, but, without childcare that caters to the specific needs of disabled children, without employers who are willing to be flexible, and without a coordinated approach to NHS appointments, the working world doesn't work for the parents of disabled children. Instead, many are forced into poverty.

There are around 1.7 million parents who have a disability themselves,[26] including one in four single-parent families.[27] The needs of those parents vary considerably so it feels trite to lump disabled parents into one category, but, as most of the publicly available research does that, I will have to follow suit.

Disabled people are labelled with many negative stereotypes: that they are a burden; that they are lazy and stupid. Add to that the stereotypes working mothers are labelled with – not committed, other priorities, may turn up to meetings with porridge in their eyebrows – and you have a veritable stereo-type party. Not the good type of party where you dance until your feet hurt and laugh until you're hoarse, but the sort of party where nobody turns up and you get food poisoning from the out-of-date sausage rolls.

Nichola Garde is a mother with two children. She has dwarfism. 'When you are employed as a disabled person, you have to work a little harder to be seen and to show that you have earned your employment there – that you're not just the token disabled person,' Nichola told me. 'In all professional and personal environments, I have felt that I work a bit harder to be seen and heard, while also taking care not to be too loud and overbearing. You need to be confident but not so confident that people begin to think you have a chip on your shoulder. It's quite an exhausting balance.' Nichola said that she was very aware that being a pregnant disabled person would create additional challenges for her at work, but, as someone who had lived her whole life in an environment not built for her, she had grown very used to constantly problem-solving. Despite this, she still struggled: 'When you become a pregnant disabled woman, your exhaustion and vulnerability is pushed to a limit where just getting out of bed requires courage and stamina. The physical environment of the workplace can be really hard to navigate as a disabled person. When you're carrying round an extra person, this becomes even harder.'

If you're a disabled pregnant woman, you have an increased risk of problems with the pregnancy, so you spend way more time at hospital. This can put immense pressure on the rela-tionship you have with your employer. Nichola recalls: 'My constant need to prove that I was as capable as my able-bodied colleagues put a huge strain on my body and mind. Taking public transport when you are disabled is a huge physical challenge. Also, ableist thoughts around disabled people becoming parents can attract intrusive questions from strangers: "Is she yours?" "How did you get pregnant?" "Is she going to be ... you know ... like you? (With sympathetic head-tilt.) While I'm happy to answer any question around my disability if it helps towards a better understanding, this is not so easy with a toddler at your side, and all before work and coffee.'

After a while, Nichola could sense her mental health starting to deteriorate: 'Ableism can cause you to doubt your own capability or self-worth as a parent. The feeling that society is judging you as a mum is magnified when you are looking through the lens of a parent with a disability.'

According to the Equality and Human Rights Commission, those with a long-term physical or mental health condition were more likely to say they felt forced to leave their job, or to report a negative impact on opportunity, status or job security once they became mothers. They were also more likely to report a disagreement with their employer about when to return to work following maternity leave.[28]

Young mums are often stereotyped as uneducated, unemployed, feckless teenagers, a stereotype that politicians have repeatedly upheld. In 2009, Tom Harris MP wrote an article for *The Guardian* entitled 'The return of morality: the army of teenage mothers living off the state is a national catastrophe'.[29] Also in 2009, Gordon Brown said that teenage mums could access supervised homes 'where they learn responsibility and how to raise their children properly',[30] when the truth is that many young mums are perfectly responsible, are trying their hardest to earn a living and just want to live in a system where they feel supported.

Laura Davies has a son called Max who is nine years old. 'I've grown up to be told that young mums are irresponsible, benefit-scrounging kids. That they wander around with buggies full of babies, with no ambition in their lives. They go on to tell me that they have no focus, no drive and are in it for free housing, free money and an easy life. When I was 19, I started university, had a long-term job in a demanding sales environment and a steady boyfriend. When I was 19, I also discovered I was pregnant. Becoming pregnant at 19 wasn't part of my big life-plan, but life doesn't always go to plan.' Laura experienced discrimination at work and in the education system: 'Working in a male-dominated sales environment, I was already at a disadvantage. But, as soon as I added a pregnancy to the mix, I felt vulnerable, as if I had a walking target on my back. I didn't feel as though I was respected as a member of the team, and some male colleagues were allowed to leer at me, making snide remarks about my pregnancy. To everyone else it might have been "workplace banter" but in reality it hurt to hear how some of my peers thought I was ruining my life.' Laura's employer refused to do a risk assessment for her, despite her working on her feet all day. She was made to feel as though she was lazy if she asked to sit down for a few extra minutes.

When Laura returned to work, her flexible-working request was outright denied, forcing her resignation. Simultaneously, she was studying at university, and it was agreed she could defer her second year to have her son: 'They seemed really enthusiastic and supportive, but, as I prepared to return, the atmosphere shifted. They had promised all my lectures would fit around the on-site childcare. They lied. I was given all evening lectures and had to beg for support. I ended up in an incredibly hostile environment where I knew I wasn't welcome, but I was paying all that money so I deserved to be there. It all came to a head when, six weeks before my final hand-in, I failed an essay. It wasn't even a major fail, just a couple of marks off a pass. The head of the course called me in and asked whether this course was right for me. He said I should probably quit the degree before I failed – the degree that I was six weeks away from finishing. Yes, I was never going to be a first-class honours student, but they suggested that I would be better off focusing on being a mum as opposed to learning. Clearly, they thought I couldn't do both.' Laura didn't give up. She found support from another lecturer, who didn't teach on her degree but offered extra help over the summer holidays, and Laura finally got her qualification. 'I realised I had no one on my course who thought I was going to pass. They didn't actually want a young mum there. I wasn't the aesthetic of an arts student. I submitted a complaint, but I didn't have the energy to follow it through. I was tired and broken. Being forced to battle prejudice and fight for my degree while caring for a tiny baby at the age of 19 – it was tough. I have a degree, and I goddam deserve it. But it took a hell of a fight.'

Although students are protected by the Equality Act 2010, bringing a case can be challenging because students don't have the same protections and legislative infrastructure, such as flexible-working protections, that employees have. Research by the National Union of Students found that 59 per cent of students who had been pregnant while studying did not feel supported by their college or university.[31] That's a pretty damning statistic.

Other young mums talk of the constant discrimination they face from health professionals, the media and politicians. 'You should have kept your legs shut' is a recurrent theme, alongside an assumption that young mums are uneducated and living unstable, directionless lives. But, actually, much of the research doesn't show this to be the case at all. A 2006 research report by the Joseph Rowntree Foundation explored the views and experiences of young mums from deprived backgrounds who had all planned their pregnancies. Most of the women talked about how motherhood had made their lives more positive, had given them renewed purpose and had helped to turn their lives around.[32] Other research compared the long-term outcomes of women who became pregnant when they were teenagers and had a miscarriage with those who went on to be young mums. It found that by the age of 30 there were no significant differences between the two groups regarding income, employment and qualifications.[33]

The research demonstrates that being a young mum is not the problem in and of itself. The problem is the discrimination young mums encounter and the systems they interact with. Or, as Joëlle Bradly, a young mum campaigner also known as Prymface, says: 'What's important to take away from this is not that being a young mum is easy and makes no difference to your "life outcomes" but that having a baby while still young can actually spur young people on to overcome any struggles.'

These challenges often result in young mums and their families living in poverty. Research by the Young Women's Trust in 2017 found that almost half (46 per cent) of young mums skip meals so they can afford to feed their children, and more than a quarter have had to use food banks.[34] The Equality and Human Rights Commission research showed that you are six times more likely to experience pregnancy or maternity discrimination if you are under 25 when you have a child.[35]

Single mums face similar stereotypes and prejudice. All the data shows that the stereotype of the benefit-scrounging single mother is a lie spun by the right-wing press. Seven in ten single parents are in work, grafting their backsides off to put food on the table. It's not at all easy: they have to deal with exorbitant childcare costs without a second earner in their household (on average, childcare is 67 per cent of a single parent's total income) and a working culture that expects long hours and unpaid overtime without a second person to catch the chaos when it's unleashed.[36]

> 'The fact that the sole parent is filling all adult roles in the house (breadwinner, home-maker, child-raiser) is fairly obvious; there is nobody else to fill them (I've tried asking Jack, 3, to put the laundry on and renew the car insurance – the results have been mixed). And, while there is some comfort in knowing you're steering your little family ship all by yourself, keeping it afloat can be tricky.'
>
> Rebecca Cox, *Harper's Bazaar*[37]

Anyone who manages to keep their ship afloat as part of a couple can but marvel at the warrior women who do it on their own. But they don't want our sympathy – they haven't got the time for it. What single mums want is respect and a system that works for them.

Ayesha is a self-employed single mum of three children. She works in TV production, which demands long and unusual hours, so her children go to the local after-school club, which runs until 6 p.m. on weekdays. Everything was just about slotting into place until the after-school club decided the whole term needed to be paid upfront: 'I can't afford that,' Ayesha told me. 'I don't have that sort of money sloshing around, so now I have no childcare next month and I have a job that I will lose if I can't find someone to look after my kids. My mum isn't well enough and I have no one else I can ask. I called a childminder but they are way too expensive – more than my pay. I have four weeks to secure something and I don't know what I am going to do. I'm trying to pay the bills, I have an ex who doesn't support us financially, I have no savings as I use every penny to make ends meet, there's £200 in my bank account and sometimes I don't know if I will be able to pay the rent – and I'm one of the lucky ones. I have a good job that pays pretty well. I know so many single mums who just aren't coping at all.'

Yes, there are single dads, too, but 90 per cent of single parents are women, and, while single dads are revered, single mums are chastised and belittled.[38] They are the fall guys (or fall women) for the world's ills (alongside immigrants and the EU). Lone parents are paid, on average, £2.14 less per hour than the *second* earner in a couple,[39] resulting in one in three children with a working single parent living in poverty in 2018.[40] A Joseph Rowntree Foundation report found that jobs with decent pay and flexibility are 'few and far between' for single parents. Single mums are also more likely to face discrimination in the workplace due to conscious and unconscious bias. The Equality and Human Rights Commission found that single mums were more likely to face negative consequences in the workplace and were more likely to be under pressure to resign than mothers who were married or were living with their partner.[41]

I caught up with Ayesha just before I finished writing this book to see how she was getting on. She'd been forced to remove her children from the after-school club due to the upfront fees, which meant she had to hand in her resignation on a really fantastic contract she had with the BBC. 'I'm broken and I am really struggling mentally,' she told me.

Even before the pandemic, poverty in the UK was on the rise, leaving more and more people beholden to food banks and credit, a cycle that is almost impossible to break once you're held in its trap. I wouldn't be so bold as to blame zero-hours contracts for this rise in poverty, but they don't help, and women, particularly single parents, are more likely than men to work on zero-hours contracts or do agency work.[42] One of the key components of these types of contracts is that the worker doesn't usually have fixed hours of work, so arranging childcare is enormously problematic. Zero-hours contracts facilitate employers' ability to drop workers like hot bricks, which means childcare might be booked then not used, but due to the late notice it will still have to be paid for.

Women on zero-hours contracts cannot take paid time off for antenatal appointments – these must be arranged outside of working hours. Such appointments are absolutely vital for the health of a mother and her baby; not giving women access to paid time off creates a financial barrier, and those living hand to mouth are less likely to attend as they simply cannot afford to do so. The other key challenge for workers on zero-hours contracts is that they have no right to return to their old job if they have taken time out to give birth and care for their baby, yet simultaneously they cannot access the Shared Parental Leave scheme, which is set up for employee couples, so the burden of care rests entirely with the mother. It is the mother who is forced to walk away from her job to do the caring without the safety net of having a job to return to. If an agency worker or someone on a zero-hours contract faces discrimination due to pregnancy or motherhood, then she is often left powerless to challenge it as there is rarely an official reporting process, and any complaints are likely to result in being given no further work.

Shelly is a mother to two young children and a tutor who works with kids who have been permanently excluded. She is registered with an agency on a zero-hours contract basis and she told me she will get a call from them about once every three weeks, when they expect her to drop everything and be immediately available. If she says she can't work, usually because of childcare issues, she is penalised, and work will be given to other agency workers before it's given to her. She can spend months waiting for another call. 'The women who call me, they know they have the power in that relationship. They expect to say "Jump" and for me to say "How high?"' she told me.

It's impossible to cover all of the challenges faced by under-represented mothers in one chapter. Here I am barely scratching the surface, but, hopefully, this starts to explain why looking at issues only through the lens of white, middle-class, able-bodied, women will not solve the problems for all mothers, and in some cases may even make things worse. In the words of Kimberlé Crenshaw: 'Treating different things the same can generate as much inequality as treating the same things differently.'

Hot tips

If you are working on a zero-hours contract, you are still protected from pregnancy discrimination. Due to zero-hours contracts stating that hours are given only when they are available, women feel they do not have any legal rights if those hours suddenly dry up after announcing a pregnancy. But, if you can demonstrate that an employer stopped offering hours after a pregnancy is announced but was offering hours before, then you could potentially have a legal case. Call Pregnant Then Screwed – we can help.

If you are a student and you face any form of pregnancy or maternity discrimination, you have up to six months to raise a claim and are covered by the Equality Act 2010, though bringing a case can be challenging because you don't have the same legislative infrastructure that employees have, such as flexible working protections. There's more information about how to take legal action against a school, college or university for discrimination on the Citizens Advice website.[43]

14

Master of Your Own Destiny: Is Self-Employment the Solution?

On the face of it, self-employment, working freelance or running your own business can seem like the silver bullet when you're trying to balance caring and work. But in reality, for many, it's less of a silver bullet and more of a slightly rusty wrench.

'The Rise of the Mumpreneur' is a particularly grating phrase that I have stolen from the *Telegraph* and the *Daily Mail*, where self-employed mothers are paraded around like prized hens. These are the success stories – the women juggling a business and children. All hail the women who can do it all.

For me, the rapid rise of the mumpreneur is not something the Government or the media should be proud of. It is the mark of a badly functioning labour market. When droves of mothers are choosing to leave the stability of a job with sick pay, holiday, a pension, maternity leave, parental leave and colleagues, then something has gone horribly wrong. Why would anyone choose to do something so risky when they have recently become a mother – unless they had no other choice – especially when 60 per cent of new businesses fail within three years, leaving some mums in a right old pickle.[1] We also know that around half of all self-employed people survive on poverty wages, according to the TUC. Yet, despite this, the number of mums who set up their own businesses almost doubled between 2001 and 2020, and it is expected we will see a leap in these figures due to the pandemic.[2]

For those who were already self-employed when they embarked on the journey of motherhood, it can appear from the outside that the hard graft is done – you've already taken the plunge and things are going pretty well; you have the connections and a good reputation. You just need to slot a baby into the mix. Surely that will be pretty straightforward when you have the ultimate flexibility to choose when and where you work, right? But the reality can be quite different. 'When you work freelance, you don't go back post-maternity leave to a desk or workload. You go back to the potential of a workload. And, if you're off your hustle, that potential is dramatically diminished,' said Katherine Ormerod, editor of Work Work Work, in a blog she penned about her own experience as a self-employed mum. 'What it has meant for me is paying a huge amount for childcare, creating time and space to work, without actually having any work to do.'[3]

The reality is that many self-employed women don't actually stop working once they have a baby. They can't. If they stopped working, then everything they had spent years building would likely collapse, so swollen and cracked nipples are smothered in Lansinoh while responding to emails and praying your new baby will do an extra-long nap so that you can hit your client's deadline.

Gemma Stokes set up her business, a research agency, in 2012. When she had her first son, she was employing four people full-time and giving regular work to six freelancers (all mums). The business was growing fast, making it really difficult to take any maternity leave, so she returned to work the day after a C-section. This sounds extreme, but it's not at all uncommon – in 2017, a bunch of NHS doctors funded a study of 104 self-employed mums and found that almost half took no maternity leave at all.[4] Gemma's husband also ran his own business (a building company) so Gemma was left holding the baby when her husband would leave at 6 a.m. each day. Eight weeks after giving birth, she developed mastitis, and it was ugly. She had to visit the hospital every other day to have her breast drained. Ultimately, this took its toll on her work and her mental health. Eventually, she managed to sew together a patchwork of childcare, but it was incredibly expensive. Any money she made from the business would go on childcare costs, which felt enormously deflating. Then, when her first son was ten months old, she discovered she was pregnant again. It was a tough pregnancy; she was admitted to hospital twice due to morning sickness. Again, she returned to work the day after a C-section with no space in between, and this time things really started to deteriorate. Her second child was a terrible sleeper, waking every hour – she was exhausted and desperate, and developed post-natal depression. 'I didn't notice it at first. It just crept in. I would feel overwhelmed with the simplest of tasks. I would cry at night or burst into tears while out walking the dog.' Post-natal depression is far more common among self-employed mums than other mums, and the same study by NHS doctors revealed that over half (59 per cent) had suffered from anxiety, general stress or depression caused by the amount of responsibility associated with running a business and having a newborn baby.[5] In the end, Gemma and her family decided it was too much, so they picked up their life and moved to France. This reduced their childcare bill enormously (French childcare is way cheaper than childcare in the UK) and it meant Gemma could develop a remote team of workers in the UK to keep her business going.[6] Her mental health started to improve and life started to look a little brighter. When Gemma sent me her story, she had this to say: 'I feel angry that women have to go through this. I think female business owners fall through the cracks of childcare. It's a nearly impossible task to keep a business running when you have a baby.'

Perhaps these stories go some way to explain the 43 per cent gender pay gap among the self-employed.[7]

Of course, there are the success stories. There are plenty of women who are forced into self-employment because they had no other choice and it was the push they needed to carve out their own destiny and to succeed on their own terms. Some even combine their previous skills with their new preoccupation of motherhood, such as Molly Gunn from Selfish Mother, whose apparel business has been so successful she has raised over a £1 million for charity from sales. Or Gemma Metcalfe-Beckers from Muthahood, whose 'Strong Girls Club' T-shirts can be seen draping the bodies of fierce girls and women. Gemma told me she had always wanted to be at the school gates and the school assemblies, so, when her employer couldn't give her the flexibility she needed, it drove her to set up her own business. She says it's not all rosy and you need to be ruthless with your boundaries: 'I think, with everything in life, understanding that there are highs and lows is important. Don't always expect the grass to be greener if you decide to start a business. It has its positives, but there are plenty of challenges – they're just different challenges to those that present themselves through employment.'

Women-led and women-owned businesses contribute a

staggering £221 billion to the UK economy. Just imagine what we could achieve if the structures and systems were implemented to properly support entrepreneurial mothers.

Self-employed? Some hints and tips

Thankfully, there are some pretty spectacular humans out there who have set up groups to build support and solidarity for self-employed-mums. The Guilty Mothers Club, run by the obscenely wonderful Helen Bryce, is one such group; though based in Manchester, most of her work is virtual so people can join across the UK. Doing It For The Kids is run by the hilarious Frankie Tortora. Based in London, she runs regular meet-ups, organises days where mums can get together in a co-working space with a crèche, and her website is full of helpful tips and advice on everything from doing your tax return or entertaining your children while you take a client call to 'How to eat anything other than biscuits', which, if you work from home, is a genuine challenge. Mummy's Day Out, run by the powerhouse that is Rachael Buabeng, brings mothers together to empower them in motherhood and business, promoting the positive image of Black British motherhood.

If you are self-employed, you can only access Maternity Allowance, rather than Statutory Maternity Pay. Unfortunately, this means you do not get the six weeks at 90 per cent of your salary that employed women receive. The law says you can have ten 'keeping in touch' days, which means that while you're receiving Maternity Allowance you can do only ten days of paid work. If you work more than ten days then you should stop your Maternity Allowance. Clearly, that is nowhere near enough time to keep a business afloat. Obviously, I am in no way advocating you break the law (*cough*) but there are ways of being creative with that time.

Applying for Maternity Allowance is quite frankly an absolute ball-ache, so start doing all the reading and pulling-together-the-stuff-you-need as soon as possible. You can't apply until you're 26 weeks pregnant and have a MatB1 form, so make sure you get one of those from your midwife at your 20(ish)-week scan. The paperwork is bewildering and laborious. There's a 'Test Period' table that makes little sense to anyone, but you can try calling the Department for Work and Pensions as their advice can be really useful (if you can get through). Whatever you do, get it right the first time – do not give them any reason to send it back to you, because it takes an absolute *age* for anyone to actually look at your form. Send it Recorded Delivery and drive them bonkers by chasing it up. Good luck.

The way to receive the maximum allocation of Maternity Allowance is to ensure you are up to date with your Class 2 National Insurance contributions. You pay these contributions as part of your annual self-assessment, so the likelihood is you are not up to date with them unless you happen to be 26 weeks pregnant just as you've completed your tax return. You will therefore probably be offered a measly £27 a week by the DWP. Don't panic. All the DWP has to do is send a letter to HMRC saying you owe them some cash so that you're up to date with your Class 2 National Insurance contributions – you pay the bill and voilà! You will now be eligible for Maternity Allowance, which is £151.20 per week (this figure will increase in April 2021) or 90 per cent of your average gross weekly earnings, whichever is lower.

Get a pension. Do it. Seriously. It's very easy to ignore (and

I am a massive hypocrite here because it sat on my to-do list for 18 months) but you will get old and you will want to retire and you really must make sure you don't retire into poverty if you can avoid it. Do not rely on a man, or anyone else – just get a bloody pension. Do a bit of research, get a financial adviser or just go online and find a simple pension to start paying into – whatever you do, just make sure you get one. Now. Right now. Do it.

15

What Are They Doing Over There?

The story goes that a Swedish tech CEO had recently recruited someone from America to come and work for him. The American flew into Stockholm and the tech CEO offered to show him around his new home city. As they wandered down the cobbled streets of the tangled old town and into the cosmopolitan city on a beautiful day in June, the American turned to the Swedish tech CEO and said: 'What's up with all the gay nannies?' The tech CEO looked perplexed: 'I'm not sure what you mean?' The American pointed to the 30-year-old bearded men bouncing babies on their knee while drinking their morning lattes; and other men pushing prams loaded with shopping, sometimes pausing to contort their faces into new surprising positions for the entertainment of their passengers. 'Oh, you mean the dads?' replied the tech CEO.

It was the moment when two worlds collided. The notion that a large number of dads would be off work taking care of their own children was so alien to an American that he couldn't actually compute what he was seeing. Yet, for the

Swede, dads looking after their own children was completely normal and ordinary – as it should be.

Parental experience is influenced by a constellation of work–family laws, policy, gender stereotypes, social expectations and labour-market behaviour. The experience of mothers in the workplace also fluctuates enormously depending on where you happen to live when you get pregnant. Across the world, politicians grapple with the motherhood penalty, some with more resolve than others, but there isn't a single country that has managed to solve it. Of course, some are closer than others, with Scandinavia leading the way. The region is seen as the equality nirvana, the place where all good people go when they die, a haven of respect and equity. On the other end of the scale is America – the good old US of A, the land of the free and the home of the brave. You'd have to be bloody brave to put up with their complete lack of support for women who give birth. In America, capitalism waits for no one.

America is the only industrialised nation in the world that has no statutory national policy of paid maternity, paternity or parental leave. This results in one in four women returning to work ten days after giving birth.[1] TEN DAYS. Can you imagine? I could barely get dressed ten days postpartum. Worse than that, my undercarriage was so sore that I couldn't urinate without crying. Suffice to say, I was not in a fit state to be in an office, and I'd had a relatively straightforward birth.

The USA's Family Medical Leave Act of 1993 gives women 12 weeks' job-protected *unpaid* leave, but many workers don't qualify for it. In fact, millions of American women aren't offered a single day off work after the birth of a child. Under US employment law, there is no requirement that employers offer paid holiday, either, though around three-quarters of private-sector workers are in receipt of some form of paid holiday,[2] which usually averages a total of ten days.[3] Therefore, for many women, giving birth means their measly annual leave entitlement is swallowed up recovering from the birth. This position isn't only brutal for a new mother; it is so damaging for babies that research shows it could be killing them. McGill University research shows a 'strong link between paid parental leave and child survival'.[4] One 1995 study found that every extra week of maternity leave correlated with a 2–3 per cent decline in infant deaths.[5] A 2011 study indicated that paid parental leave could reduce infant mortality by 10 per cent.[6] The United States' infant mortality rate is high for a developed county – twice that of Sweden.[7]

Sharon Lerner wrote a piece for *In These Times* in which she explored the experiences of some of the mothers who had returned to work less than two weeks after giving birth. In the article, she talks about Leigh Benrahou, a mother who went back to work just a few days after her son, Ramzi, was born prematurely: 'I remember walking real slow and wearing stretch pants and just making it happen,' she says hazily. She spent those early days cutting a path between the college, the hospital's neonatal intensive care unit (NICU), where Ramzi spent four months and underwent two stomach surgeries, her 3-year-old daughter's daycare centre, and her home, where, despite her exhaustion, she found it difficult to sleep.

At work, Benrahou tended to the needs of her students, whose questions about enrolment requirements and course changes occasionally provided distraction from her own, far graver problems. But mostly it was surreal – and painful – to be there. Climbing stairs was difficult because of her recent surgery. And pretty much every time she closed the door to pump breast milk, she wound up crying. Harder still was being away from her tiny baby, whose health was still so uncertain. Every time she got a call from the hospital when she was at work – and there were many – her stomach clutched.

'They say it's like being on a roller coaster [having a child] in the NICU,' says Benrahou. 'But a roller coaster is fun. I wanted to throw up all the time.'[8]

Like many American women, Leigh was forced to battle ahead. Desperately trying to keep a roof over her family's head meant leaving her sick child on his own in hospital – but what choice did she have?

Research from the US Department of Labor shows that if a mother is offered paid maternity leave then she is significantly less likely to quit her job before or after the birth of her child.[9] Paid maternity leave is good for companies as staff are more likely to return to their jobs; it also reduces infant mortality,[10] improves a child's overall health and reduces the likelihood of post-natal depression.[11]

The lack of paid maternity leave in the USA means that maternity discrimination is less common, but pregnancy discrimination is rife. The *New York Times* reported in 2019 that: 'The number of pregnancy discrimination claims filed annually with the Equal Employment Opportunity Commission has been steadily rising for two decades and is hovering near an all-time high.'[12] As the health system in the US is privatised, most women use medical insurance to cover the cost of the birth. The problem is that your health insurance is often tied to your work, so, if you get kicked out of your job, not only do you suddenly have no income, but you can easily end up with a colossal medical bill. The average cost to give birth in the US, if you don't have any complications, is $10,808, but costs can be even higher with operations and aftercare factored in.[13]

America's legal system doesn't oblige employers to make any accommodations for pregnant employees. If a pregnant woman refuses to lift heavy objects or to work with dangerous chemicals, then an employer can ask her to leave. These issues, coupled with an expensive, inaccessible childcare system and a working culture that demands long hours from its employees results in 43 per cent of women with children leaving their jobs. The gender pay gap in 2020 was 19 per cent and in 2019 Unicef ranked America last when measuring a country's 'family friendliness'.[15]

With America sitting at one grubby end of the scale, it's only sensible to make a dramatic leap to the other end. (Look, America, this is what you could have had.) Sweden was the first country to legislate for paid maternity leave, and this was reformed into a shared parental leave system back in 1974, a mere forty-one years before the UK introduced its version.[16] Since then, the Swedes have constantly been ahead of the game. They currently offer both parents 480 days of paid parental leave, with 90 days reserved for each parent. (Only single-custody parents are allowed to take the whole allocation themselves.) The days don't expire until the child is eight years old and parents generally get 80 per cent of their salary for the first 390 of them. A reduced amount is then paid out for the remaining 90 days. Once you use all your parental leave days, you are then legally entitled to decrease your working hours by up to 25 per cent.

At the heart of the Swedish parental leave system is what's

best for the child, rather than what's best for the parent, but this earmarking of 90 days for each parent triggered a culture shift where it has become frowned upon for dads not to take their allocated leave, and close to 90 per cent of Swedish fathers use it. In the scheme's first year, over forty years ago, men took only 0.5 per cent of all paid parental leave; now they take a quarter of it.[17] At the same time that dads started to take more of the leave, divorce rates decreased[18] and Swedish women saw both their incomes and levels of self-reported happiness escalate.[19] And, in 2010, the *New York Times* printed an article entitled 'In Sweden, men can have it all', which is probably the best article title that has ever been written.

Once both parents return to work, they are offered very affordable, high-quality childcare (as detailed in Chapter 9). On top of all of this, flexible working in Sweden is the norm, Sweden was ranked the best country in the world for work–life balance by HSBC[20] and the OECD has shown that only 1.1 per cent of Swedes work very long hours[21] while 11 per cent of employees in the OECD and 12 per cent of employees in the UK[22] work 50 hours or more per week.[23] The average working day for a Swede is 9 a.m. to 4 p.m. but some companies offer flexitime, which means employees only have to be in the office from 10 a.m. to 3 p.m. Taking a day off to care for a sick child is a perfectly normal thing to do and you are reimbursed 80 per cent of your pay.

And then we wonder why Sweden is a leader among advanced economies in female labour participation. As of 2019, according to Eurostat, more than 77 per cent of women in Sweden worked. In the United States, that figure was 66 per cent, a massive 11 per cent difference. In the

UK, 71 per cent of women were in employment during the same period.[24] This is despite Sweden paying families a basic income whether they work or not, something the Americans have never done, while in the UK child benefit is means tested.

It's pretty clear that there is a direct link between family-friendly policy and female labour participation, and there is little evidence that an increased welfare state discourages people from working. Taxes in Sweden may be high, helping to fund the high-quality, cost-effective childcare, fantastic parental leave system and universal child benefit, but the majority of Swedes don't begrudge paying them. 'I am very happy to pay high taxes because I know I am getting value for money, and I want to live in a country that is striving to reduce social inequality,' said Irja, a 38-year-old finance manager with two young children, when we met at an event in Skellefteå, northern Sweden. Looking at the different outcomes between the Nordic countries, where taxes are high and the money is spent on the welfare state, and the UK and America, where taxes are low and the welfare state is being scaled back, families have very different experiences.

In comparison with all Nordic countries, social inequality in the United Kingdom and the United States is considerable,[25] and, while child poverty in the UK has increased year on year since 2011,[26] in Sweden it has been decreasing year on year.[27] In response to Sweden's falling child-poverty figures, Ola Mattsson, head of Save the Children in Sweden, said: 'It goes hand in hand with a positive economy, with more parents in work.'[28]

Despite the high taxes, Swedish families still have more disposable income than we do in the UK. That's true of all

Nordic countries: taxes are much higher – a notion that makes us Brits baulk – yet the average person has more disposable income.[29] They have a stronger welfare state, they have more money in their pockets to spend on whatever they like, and they are a whole lot happier. According to the 2019 World Happiness Report, Sweden is the seventh happiest place in the world (Finland was the first). The UK was fifteenth and the United States nineteenth.[30] Could it be that a political system that prioritises the reduction of inequality and the welfare of all its citizens makes people happy?

Sweden isn't all a bed of roses for women, though. The gender pay gap in Sweden is 11.8 per cent – a great deal better than the UK (15.4 per cent) but still a sizeable chunk.[31] The problem seems to lie in the private, rather than public, sector, where only 36 per cent of roles are held by women.[32] When I spoke to a Swedish audience about this in 2017, a number of women came to talk to me after the event and expressed their delight that someone was reminding Swedes that the struggle for gender equality wasn't over. They said that, when they had raised concerns with colleagues or employers, they were often met with the same response: '*Pah! You think this is bad? Try living anywhere else. Have you seen how they treat mothers in America?*' They would feel as though people weren't willing to properly discuss the issue because Sweden is hailed as a global-equality nirvana, when in fact a report from 2011 found that almost one in four mothers has faced discrimination in the workplace after having children.[33] That's much lower than rates in the UK (77 per cent of working mums have experienced discrimination) but still it's higher than it should be.

'We do have the idea of being gender equal … but we have a long way to go before we *are* gender equal,' said Anneli

Häyren, from the Centre for Gender Research at Uppsala University in Sweden, to the BBC. 'I think it will take quite a lot of time – another 50 years at least – until we get there, and that is only if we keep working at it.'[34]

According to a 2018 report, women in the Nordic countries (Iceland, Finland, Denmark, Norway, Sweden and the Faroe Islands) are more likely to work part-time than men, and they spend more hours doing housework or caring for elderly relatives than men do.[35] Despite great policies to try to rebalance entrenched gender stereotypes, these still pervade. But that doesn't mean the policies aren't working – on the contrary, the evidence is unequivocal: there is a direct correlation between family-friendly policies – including affordable, good-quality childcare, properly-paid, ring-fenced paternity leave, flexible working as standard and a welfare state that puts the economic stability of families at the centre – and a smaller gender pay gap, more women in work, fewer instances of pregnancy or maternity discrimination, lower social inequality and increased happiness and well-being of citizens. In 2015, Save the Children ranked the best countries in the world in which to be a mother, and it was no surprise that Norway, Finland, Iceland, Denmark and Sweden were the top five.[36] The UK was number 24. Way to go, Blighty!

Moving across the water to the land of mystery, kimono and sushi, we come to Japan. In 2018, it was uncovered that Tokyo Medical University and at least eight other institutions were rigging exam results to ensure very few women successfully gained a place in medical school – despite the women doing better than the men in the exam. During the investigation, the assessors made it clear they felt a place in medical school would be wasted on women as they would inevitably get pregnant.[37] It's certainly true that many Japanese women fall out of the workplace when they have kids; in part due to the obscene overtime expected by employers, which can make combining parenting and a career completely unfeasible. Nearly a quarter of Japanese companies require employees to work more than 80 hours of overtime a month.[38] There's even a Japanese word for working yourself to death – *karoshi*. And, while Japanese employees are working themselves to death in the office, Japanese women are slogging it hard at home. They spend, on average, three hours 44 minutes a day on the household chores and childcare, compared to just 44 minutes done by men.[39] According to the *Japan Times*, in 2019, 70 per cent of men did no housework whatsoever, nor did they take part in child-rearing, irrespective of whether their wife worked or not. Research has shown that, if Japanese men are given more free time, they spend it doing relaxing activities, such as watching TV, while women spend it doing household chores.[40] Japan desperately needs more women in work as they have a scarcity of workers, so the government implemented some Swedish-style changes without really considering their execution, and it all went a bit tits up.[41]

In October 2019, Japan offered free childcare to kids aged 3–5 years, and from age two for those on low incomes, but they seemingly forgot to consider capacity, and, as parents scrambled to get their kids a free childcare place, waiting lists shot through the roof, leaving many without any childcare solution at all.[42]

Japan also implemented a generous parental leave policy in 1992, though until 2001 an employee could be fired for using it. Both parents are offered up to a year of leave paid at 60 per cent of their salary, but, despite this, only 6 per cent of dads take paternity leave and most take only a week off,[43] even though a 2017 Japanese government-commissioned study found that just over a third of new fathers wanted to take paternity leave.[44] The problem is that, in this work-first culture, employees know that any time away from their job will likely result in negative consequences so it simply isn't worth the risk.

Over in Australia, the situation also seems pretty dire. Australian women receive 18 weeks pay at the national minimum wage (about £390 per week). Companies have a legal obligation to provide 12 months of maternity leave, but it doesn't have to be paid. Dads get two weeks' paternity leave at the same rate of pay.

Childcare in Australia is expensive, costing about £55 a day, there are few childcare professionals, and places can be hard to secure.[45] On top of this, discrimination towards pregnant women and new mums is rife. In 2014, research showed that 49 per cent of mothers reported that they had experienced discrimination in the workplace. This includes a colossal 37 per cent who were threatened with dismissal, were dismissed or whose contract was not renewed.[46]

Aoife O'Donoghue worked in digital media for a big corporate in Perth: 'There I was, in labour with my first child – it was the longest 42 hours of my life. Plenty of times during that eternal two days notifications chimed on my phone, and in the early stages of labour I would read them to try to distract myself. There was important stuff, like messages from my family back home in Ireland. There was the usual pointless and inane stuff. Then there was an email I never would have expected to read in *that* moment. (If I had expected it then I would have avoided my phone like the plague!) Ding! It was the HR department at my work.

Another company restructure was imminent: "Your role will be made redundant." WHAT?! That's right. I was literally in labour when they told me I didn't have a job.'

Before Aoife had her baby, her performance rating was 4 out of 5. Once the redundancy process was announced, and while she was still on maternity leave, a manager whom she had never met dropped her rating to 2 out of 5, i.e. under-performing. 'I later learned that five other women were made redundant from the same department; they were all on maternity leave.'

The dads get a pretty raw deal in Oz, too; more than a quarter of fathers and partners who took their two weeks' paid parental leave reported that they experienced discrimination.[47] This all seemed rather bizarre to me in a country that has a reputation for its beer-drinking, laid-back, throw-another-shrimp-on-the-barbie culture, but then I looked at the work–life balance stats in Australia and was stunned: Australia is in the bottom third of OECD countries when it comes to work–life balance.[48]

Aoife also told me about a company she had worked at where the presenteeism was unreal: 'When it came to 5 o'clock and people started to leave for the day, do you know what would happen? Each person who left would be clapped out. Everyone would point at the clocks, laugh and applaud. Not in a good way, like, 'Yes, go to your family, friends, life!' They were clapping in a sarcastic way, like, 'You're soft.' Rather than put a stop to it, the managers encouraged it. They liked it! Can you imagine the pressure there was to not be the first to leave, ever, let alone consistently? How on earth could they call themselves family- or parent-friendly while exerting this peer pressure to stay late?'

If we look at maternity rights globally then things are

pretty bleak. In 2014, there were 830 million workers around the world who were still not adequately protected by law from pregnancy or maternity discrimination. Globally, just over two-fifths of employed women enjoy a statutory right to maternity leave and just over a quarter of employed women (330 million) worldwide receive maternity pay.[49]

So, there really is a whole lot to be thankful for over here in Blighty – aah, but wait! That isn't the end of the story, because, in other areas when we compare the UK with developed countries, we really do suck. The UK is the third worst-ranking country in Europe in terms of paid parental leave,[50] and, in 2019, Unicef ranked us as the least family-friendly country in Europe, mainly based on our paid-parental-leave policy and the use and accessibility of our childcare system.[51]

The evidence that policy has a direct influence on the motherhood penalty is clear. We can see that implementing family-friendly policies does not damage an economy; indeed, Iceland, the world's best place to be a woman,[52] successfully rebuilt its economy after the 2008 economic crash with gender equality as a core feature of its domestic and foreign policies.[53] Not that GDP is the most important thing, as Robert Kennedy rightly said, 'GDP measures everything except that which makes life worthwhile,'[54] and the evidence shows a direct correlation between the countries that implement family-friendly policies and citizen well-being. Governments across the world may talk the talk about gender equality – on International Women's Day 2020, Boris Johnson said 'there is so much more to do' to make gender equality a reality – but just saying the words does not make it so. As the Nordic countries have shown us, it takes serious commitment, vision, ambition, political struggle and hard action from governments, businesses and women's groups to reduce the motherhood penalty, but the results are a happier and more inclusive society.

16

Where There's a Will There's a Way

'Mothers are left stranded, madly holding a lump of London clay, some grass, some white tubers, a dandelion, a fat worm passing the world through itself.'

Zadie Smith, *NW*

It's not mothers who need to change. We've tried that. We've bent over backwards to try to make it work. We've forced our childbearing hips into pairs of corporate trousers that were never designed for us, and, quite frankly, it has given us thrush. The ideal-worker mould, invented by ravenous capitalism, only works for a small number of people; but, in a desperate attempt to comply and not cause a fuss, we've sacrificed everything – time with our children, sleep, money, our health, our sanity. Enough is enough.

Society believes that to become a mother means you must relinquish your own power in service of your children, yet we don't expect the same of men. But what this fails to acknowledge is that becoming a mother refines your power;

it radicalises you. It's like an elite training course, more brutal than the US Navy SEALs, more emotional than a Gwyneth Paltrow speech, more joyous than Ecstasy (well, almost). We spend maternity leave cocooned in our chrysalis, but we emerge – and, when we do, we are transformed. But, instead of this metamorphosis being recognised and appreciated, we find that we are dismissed and discounted.

We continue to steamroll ahead with a system that isn't fit for purpose any more, a system that works only for a very small proportion of people, and instead of changing the system we try to change women. It is now estimated that almost 5 per cent of American companies with more than 500 staff offer egg-freezing as part of their recruitment package and UK companies are exploring options to do the same.[1] It's all a smidge dystopian.

A well-functioning society values care highly. It restricts capitalism so it can't consume itself (and us) and it allows humans to prioritise the care of others when they need to. For all those CEOs, politicians and keyboard warriors who think care is the enemy of the economy, think again. Care is the invisible scaffolding holding it all together. Without care, our society and our economy fall apart. It took a global pandemic for this to be recognised. We stood on our doorsteps at 8 p.m. every Thursday from March through to July 2020 gleefully clapping and cheering for those who were putting their own lives in danger to care for others. It seemed that we had finally got the memo. Simultaneously, the Government refused to discuss a pay rise for NHS workers, the prime minster appeared to blame care workers for the spread of the virus by saying many hadn't followed 'correct procedure' and the Government excluded migrant social-care workers from the fast-track visa system, forcing many out of the country.

We watched in horror as childcare was ignored by minister after minster while Pregnant Then Screwed research revealed that 46 per cent of mothers being made redundant said a lack of childcare was the reason. Clearly, we had learnt nothing at all.

There has never been a more urgent time for us to create a society and a labour market that works for mothers. There were 4.3 million children living in poverty in the UK in 2019–20. That works out at nine in a classroom of thirty.[2] Child poverty has been rising year on year, with a 30 per cent increase between 2010 and 2019, despite a commitment from the Government to end child poverty by 2020.[3] Children aren't poor by themselves; they are poor because their mothers are poor. As we head for the worst global recession since records began, it is inevitable that this figure will increase, but, if our government were to take a leaf out of Iceland's book and placed gender equality at the heart of its policy-making, it could be a very different story.

Short of stealing Jacinda Ardern, Katrín Jakobsdóttir or Michelle Obama and holding them hostage in Number 10 until they fix everything, this whole issue can seem like an impossible challenge. It is not impossible, but first we need political and public determination. Sadly, the political and public impetus for radical change often feels like a post-dunked digestive biscuit – very soggy, and with the slightest shake of the wrist it could plop back in and disintegrate to mush, ruining your whole cup of tea. You start to wonder whether you would have been better off with a Jammie Dodger. (I might be getting a little carried away with this metaphor now.)

It doesn't bode well when our current prime minister, Boris Johnson, wrote an article in 2006 saying the children of working mothers are 'more likely to mug you'.[4] He also called the children of single mothers 'ill-raised, ignorant, aggressive and illegitimate' in a column he penned in 1995.[5] Since then, his unmarried partner, Carrie Symonds, has given birth to his sixth (he says) child. Of course, people's opinions change over time, and these comments were made a long time ago, but it's not just the opinions of Boris Johnson we need to worry about. The British Social Attitudes Survey 2018 found that one in three people thinks that mothers with children under the age of five should stay at home.[6] In 2019, the survey also found that one in ten believes that new parents should not have a legal right to paid leave.[7] That's a large proportion of our society who believes mothers should be doing all of the domestic and invisible labour but should receive nothing in return. I'm going to go out on a limb and call that misogyny.

These views regularly make an appearance when I write an article for an online national newspaper, and, as I am the sort of sadist who likes to read the 'below the line' commentary, I thought I would share a few for your reading pleasure:

'The sense of entitlement that women display is breath-taking in its arrogance.'

'As a woman, a mother and (previously) an employer, I would say that the pendulum has actually swung so far in favour of pregnant women that it's no surprise that many small employers dare not risk taking on young women.'

'Oh, the joys of being a single mum ... You make your bed then you lie in it. Not my problem, sorry.'

'You want to close the "Wage Pay Gap"? Fine … Be prepared to work VERY LONG hours (for no extra pay). Forget about "family friendly"-hours nonsense. Be prepared to DIE at work … just like men do.'

'If these women were attractive enough, they'd have had kids with a man who could provide for the family. It's unfortunate but you will have to find gainful employment if you let yourself go.'

Pushing for change can feel like pushing a very large rock up a very large hill, with the constant worry that if the wind gets stronger the rock will squash you. So, rather than starting with the how, let's start with the why. Why should we bother? Why should the likes of Jacob Rees-Mogg give two tweed jackets that our workplaces don't work for mothers, and that care is systematically undervalued?

The economic argument is really powerful. Our current set-up means that we're not making the most effective use of our resources. We have hundreds of thousands of highly trained, extremely skilled women who have been through the British education system at the taxpayer's expense, who are no longer able to use those skills in the workplace even if they want to. As the Swedes say, 'We can't afford to have the most educated housewives in the world,' so in Sweden the state intervened to ensure parents are enabled to work and care for their kids. This isn't feminism; this is just good economics.

All we have to do is look at the incredible things some mothers have achieved, despite butting up against structures and systems that don't work for them, to appreciate how humanity is losing out by keeping them tied to the kitchen sink.

Marie Curie, mother of two, pioneered research into radio-activity. Jennifer Doudna, mother of one, is a leading figure in the development of mediated genome editing. Professor Sarah Gilbert, the Oxford University scientist behind the Covid vaccine, is a mum of triplets. Maria Goeppert Mayer, mother of two, was a theoretical physicist and Nobel Prize winner, who proposed the nuclear shell model of the atomic nucleus, despite universities refusing to employ her because she was a woman. Ethiopian supermodel Liya Kebede, mother of two, set up a charity that has overseen the birth of 7,000 babies in Africa, and not a single woman or child has died in their care. And let's most definitely not forget Nancy Johnson, mother of two and inventor of the ice cream freezer in the eighteenth century, bringing ice cream to the masses. All I can say is, thank you, Nancy, thank you. Just imagine what us mothers could do if we had equal access to the labour market and were enabled to share care equally with men.

All the research supports the benefits to our economy if we can achieve gender equality in the workplace. McKinsey Global Institute reckons that improving gender parity could add £150 billion to the UK economy by 2025. This figure roughly equates to the size of Britain's total annual Government expenditure on education, defence and transport combined.[8] Meanwhile, if male and female rates and levels of employment were completely equal, a total of £600 billion could be added to our economy by 2025.[9]

Then there's what would happen to our economy if we alienated women from it entirely – well, quite frankly, it would dry up like a cheap raisin left at the bottom of your handbag. The more barriers we place in the way of mothers being able to work to their full potential, the less resilient and robust our economy. Fact. And it's a fact that the Government failed to acknowledge in the post-pandemic economic recovery plan, despite Covid-19 having a disproportionately negative financial impact on women. Indeed, UN Women believe that the pandemic could have wiped out twenty-five years of hard work improving gender equality.[10] The barriers to maternal employment became even more obtuse due to all the extra childcare that needed doing, as schools and child-care facilities closed, then opened, then closed again, then half opened, then whole year groups were sent home because little Johnny had a cough from playing pass-the-snotty parcel, and no one could get a test. Yet barely any thought was seemingly given to how investment and cuts would affect men and women differently. On 30 June, cocksure and confident, the prime minster rolled out the tired old trick of investment in physical infrastructure – 'Build, Build, Build', it said on the slightly wonky lectern sign – surrounded by hard hats and high-vis jackets. This focus on physical infrastructure to the detriment of social infrastructure is a plan made by men that predominantly benefits men, with 90 per cent of the construction industry being male.[11] It also failed to acknowledge that physical infrastructure and social infrastructure must go hand in hand for society to thrive. The Women's Budget Group found that investing in care would create 2.7 times as many jobs as the same investment in construction, and 50 per cent more can be recouped by the Treasury in direct and indirect tax revenue from investment in care than in construction.[12] Far from being a soft option, research by economists has proven time and time again that investment in care makes economic sense and it is critical for the well-being of our society.[13] Perhaps the slogan should have been: 'Care, Care, Care'.

Employers also benefit from looking after pregnant women and new mums at work. The cost to UK businesses per year of kicking women out of their jobs is £278.8 million, based on recruitment and training costs as well as lost productivity. That cost doesn't take tribunals into consideration or the long-term damage to a company's reputation should the media or campaign groups like Pregnant Then Screwed get hold of the story.[14] Pregnancy or maternity discrimination makes no real sense from a business perspective. You've invested all that time and money in someone and then you're just going to cut them from your business because they won't work the exact hours you want them to or because you think their brain will be addled because they've given birth? Great business move. Genius.

It is expected that women will control 75 per cent of all household spending by 2028 so you're going to need some women on your senior team if you're eager to make products that women want to buy.[15] If you kick them out at middle-management level because they dared to procreate, how do you expect to have dedicated and knowledgeable women in decision-making roles? Men definitely don't understand what motivates a woman to make a purchase more than a woman does, and you're going to need disabled women, Black, Asian, and Minority Ethnic women in senior positions for the same reason.

Gender-balanced leadership teams are more profitable. Fact. McKinsey found that companies in the top quartile for gender diversity on their senior team were 25 per cent more likely to have above-average profitability than companies in the bottom quartile.[16] They also found a 47 per cent increase on returns for companies with the most women on their executive committees compared to those with none.[17] London-listed companies are more profitable when women make up more than one in three executive roles; in fact, their profit margin is ten times greater than those without it, according to the

'Women Count 2020' report by Pipeline.[18] Despite all of this evidence, 15 per cent of companies in the FTSE 350 have no female executives at all.[19] A 2018 Government-backed report looked at the most commonly used excuses by FTSE 350 companies to explain why they have so few women on their board. My favourite is, 'Well, we already have one,' swiftly followed by the notion that women struggle with 'complex issues'.[20]

Of course, there's more to life than the economy and business profits. Our collective reasoning for addressing the challenges women face in the workplace should be about more than money. You know, there's that whole ethical thing as well. Women deserve equal opportunities. But also, if you're going to callously toss a pregnant woman or a new mum out of your business when they are most in need of your support, then I just hope you can sleep at night. I doubt your other colleagues care much for your behaviour, either; it's not exactly an aspirational method for winning friends and influencing people, now, is it? But it's not just about ensuring you're doing the right thing by your employee. Getting rid of a new mother from your business can have a disastrous effect on her whole family. Losing your job when you're pregnant makes getting a new job very difficult. Attending interviews after spending months completely immersed in the joy and exhaustion of new motherhood can leave you at an enormous disadvantage compared to other candidates. I've heard from too many women who got kicked out of their jobs at this stage of life and ended up homeless – far too many.

There is also ample evidence that women's earnings have positive spill-over effects on the well-being of children, as more of women's earnings than men's are spent on their kids; this is particularly pertinent for single mums.[21] Ultimately, if we consider child poverty to be a national scandal and we want to improve child well-being, then we all need to work hard to tackle the motherhood penalty. Ensuring mums have equal access to the labour market is not just the responsibility of employers; it is the responsibility of policy-makers. This isn't about enhancing the law or papering over the cracks; we need radical legislative reform as well as innovative thinking and transformative action from politicians. We need a change in the way we think so that we can break free from the rigid shackles of established practice and entrenched stereotypes. We need public and political will. It's not going to be easy, but if we get it right the rewards will be resplendent.

Throughout this book we've already explored some of the building blocks for change, but here is Our Graham with a quick reminder.

Flexible working

As we know, it isn't just mums who want flexible working. Pretty much everyone is seeking a nugget of pliability in their weekly schedule, because, guess what? We all have actual lives outside of work, and no one wants to live their life afraid that they might be nine minutes late into work one day because their toddler refused to wear shoes that morning.

The problem for mothers is two-fold: they don't just *want* flexibility; they need it if they are to manage their personal and professional responsibilities because they also do the majority of the domestic labour and care work. But, because part-time work is viewed through a punitive lens, it means that your chances of progression are vastly reduced. Mothers will always lose in a culture that values long hours, even if every company offers some employees a form of flexible working.

We work way too many hours in the UK, and it's creating a mental health crisis. Time and time again the research shows that long working hours correlate with high rates of anxiety, poor sleep and poor mental health, thereby killing our productivity, alienating mothers from the workforce and making us all absolutely miserable. Yet employers continue to reward their employees for seat-warming rather than performing. It's a difficult mental shift to make for employers; measuring productivity is way harder than measuring time sitting at a desk.

Alex Soojung-Kim Pang is the author of *Shorter: Work Better, Smarter and Less – Here's How*, which advocates for humans to work fewer hours, to the benefit of the economy and all people. Alex studied more than 100 companies around the world and across different sectors that have shortened their days or weeks without sacrificing productivity or profitability – and often improving both. He says that, if done right, shorter hours can help companies flourish. He cites various examples including Microsoft Japan, which reported that productivity rose nearly 40 per cent during a summer trial of four-day weeks, while Woowa Brothers said that its revenue grew ten-fold during three years of shorter hours. Japanese groupware company Cybozu said that shorter work weeks have helped it to compete with Microsoft and Samsung for top talent. At the Glebe, a Virginia nursing home, annual turnover among nurse aides fell from 128 per cent to 44 per cent after it moved to a 30-hour week.[22] In 2016, Blue Street Capital decided to cut the length of its working day to five hours – over the first year, sales increased 30 per cent.[23] Perpetual Guardian, a New Zealand-based finance company, trialled a four-day working week with no reduction in pay and found that its 240 staff were happier and 20 per cent more productive.[24]

There is a tonne of research to support the theory that reducing working hours increases productivity and profits while decreasing staff turnover. It also decreases the motherhood penalty. Alex told me: 'In an environment where being able to work long hours no longer offers a competitive advantage for workers (and indeed can be seen as a sign of bad self-management rather than devotion or professionalism), companies want people who are well organised, ruthless about their time and experienced enough to know how to change how they work. For many companies, working mums fit that bill.' He believes that a four-day working week would see mums flourish in the labour market. When we take presenteeism and proximity bias out of the workplace, we are simply left with skills and productivity. Output over input. That's good news for mums and good news for companies.

In Denmark, work–life balance is not just a corporate T-shirt slogan, and you're unlikely to find anyone in an office past 4 p.m. Only 2 per cent of employees work very long hours compared to the OECD average of 13 per cent; and yet Denmark has the second-highest productivity in the world.[25] The TUC found that full-time working staff in Denmark are 23.5 per cent more productive per hour than UK workers.[26] Seventy-two per cent of Danish women have paid jobs outside the home (far above the OECD average of 59 per cent), thereby demonstrating what I keep saying – the UK obsession with presenteeism is the death knell for productivity and gender equality. I enjoyed a story that Anne-Marie Slaughter relays in her book *Unfinished Business* of when she asked the Danish Consul General why the Danes are so happy and his response was simply that 'Danes think people who work all the time are boring.'

The idea that the UK Government, in its current guise,

might legislate for a four-day working week seems absolutely bonkers to anyone with a pulse, but in September 2021 Scotland joined Japan, Iceland, New Zealand and Spain in stating that they would trial such a scheme, moving to a four-day working week for some office workers without loss of pay. So, if all goes well, maybe this really could be the future for all of us.

In the meantime, alongside a bunch of other organisations, we have been campaigning for all job adverts to include flexible working options, unless there is a good business reason not to. This would make flexible working the default way of working, rather than it being seen as a perk for favoured employees. Once flexible working is truly embedded in our culture then mothers will no longer be penalised for working in this way. The result will be increased productivity, improved well-being for all humans and better gender equality in the workplace. Winner, winner, chicken dinner.

But implementing policies that will abolish presenteeism, or will create a culture shift in the way we view flexible working, is only one slice of a delicious cherry tart. If you have children, you can't work unless someone is dutifully caring for your kids. And so that leads me on to . . .

Childcare

Without childcare, it all falls apart. Covid-19 was testament to this fact. As lockdown kicked in, and schools and childcare facilities closed their doors, many harassed parents attempted to log on to their laptops and complete a day's worth of work while the kids demanded constant snacks, refused to wear clothes ever again and repeatedly terrorised the neighbour's cat. (Well, that was my experience of lockdown, anyway. Huge apologies to Jiggles the Cat.) Couples across the land were forced to enter into new, heated negotiations about the balance of home schooling and work, while others were unable to do their paid job if it could not be done from home. Arguments erupted about whose job was more important, while employers became increasingly agitated. Perhaps it's no wonder that divorce enquiries increased by 42 per cent after coronavirus restrictions started.[29]

It wasn't just the fact that parents (mostly mothers) were unable to do their jobs properly, but that this lack of childcare put them first in line for redundancy. Research by Citizens Advice in August 2020 found that three in ten people with children under 18 (31 per cent) were facing redundancy, compared with less than one in ten (7 per cent) of those who don't have children under 18. Parents were three times more likely to lose their jobs.[30]

Childcare is the invisible gender peace agreement. It's the infrastructure that underpins all working families and our economy, but it can only be truly effective if it is accessible, flexible, good quality and affordable. To achieve this, childcare needs to be subsidised from when Statutory Maternity Pay that ensures it is affordable for all families (no more than 10 per cent of household income, and free for any household with an income below £35,000), and all childcare workers must be paid the same salary as primary school teachers.

For me, the answer doesn't lie just in fixing our childcare sector, but is about a more holistic approach to the whole challenge. If we ensure all children can access really good-quality and affordable care for 30 hours a week, with childcare workers paid fairly for the very difficult and important job they do, but we also reduce the number of hours everyone is working so that 30 hours is ample coverage, then it all starts to slot into place.

Paternity leave

Women experience a fall in pay with childbirth, and this penalty increases in line with the number of children they have. The impact is persistent and cumulative throughout a mother's career. Meanwhile, the opposite happens for men: dads receive pay rises and promotions. The gender pay gap between mothers and fathers is far greater than that between men and women.[31] The thing is, many dads are desperate to spend more time with their kids and less time at work, but as they are the main breadwinner they feel unable to take a step back.

If we create a system where fathers are just as likely to take time out to care for their children as women are, then there will be less discrimination in the recruitment process towards women of childbearing age. Candidates will have a greater chance of being judged on their skills and abilities, rather than factoring in whether they look ripe for procreation. Better policies and practices would be implemented to accommodate parental leave and caring. And it would start to shift the deeply entrenched stereotypes of whose responsibility it is to do the caring.

We know that ring-fenced, properly paid paternity leave increases the number of dads taking time out in those early days because we have the evidence from other countries to prove it. We know there is a direct correlation between fathers spending more time with their children when they are babies and them remaining very involved as their children grow.

We know that paternity leave is good for children, good for fathers, good for the mental, physical and economic health of mothers; it's even good for marriages. We know that, when dads take paternity leave, they are more likely to share the housework, thereby improving the gendered division of domestic labour,[32] and we also know that the sons of dads who share household tasks equally are more likely to accept and promote the idea of gender equality, while daughters are more likely to aspire to leadership positions.[33]

The Government keeps talking the talk about reducing gender inequality, but, until men are taking time out of the workforce at the same rate as women and doing the same amount of work in the home, then we are not going to close that gap. To increase paternity leave and reap the benefits we need to follow the lead of countries including Iceland, Finland, Sweden and the province of Quebec, and give both parents access to ring-fenced, properly paid parental leave.

Access to justice

Until the above is in place, the least we can do is ensure pregnant women and mothers can access the justice they deserve when they experience discrimination. Until companies are held accountable for their actions, pregnancy and maternity discrimination will continue to wreak havoc on women's careers. The problem is that companies aren't being held accountable, because our justice system is failing women.

Increasing the time limit to raise a tribunal claim from three months to one year is imperative. The bare minimum we can do is give women the time they need to start legal proceedings after they've been screwed over by their employer when they're at their most vulnerable. Do we really want to force pregnant women or exhausted post-partum mothers to undertake exceptionally stressful tribunal claims? Because that's what's currently happening, and the result is that women are choosing to protect their own mental health and the health of their growing baby rather than accessing the justice they deserve.

Legal Aid for employment claims must be reinstated, unless we want justice to be available only to the privileged. A truly fair justice system would ensure everyone can access good-quality legal advice and support.

We need to take the pressure off vulnerable pregnant women and new mums to exercise their legal rights. In Germany, they switch things up a bit, so if an employer wants to make a pregnant woman or new mum redundant then they have to seek permission from a competent authority, thereby forcing the employer to go through their own 'mini tribunal', so to speak. When Covid-19 triggered mass redundancies and I posted about parents being the first to go because of their caring responsibilities, a German worker responded saying, 'It's funny because in Germany it's the exact opposite: parents are the first to be protected.'

Our ineffective justice system means that the power lies with the employer. They can hire and fire pretty much as they wish, knowing that the likelihood of anyone using the legal process to challenge their behaviour is slim. If someone is brave enough to defend themselves, then they can be silenced via a non-disclosure agreement. Women who face discrimination deserve the right to tell their stories and to be heard, but instead employers invoke the final legal weapon at their disposal and force them into silence. We will never really know the true extent of pregnancy and maternity discrimination in this country because the whole horrific affair is shrouded in silence.

Quotas

Quotas, a process to define a percentage of places that must be filled by women, are not a popular concept. People object to them – many think they are patronising. They want their achievements to be based on merit alone, and I get that; I can understand why they're off-putting. But the fact is that they work. In the UK, both Labour and the Liberal Democrats have used all-women shortlists to increase the number of women who hold seats in their parties. Before 1997, 9.2 per cent of MPs were women. Labour used all-women shortlists for the next election and the numbers shot up to 18.2 per cent – the Labour Party went from having thirty-seven female MPs to 101 in just one election. Meanwhile, the Conservative Party, which didn't use all-women shortlists, had seven fewer female MPs after the same election.[34] This overall leap in female representation changed the political dialogue. Issues that are particularly pertinent to women were now firmly on the political agenda, including maternity leave[35] and childcare.[36]

The argument against quotas is that they drive bias into the system, but what they actually do is counter the existing bias. There are more men called Steve running FTSE 100 companies than there are women. Do we really believe that this is because all women are less capable than men called Steve? Or do we believe it is because the system promotes and supports the ambitions of men called Steve more than it does women? It's a similar argument for including quotas on race – indeed, there isn't a single Black, Asian or Minority Ethnic female CEO of a FTSE 100 company.

Quota systems to encourage diversity in employment already exist in countries including France, Italy, Germany, Spain, China and India.[37] Norway, Iceland, Germany, France and Spain have mandatory quotas for women on company boards – they must be 30–40 per cent women. In those countries, the number of women on boards is much higher than the average across European countries.[38] They're a blunt tool, though. Creating quota systems at the top of the business pyramid can mean that women are shoehorned into positions before they're ready. Quota systems don't automatically solve discrimination and the structural issues women encounter lower down the chain. They must be part of a process for dealing with the motherhood penalty, or racism and disability discrimination, and not the only tactic used.

These changes may sound radical if you've swallowed the neoliberal Kool-Aid, but they're the very least we can do if we're serious about improving women's access to the economy. Mothers must be handed the power to choose what is right for themselves and their family, but our current set-up means that choice is decidedly restricted.

Women bear the cost of child-rearing: we step back from our careers, using that energy and time to ensure our children have the love, encouragement and support they need to thrive. This unpaid work contributes to the creation of wealth, but it goes unrecognised. Birthing and raising children has an obvious benefit for employers, as it reproduces the labour force. It benefits the government by creating good, taxpaying citizens who will contribute to the economy in a variety of ways.

When Faryal Makhdoom Khan, an ex-model and the wife

of Amir Khan, said on *Good Morning Britain* that housewives should be paid £100,000 a year, she was humiliated in the press and bullied on social media by men and women alike, because people are blinded by capitalism and patriarchy. The work that happens in the home is considered of no value, yet without it children would roam feral, babies would be left to fend for themselves, dust would gather in every crevice, clothes would be crumpled and smelly, dishes would pile up, smeared in encrusted bean juice. The point is that, while stay-at-home parents (usually women) and those with a career (usually men) are both spending their days working very, very hard, one of them is being paid for it and the other isn't. Can we all agree that looking after children is a job, and one that has enormous benefits for the economy and society? Who has decided which work commands an income and value, and which work does not?

The unpaid work that women (mainly) do saves the Government a fortune. According to Penny Wincer: 'Carer's allowance for full-time carers of disabled children is £66 a week – that's 39p per hour – to provide care that keeps another human alive.[39] That is how undervalued care work is.' She says that these carers save the Government £132 billion a year, which is more than the budget of NHS England.[40] Unlike other countries, including France, Germany, Norway and Sweden, the UK does not give parents an automatic allowance if they decide to stay at home and care for their children.

Salary.com worked out that a stay-at-home parent's pay should be £124,455, based on a salary that is similar to a handful of jobs that stay-at-home parents participate in on a daily basis and their average working week being 96 hours.[41] As a minimum, if the Government is subsidising childcare facilities to enable parents to work and if a parent chooses not to use that subsidy and instead looks after their child themselves, shouldn't they then be given the money that has been allocated to them?

In 2013, George Osborne said that caring for children and not doing paid work was a 'lifestyle choice', sparking understandable outrage.[42] Let's not forget that Save the Children found that half of stay-at-home mothers want to work but can't because of the cost and availability of childcare.[43] Mothers are caught between a rock and hard place. They can't afford to participate in paid work; they can't afford not to participate in paid work. If they stay at home and care for their children, they become invisible and their labour is undervalued. How about the Government grants families a payment for each child and families choose whether to use this to pay for childcare or to care for their child themselves?

Creating an economy that works for mothers is a nuanced and complex issue, and solving it will take many different, radical measures. We need to implement all of the measures mentioned above and more. We need to reinvent the labour market so that it works for everyone, not tinker around the edges or paper over the cracks. We need the Government and employers to put their money where their mouth is, not just go for the easy stuff that gives them a quick PR win. I'm calling on employers to stand up to the Government on our behalf – are you not sick of being blamed for the gender pay gap, when only a portion of the blame should rest on your shoulders? Do you not want your business to operate in a society where your talented staff aren't forced out of the workplace due to the extortionate cost of childcare and antiquated legislation that places the burden of care on one parent?

Change can be triggered by our collective voices, and the voice of employers is critical if we are to make ourselves heard, but we also need more mothers involved in policy-making – mothers from different backgrounds with different life-experiences. And not just because this would inevitably mean better policies for families and women, but because women make excellent leaders, exemplified by the fact that countries with female leaders suffered six times fewer Covid-19 deaths.[44] Before the 2019 general election, 20 per cent of MPs were mothers, while mothers form 40 per cent of the general population. This isn't representative. At a local level, in 2019, 96 per cent of local councils were led by men.[45] The faces of women were clearly missing during the global pandemic – indeed, out of twenty-two minsters running the show, only three were mothers (Priti Patel, Elizabeth Truss and Anne-Marie Trevelyan) and there wasn't a single woman on the pandemic 'war cabinet'. It showed in their policy-making.

The world of politics can feel like a pretty grim place for a woman, with harassment, abuse, death threats, long hours and extended periods of time away from home. It's not just the labour market that needs radical change if we are to reduce the motherhood penalty; it's also the political system. Though, interestingly, research has found that women experience fewer difficulties in combining parenting with a political career in countries where female employment is higher.[46]

This book is a call to arms for women. My hope is that you read these words and are inspired to pull on your William Wallace battle suit to help to make change happen. Don't worry, I get it – you're knackered, you have no time, childcare is expensive, all your energy is absorbed with repairing your own mental health or caring for someone, you smell of a child's bodily fluids and you forgot to brush your teeth this morning. It shouldn't be on our shoulders to fix this problem, but it is, and small steps can make a big difference. Sign petitions; write to your MP; establish a women's group within your company to lobby your employer for change. When people tell you that women have equality, remind them that the number of women forced out of their job for daring to use their uterus has almost doubled in ten years. Talk about your experience publicly if you feel able to; offer support to others who face discrimination. Stop praising men for caring for their own children while judging mothers for working/not working/losing their shit in public; raise your sons and daughters so that they see a positive gender-balance of domestic duties; ask your sons if they want children and what kind of father they want to be; talk to them about inequality and how we fix it. Give your son a doll and let him cuddle it, feed it and push it around in public. Impress upon new mothers that they are not a burden, they are phenomenal – it is their employer and the system that is the problem. Stand for election – you, yes, you! If you don't think you're good enough, just stop and look around you, or google Greg Knight MP's 2017 campaign video – if nothing else, it will give you a good laugh. But, ladies, the changes will not happen without us pushing for them, and so, in the words of Shirley Chisholm, the first Black woman to be elected to the United States congress: 'If they don't give you a seat at the table, bring a folding chair.'

If there were ever a person who would make me want to shove something painful down their oesophagus, it's Harvey Weinstein, so I'm not too thrilled that his name is infiltrating the final paragraph of the final chapter of this book. There's just something so poetic, so poignant about his downfall. A man who was the embodiment of patriarchy, and who used his power to abuse others, was exposed, and ultimately convicted and imprisoned, because of the tenacity and teamwork of women. His actions triggered an outpouring of women's rage on a global scale and the world hasn't been the same since. It's up to us to create the #MeToo movement for mothers. Most people have no comprehension of the many challenges women face when trying to be a good mum and earn a living. They know nothing of the discrimination that takes place behind the closed doors of companies. These issues will continue to be ignored if we allow it. So, put down that gyrating toddler, ignore the splattered bean juice and tumbling stair pile, stop worrying that the kids haven't got any clean clothes to wear tomorrow and start hatching a plan for change. Because, honestly, I can't do this without you.

17

Lockdown

'I must give the British people a very clear instruction: you must stay at home.'

Boris Johnson, 23 March 2020

Initially, there was a sense of excitement. Well, not quite excitement, more a Blitz-esque show of isolated camaraderie. The instructions were clear: you must stay at home. Kids and all. But don't worry because Joe Wicks will be limbering up from 9 a.m. to ensure we don't vegetate into a state of pandemic catatonia, and on Thursday evenings, from the comfort of your own doorstep, you can see other humans blithely bashing the bottoms of stainless steel saucepans.

I remember fantasising about all the things I could teach my kids with this new time we had together. They would listen intently, agog at my wisdom, as I coached them in everything from third-wave feminism to making the perfect cup of tea. Both boys would be so grateful, so full of my dedicated council, that I could happily leave them to frolic in the garden for the rest of the day while I completed my full-time job.

I'm sure you won't be shocked to hear that the reality was very different. About two weeks into lockdown, after notching up at least 30 gazillion hours of screen time, my youngest child interrupted a meeting I was holding with an MP by bending over, presenting his bare bottom to me, and brazenly announcing that he had done a very sticky poo that had gone EVERYWHERE and my services were required to clean it up. Home schooling became a mythical unicorn that was replaced by my repeated attempts to stop my children from continuously playing with their own penises and punching each other in the face. My new barometer of success was getting through the day without sobbing or screaming hysterically.

And, well, that is where it all began for many of us. As the pandemic unravelled, so did the minds, the mental health and the careers of mothers. We felt abandoned, and our needs were sidelined and ignored, which was unsurprising considering the decision-makers were nearly all men. The daily 'war cabinet' set up by the Government to make strategic decisions about the pandemic didn't include a single woman,[1] never mind a mother. Only one woman, Priti Patel, was trusted with the job of leading the daily briefings to the nation as this emergency situation unfolded, while 11 male ministers were on regular rotation.[2] Analysis of the SAGE meeting minutes by the London School of Economics found that although pregnancy was mentioned, there was no mention of gender.[3] It was as if the gendered impact of policies such as school closures didn't even register.

Pretty much every financial scheme the Government issued failed to consider the needs of mothers. The job retention scheme initially forgot to consider that if you were paid 80 per cent of your usual wages while you were pregnant then you might not qualify for statutory maternity pay as you may not meet the minimum required earnings. The self-employed income support scheme (SEISS) discriminated against new mothers in the way it was calculated – if you had taken a period of maternity leave in the previous three years then you would receive a much-reduced payment compared to your childless or male colleagues. Despite the Government denying there was any unfairness in the calculation method, Pregnant Then Screwed took the Government to court, where it was ruled as discrimination.[4]

When schools closed and the kids were at home, there was an unspoken assumption that women would scoop up the majority of the additional unpaid work, forcing hundreds of thousands of working mothers to reduce their hours or take unpaid leave, as there was no mandatory, targeted support for parents, unlike in countries such as Germany[5] and Portugal.[6] This gender-blind policy-making meant that women could neither support their families nor contribute to the economy. If they tried to do both, their mental health took an inevitable beating.

During the pandemic we set up a voicemail inbox that we called the 'Scream or Shout Line'.[7] It was there for mothers to document how they were feeling, to let rip and to tell the world what lockdown was really like for mums. The messages were full of so much anguish and chronic desperation that I would find myself sobbing every time I listened to them. One woman simply said over and over again: 'Please. Please. Please. Make this stop.'

Most shockingly of all, it took the Government nine months to publish any specific safety guidance for pregnant women in the workplace; meanwhile, thousands were forced to choose between the health of their unborn child and their livelihood.

Others, such as Mary Agyapong, a 28-year-old pregnant nurse, and Becky Regan, a 29-year-old pregnant healthcare assistant, tragically lost their lives. But it wasn't just the Government who failed to consider the needs of pregnant women. They weren't included in clinical trials for the vaccine, either; this wasn't unusual, but with well-documented evidence that pregnant women are disproportionately impacted by respiratory diseases, why were they still excluded from this life-saving research?

The risk associated with including this vulnerable group was removed from the drug companies and placed squarely on the shoulders of pregnant women, who were left to decide whether they were willing to take the vaccine without the data to confirm it was safe to do so. And thankfully, they did, which provided enough real-world data for the Department of Health to start recommending the jab to this group of women four months after the first jab had been administered in the UK.

Once that hurdle had been overcome, a new one arrived, with some pregnant women reporting that they were being sent away from vaccine centres, while just under half said they had been given conflicting or misleading information about the vaccine from health professionals.[8] As I write this in December 2021, the Government has still not invested in any specific communication to explain how the vaccine works in pregnancy – despite it being a year after the first person had been vaccinated in the UK. Between July and September 2021, 13 pregnant women died with Covid-19. During this period, 85 per cent of pregnant women were unvaccinated.[9] All the while, guidance for employers about the safety of pregnant women at work remained unclear, with the Government website stating that those over 28 weeks' gestation should take a 'precautionary approach', of which there is no legal definition.

When Jasmin, a pregnant care worker, raised concerns with her boss about her safety at work – as infection rates increased yet people abandoned both mask–wearing and social distancing – she was threatened with her P45:

> My boss just kept saying it was fine, that I was at no greater risk than anyone else. He said that if Carrie Symonds had been infected with Covid while pregnant and she was fine, who was I to think I should get special treatment? So I went in every single day, and I worked in close proximity to other people who could be infected with the virus, with just a flimsy paper mask and a plastic bib to protect me and my baby. I was made to choose between my livelihood and my health, and if I didn't earn any money I would lose my house – what sort of start would that be for my precious baby daughter?'

That sort of anxiety plays havoc with your head, and although Jasmin was lucky enough to not become infected with Covid, her mental health was on the floor; by the time her baby arrived she told me that she felt so anxious that she couldn't leave the house.

And I haven't even got to the absolute hellhole that was giving birth during a pandemic. Looking back at that period now, as I write this new chapter in December 2021, I am absolutely staggered that we were mostly okay with forcing pregnant women to go for scans, to endure early labour and sometimes actually give birth on their own without someone they know and trust in the room supporting and advocating for them.

Pregnant Then Screwed research from October 2020 found that nine in ten pregnant women said hospital restrictions had negatively impacted their mental health.[10] Which isn't at all surprising, particularly when we know that the outcomes for mothers and their babies are better when they have a birthing companion.[11] We also know that from 8 October to 8 December 2020, 7 per cent of women gave birth on their own due to these restrictions[12] – sometimes because their birth partner had been contacted too late; sometimes because the mother had tested positive for coronavirus; sometimes because there was confusion among the staff about the restrictions, which is what happened to Jami-Lay:

'I birthed my girl alone on the ninth of April, via a cat[egory] 1 emergency C-section after a short induction, because of Covid restrictions. Not because me or my partner had Covid, or that we had been in contact with Covid, but the reason my partner wasn't allowed in during the most traumatic time of my life (even though he made it to the hospital and was fully dressed in scrubs) was because someone in the operating room said no. It seems that there wasn't enough clarity on restrictions, so they just didn't let him in. At the time I was terrified and thought there was something wrong with me and the baby, and that's why they stopped him from entering the theatre. However, I've since found out that there must have been a mistake and confusion over the guidelines.'

Too many women had to endure the traumatic experience of attending a scan on their own and potentially being given bad news. Author and feminist campaigner Caroline Criado Perez experienced pregnancy loss in December 2020 and documented her experience in her fortnightly newsletter. She wrote:

'I didn't expect to have to lie down on an examination table and have an ultrasound wand inserted into my bleeding vagina and pressed around my painful, empty womb, while no one was allowed to touch me or hold my hand. I didn't expect to have to be told that they couldn't find my baby and that they didn't know if I was having a miscarriage or if I had an ectopic pregnancy. I didn't expect to start crying in front of strangers. I didn't expect to feel so humiliated and alone.'

And then there were the masks. Our research found that nearly one in five pregnant women in the UK were forced to wear a mask during labour.[13] Can you imagine? I struggled to keep mine on in the supermarket, let alone as a baby's head ripped my vagina open. Women described feeling unable to breathe, having panic attacks or even being physically sick during labour because they were made to wear a face covering. I heard from Tricia, who arrived at hospital in the very late stages of labour (as she had chosen to remain at home for as long as possible, worried that she would be separated from her partner once she arrived at the hospital). She was in such agony that she got down on all fours in the hospital reception area and was mooing like a cow; clearly the baby's arrival was imminent. A member of hospital staff repeatedly placed a face covering over her mouth and nose, stating that this was hospital policy, while Tricia kept ripping it off in a desperate attempt to keep her airways clear. The baby arrived 30 minutes later.

None of this is about blaming midwives or other health professionals for the horrific experiences of women during the pandemic. The fact is they were demoralised and over-stretched, with more than three-quarters of midwives saying staffing levels at their NHS Trust were unsafe, and just 2 per cent saying they felt valued by the Government.[14] Perhaps if ministers had heeded the warnings from the Royal College of Midwives in 2016,[15] and again in 2018,[16] that midwifery was hemorrhaging staff due to low pay and the abolition of nursing bursaries, then we might not have ended up in such a mess.

In a bid to marginally reduce your blood pressure, let's intersect here with a positive. You're probably thinking I've lost the plot – positives for women from the pandemic? But there were one or two. Top of the list has got to be that there were more dads and second parents at home than ever before – either because they had been furloughed or they were now working from home – and as one dad put it during an interview for *The Guardian* in February 2021: 'I had no idea about the hidden labour.'[17]

It seems that many fathers underwent a radical transformation by being forced to stay at home. A transformation that, according to research undertaken by Birmingham University, could have taken decades if it wasn't for a global disease forcing us to lock ourselves indoors together.[18] Suddenly, many dads and co-parents were thrust directly into the chaos, and they had to roll up their sleeves and get stuck in. That meant homeschooling and disciplining and making meals and never having five minutes' peace, and for many it was an abrupt introduction to all of the domestic labour that was previously unseen.

'It changed me,' said one dad when I talked about this on social media. 'I can't tell you exactly how it changed me, I just know that it did, and I will be a better dad and a better husband as a result.' And research by the Fatherhood Institute supported this, with many dads reporting that they emerged from the pandemic feeling more confident as parents and that they had better relationships with their children.[19] What is even more promising is that the number of dads who then said they want more flexibility at work so that they can be more present at home also increased;[20] but the only way that these positives lead to change in the home and workplace is if employers keep pace with their employees and respond with equally progressive policies.

As we became giddy with excitement at the notion that the pandemic could be a trigger for the flexible working revolution we had all been waiting for, our own data was showing that flexible working requests were being rejected at a much higher rate than they were pre-pandemic. Perhaps our advice-line data should have acted as a canary in the mine, because in November 2021, flexible working consultancy Timewise also found that fewer jobs were being advertised as part-time or flexible. Only 8 per cent mentioned home working, and part-time work was on offer in only 10 per cent of cases. Flexible hours were offered in only 3 per cent of job adverts.[21] What sort of madness was this after we had just spent 18 months literally living the home-working transformation that everyone had said was impossible? The very human yearning to return to normal was eating every positive we could reluctantly draw from the wretchedness that was Covid-19.

It didn't help that politicians and the media seemed to be trying to drag us all back to the office kicking and screaming, with the prime minister even saying that if you didn't go back to the office then your colleagues would gossip about you (yes, seriously!).[22] The chancellor of the exchequer added his contribution by stating that going back to the office is the only way to 'get on' in your career,[23] and Oliver Dowden MP told people to 'get off their Pelotons' and go back to work.[24]

Then, in November 2021, all the national news outlets ran

with a story about the Bank of England economist Catherine Mann, who had commented on women's careers potentially being impacted by continued home working. The headlines shifted any potential for blame onto women: 'Women warned home working may harm their career', said the BBC.[25] Women who work remotely will hurt their careers', said *The Times*.[26] While the *Daily Mail* wrote: 'Women who work from home will damage their careers and could widen the gender pay gap'.[27]

That's right, the gender pay gap is the fault of women. Rather than fixing these headlines to say: 'Companies who only promote those in the office will damage their productivity and their profits, and they will risk discrimination claims', the media had decided to place any potential downsides stemming from a new 'hybrid' way of working squarely on the shoulders of women.

Of course, it's true that 'proximity bias' is a risk to those who spend more time working at home than from the office, but it's not our fault that employers are biased! Ultimately, the likelihood is that there will be more home working following the pandemic because we've seen that it can have benefits for businesses and for employees. And this could be a good thing for women, as long as employers don't punish the ones who make use of it. However, for mothers in precarious work, or jobs that simply cannot be done from home, it is highly unlikely we will witness any benefits whatsoever.

Time for another pandemic positive. Okay, so I am clutching at straws a bit here, but some women told me it was a joy not to have to entertain people in the first few weeks after giving birth (on the flip side, I know a lot of mothers were devastated that their family couldn't meet their baby). Some women told me they did things and experienced things they doubt they would have ever done if they weren't in lockdown. One woman told me: 'We spent most of my son's first year of life outside. We went to the beach and it snowed and we ate hot donuts while I breastfed him; it was bliss.'

A number of women told me they breastfed for way longer than they ever thought would be possible, as they had so much more time and not a lot to do; plus, their partner was at home acting as an extra pair of hands while their hands cradled their baby. And then there were the women who said they were able to hide their pregnancy for longer as it wasn't visible on Zoom, so they could bag the promised promotion before risking being discriminated against for getting up the duff.

Some reported that their employer was now way more conscious that their employees were humans with real lives and responsibilities, and it was no longer taboo to talk openly about your kids or to take time off if they got sick. Certainly, the skills shortage that followed the pandemic, and the research that showed 40 per cent of employees were looking to move jobs,[28] should have given employers the poke up the bum they needed to start considering the well-being of their staff. And there were signs that some employers had started to take this very seriously. Research from Acas in September 2021 found that a third of employers reported that mental health support had improved in their workplace since the start of the pandemic.[29]

Meanwhile, the childcare sector was crumbling before our very eyes, with the Government's own data showing a net loss of 2,909 childcare providers between 1 January and 31 July 2021[30] due to a lack of investment from the Government both prior to the crisis and during it, while the cost to secure your kid a place in what was rapidly becoming an exclusive service had risen by 4 to 5 per cent.[31] The availability of this vital infrastructure was decreasing, something which should have sent alarm bells ringing through the corridors of Westminster, but when questioned on this in Parliament, the then Minister for Children and Families acknowledged that there was a net loss of providers but simply said it was largely due to a reduction in childminders,[32] as if that somehow made it all okay.

On the flip side, the childcare crisis has become an open goal for employers looking to recruit talented parents. According to a survey of 5,000 UK and US professionals by the recruitment platform Beamery, childcare benefits are valued more than other employee benefits such as gym membership, well-being benefits and even parental leave. And childcare providers including Busy Bees and Bubble have recently relaunched their corporate offer believing companies will be keen to support their staff by subsidising childcare or providing it onsite.

Then, in September 2021, a new headline hit the news. The Social Market Foundation said the UK birthrate was almost half what it was at its post-war peak in the 1960s, and the country's ageing population could lead to economic decline.[33] It was almost funny to watch journalists and politicians fumble around for an explanation as to why the UK was heading for a disastrous baby shortage. Media outlets mused that it must be because modern-day women are so 'empowered', or perhaps it was due to climate change.

That's right, the most common theory was that the ladies had stopped shagging in a bid to save the planet – how very noble of them. Except that it wasn't that, of course. Mothers across the country found themselves swearing at the news; could journalists and politicians have somehow missed the extraordinary toll the pandemic had taken on women? For many of us, we just felt that enough was enough. Why on earth would we go through the gruelling process of gestating, birthing and raising more children when we have seen how quickly we are abandoned in an emergency situation? And anyway, how can anyone afford to have children with the ever-increasing cost of childcare?

Ultimately, it seems the pandemic has drawn new battle lines between mothers and the Government by shining a magnifying glass on the inequalities we experience, not just in the workplace but in public health and beyond. In that regard the pandemic has been bleakly useful. A revolution requires visceral anger, and if there's one resounding theme from the pandemic, it's that women are livid. Unless the Government and employers step up and start making the workplace work for mothers and place their needs at the centre of future policy-making now, then we might just rebel in ways they hadn't even imagined. Maybe, just maybe, we'll stop procreating, slowing down the reproduction of the human race and ultimately crippling the economy – perhaps you'll start listening to us then, eh?

AFTERWORD

Nolite Te Bastardes Carborundorum

'A mother is always the beginning. She is how things begin.'

Amy Tan

This book was born out of anger. When I was callously tossed out of my job because I was pregnant, my heart felt as though it had been strangled with Sellotape. I've experienced the fear and devastation that pregnancy discrimination can leave in its wake. You are at your most vulnerable when they pull the rug from beneath you, leaving you swaying and wobbling as your abdomen expands, obscuring your previous ability to defend yourself. Its insidious nature leaves you cockeyed with confusion.

If you are currently wading through this treacle, then please know that there are thousands of us who have gone before you. You are not on your own. Send out an SOS and Pregnant Then Screwed will respond. I promise there is light at the end of the tunnel. Whether you decide to take legal action against an employer or not; whether you settle or not; whether you go to court or crumble into an inoperable heap – this will all get better.

I'm not going to pretend that my mental health was instantly solved by getting my career back on track. After I gave birth, I fell into a deep, dark depression that lasted 18 months. I can say with absolute confidence that being unceremoniously sacked when I felt at my most fragile contributed to the terrible state that my mind lapsed into once my baby was born. I also blame the stress of being sacked for the high-risk pregnancy that could have killed my baby. Discrimination during pregnancy and early motherhood has serious and long-term consequences for women and their families, and it is imperative we work to solve it, but with the right support you will get your life and your confidence back – and, let me tell you, there is little more satisfying than overcoming the shitty treatment of a bad employer and then a few years later being able to stick two fingers up at them as you revel in your own success. Don't you ever dare think you are to blame for this. You are not.

Don't give up.

Other Places to Go for Help

If you are experiencing discrimination at work, there are a few organisations that can support you.

Pregnant Then Screwed

If I can't put my own organisation at the top of the list in a book that I have written, where can I? Your best bet is to visit our website, pregnantthenscrewed.com, where you can find all the contact details for our different support services. But here is a bit of a summary.

Our helpline is staffed by HR specialists. If they feel you need to speak to an employment lawyer, they'll pass you on to our legal team. You can contact the advice line on 0161 222 9879 and you can ask them about any issue you have as a pregnant woman or new mum in work, including flexible-working issues, redundancy, sackings, demotions, maternity-pay issues, Health and Safety issues, bullying, harassment, holiday, or anything else that might be causing you problems or anxiety.

We run a mentor programme to support you through an employment tribunal – you need to register for that on our website and we will match you with a mentor.

If you would like to volunteer for us, then – huzzah! Please visit our website, where there is a form you can fill in at pregnantthenscrewed.com/volunteer.

You should definitely also follow us on Instagram (@pregnant_then_screwed), because that's where I do the majority of my ranting – and who would want to miss out on that?

Also, if you've been made redundant, we run a brilliant online programme called Redundancy Rehab that will help you get back on your feet.

If you run a company and want to understand how to make your workplace the best it can be for working parents, we have a sister organisation called Gendering Change: genderingchange.com.

Working Families

Working Families is a charity that provides free advice on family- and carer-related employment rights and in-work benefits.

Telephone: 0300 012 0312

Email: advice@workingfamilies.org.uk

Website: workingfamilies.org.uk

Equality Advisory Support Service (EASS)

A helpline that advises and assists individuals on issues relating to equality and human rights across England, Scotland and Wales.

Telephone: 0808 800 0082

Website: equalityadvisoryservice.com

Maternity Action

Maternity Action is the UK's maternity rights charity. They provide free advice on rights at work and benefits for pregnant women and new parents.

National advice service telephone: 0808 802 0029

London advice service telephone: 0808 802 0057

Website: maternityaction.org.uk

Politics and campaigning

If you are thinking about getting in to politics, then I would highly recommend looking up The Parliament Project at www.parliamentproject.co.uk and 50:50 Parliament at 5050parliament.co.uk. If you want to contact your local MP about any of the issues raised in this book, or anything at all, then go to theyworkforyou.com to find your local MP's details. If you want to lobby your employer for a specific change at your workplace, then look up organise.org.uk.

Mental health

If you are concerned about your own mental health, or that of a mum you know, then you can contact your GP, midwife or health visitor for advice or call one of these fantastic organisations and speak to a qualified adviser.

Association for Post Natal Illness

Helpline hours: Monday–Friday, 10 a.m.–2 p.m.
 Telephone: 020 7386 0868

PANDAS Foundation UK

Helpline hours: Every day, 9 a.m.–8 p.m.
 Telephone: 0843 2898 401

Samaritans

Helpline hours: 24 hours a day, 365 days a year
 Telephone: 116 123 (freephone)

Twins Trust

Helpline hours: Monday–Friday, 10 a.m.–1 p.m. and 7 p.m.–10 p.m.
 Telephone: 0800 138 0509

Tommy's

Helpline hours: Monday–Friday, 9 a.m.–5 p.m.
 Telephone: 0800 0147 800

If you have post-natal depression, or think you might have, there's a fantastic woman called Rosey who runs a regular #PNDHour tweet chat on Wednesdays from 8–9 p.m. You can follow her on @PNDHour.

Further Reading

Here are some books that you might enjoy that cover issues raised in this book:

Mother of All Jobs: How to Have Children and a Career and Stay Sane(ish) by Christine Armstrong

The Freelance Mum by Annie Ridout

Flex: The Modern Woman's Handbook by Annie Auerbach

Invisible Women: Exposing Data Bias in a World Designed for Men by Caroline Criado Perez

The Paula Principle: Why Women Lose Out at Work – and What Needs to Be Done About It by Tom Schuller

Forget Having It All: How America Messed Up Motherhood – and How to Fix It by Amy Westervelt

Fair Play by Eve Rodsky

Equal: How We Fix the Gender Pay Gap by Carrie Gracie

I Am Not Your Baby Mother: What It's Like to be a Black British Mother by Candice Brathwaite

Creating a Caring Economy: A Call to Action, Women's Budget Group, September 2020

Key Data

Fifty-four thousand women a year are pushed out of their jobs due to pregnancy or maternity (Equality and Human Rights Commission).

Seventy-seven per cent of working mums have encountered some form of discrimination in the workplace (Equality and Human Rights Commission).

One per cent of women who experience discrimination raise a tribunal claim (Equality and Human Rights Commission).

By the time a woman's first child is 12 years old, her hourly pay rate is 33 per cent behind a man's (Institute for Fiscal Studies).

Women in the UK do 60 per cent more domestic and unpaid labour than men. On average, men do 16 hours of the cleaning, cooking and caring for children or elderly relatives, and women do 26 hours per week (ONS).

The 'State of the World's Fathers' survey found that 85 per cent of dads would do anything to be home with their babies.

In 2017, only 25 per cent of mothers worked full-time, compared with 83 per cent of fathers with children the same age. Parents working part-time have a 21 per cent chance of being promoted, while their full-time counterparts have a 45 per cent chance of being promoted.

Part-time work is paid, on average, £5 less per hour than full-time work.

In 2019, only 14 per cent of jobs advertised as part-time or flexible offered a salary above £20,000.

Dads working full-time earn 21 per cent more than men without children.

Between 2012 and 2019, the gender pay gap declined by 0.6 per cent.

According to a report by the Papworth Trust in 2018, 84 per cent of mothers of disabled children were not working and only 3 per cent of mothers of disabled children were working full-time.

You are six times more likely to experience pregnancy or maternity discrimination if you are under 25 when you have a child.

Research by the Young Women's Trust in 2017 found that almost half (46 per cent) of young mums skip meals so they can afford to feed their children, and more than a quarter have had to use food banks.

Ninety per cent of single parents are women.

Child poverty increased by 30 per cent between 2010 and 2019.

The number of mums who set up their own business almost doubled between 2001 and 2020.

Around half of all self-employed people survive on poverty wages, according to the TUC.

Sixty-two per cent of those earning less than living wage are women.

There is a 43 per cent gender pay gap among the self-employed.

Key Data

According to research by Save the Children, there are 870,000 stay-at-home mums who want to work but can't because of the cost and availability of childcare. That's half of all mothers who don't participate in paid work.

Forty-five per cent of single parents – the vast majority (90 per cent) of whom are women – are living in poverty. Almost half of children living with a single parent (47 per cent) are now in poverty (Women's Budget Group, 2019).

Women rarely reach the highest management positions, with women holding only 6.3 per cent of CEO positions in major, publicly listed companies in the EU (European Commission, 2019).

Notes

The Interview

1. Richard Partington, 'Living costs rising faster for UK's poorest families than richest', *The Guardian*, 25 April 2019.

Preface

1. Cara McGoogan, 'Third of bosses avoid hiring women who could have children soon', *Daily Telegraph*, 21 July 2018.
2. 'Pregnancy and Maternity Discrimination Research Findings', Equality and Human Rights Commission, 25 May 2018.
3. Sean Fleming, 'These countries have the most expensive childcare', World Economic Forum, 23 April 2019.
4. '870,000 mums in England can't get the childcare they need', Save the Children.
5. 'Women shoulder the responsibility of "unpaid work"', Office for National Statistics, 10 November 2016.
6. 'Families and the Labour market, UK: 2020', Office for National Statistics, March 2021.
7. Jamie Doward, 'Working mothers "up to '40% more stressed"', *The Guardian*, 27 January 2019.
8. Claire Cain Miller, 'How same-sex couples divide chores, and what it reveals about modern parenting', *New York Times*, 16 May 2018.

9. 'The Timewise Flexible Jobs Index 2021', www.timewise.co.uk, 2021.

10. 'Gender Pay Gap in the UK: 2018', Office for National Statistics, 2018.

11. Samantha Gould, 'Pensions for girls: big questions for little people', *Now: Pensions*, 4 March 2020.

12. Sara Reis, 'DWP data reveals: women and children continue to be worst affected by poverty', Women's Budget Group, 29 March 2019.

13. 'Women in Management: Quick Take', www.catalyst.org, 11 August 2020.

14. 'Gender Pay Gap in the UK: 2019', Office for National Statistics, 29 October 2019.

15. Joeli Brearley, social media poll 'Pregnant Then Screwed', 12 February 2020. Ref. 1 – 843 votes for yes and 739 votes for no. Ref. 2 – 557 votes for yes and 99 votes for no.

16. Bronnie Ware, 'Regrets of the Dying', www.bronniewar.com.

Chapter 1

1. 'Severe Vomiting in Pregnancy', www.NHS.co.uk, 30 September 2019: 'Hyperemesis is a debilitating sickness condition that about 1–3% of pregnant women suffer with in the first 3 months'.

2. Tanya Abraham, 'Majority of Britons think gender equality has yet to be reached in seven key areas', YouGov, 8 March 2019.

3. 'Pregnancy and Maternity Discrimination Research Findings', Equality and Human Rights Commission, 25 May 2018. There were three research reports published by the Equality and Human Rights Commission. The first was released in July 2015: this research was funded by the Government and the figures are considered to be the official statistics on pregnancy and maternity discrimination in the UK.

4. 'Pregnancy and Maternity-Related Discrimination and Disadvantage – First Findings: Surveys of Employers and Mothers', Equality and Human Rights Commission, 2015: p. 9.

5. 'Three in four working mothers say they've experienced pregnancy and maternity discrimination', Equality and Human Rights Commission, 5 April 2016.

6. 'Greater Expectations: Final Report of the EOC's Investigation Into Discrimination Against New and Expectant Mothers in the

Workplace,' Equal Opportunities Commission, 2005: p. vii. The 'Greater Expectations' report revealed that almost half the 440,000 pregnant women in Britain at that time experienced some form of disadvantage at work simply for being pregnant or taking maternity leave. It was also reported that 30,000 women were forced out of their jobs. This figure included women who opted for voluntary redundancy.

7. 'Pregnancy and Maternity-Related Discrimination and Disadvantage: Experiences of Employers', Equality and Human Rights Commission, 2015.
8. 'Greater Expectations': p. 71. While 17 per cent of women who experienced problems considered filing a claim at an employment tribunal, only 3 per cent actually did so.

Chapter 2

1. Lyndal Roper, *Martin Luther: Renegade and Prophet* (London: The Bodley Head, 2017), p. 24.
2. Richard Morgan, 'Sexist Ernst & Young seminar advises women "don't show skin"', *New York Post*, 21 October 2019.
3. Lisette Voytko, '"Rage inducing": Sexist Ernst & Young seminar draws women's reactions', *Forbes*, 21 October 2019.
4. Haroon Siddique, 'Workplace gender discrimination remains rife, study finds', *The Guardian*, 13 September 2018.
5. 'Pregnancy and Maternity-Related Discrimination and Disadvantage: Experiences of Mothers', Equality and Human Rights Commission, 2016.
6. Emma Griffin, 'An Alternative History of Mothering'. Wet nurses were discussed by Jane Whittle, a history professor from Exeter University who studies a time in our culture when motherhood was not sentimentalised.
7. 'Unit 1: The origins of capitalism', www.solfed.org.uk, 29 October 2012.
8. Sheila Rowbotham, *Hidden from History: 300 years of Women's Oppression and the Fight Against It* (London: Pluto Press, 1992).
9. 'Social and Family Life in the Late 17th and Early 18th Centuries', British Literature Wiki, accessed 15 August 2020.
10. Jamie Gianoutsos, 'Locke and Rousseau: Early Childhood Education', *The Pulse*, Vol. 4, 1 (2006).

Notes

11. Jina Moon, *Domestic Violence in Victorian and Edwardian Fiction* (Newcastle Upon Tyne: Cambridge Scholars Publishing, 2016), p. 184.
12. Mandy Barrow, 'Britain since the 1930s', www.primaryhomeworkhelp. co.uk, 2013.
13. Carol Harris, 'Women Under Fire in World War Two', BBC History, 17 February 2011.
14. Penny Summerfield, 'Women Workers in the Second World War: Production and Patriarchy in Conflict', 1984, p. 94.
15. 'The Impact of WWII on Women's Work', www.striking-women. org, accessed 12 August 2020.
16. Gail Lewis, 'Black Women's Employment and the British Economy', *Inside Babylon: The Caribbean Diaspora in Britain* (London: Verso, 1993).
17. 'Gains and Losses for Women After WWII', www.striking-women. org.
18. Allyson Sherman Grossman, 'Special Labour Force Reports – Summaries: Working Mothers and Their Children', *Monthly Labor Review*, May 1981.
19. 23 European Agency for Safety and Health at Work, Directive 92/85/ EEC – Pregnant Workers.
20. 'DWP data reveals: women and children continue to be worst affected by poverty', Women's Budget Group, 29 March 2019.
21. Fiona Thomas, '"You will always be missing something": these mums reveal the hardest thing about returning to work after having a baby", *Metro,* 30 May 2018.

Chapter 3

1. Lola Borg, 'Nearly 90 per cent of mothers feel guilty. The good news? You can conquer it', *Sunday Telegraph*, 3 September 2017.
2. Dhruti Shah, 'If you want unsolicited advice, get pregnant', BBC News, 5 August 2019.
3. Hannah Sparks, 'Pregnant women are basically endurance athletes: study', *New York Post,* 11 June 2019.
4. 'Refrigerator mothers – a discredited cause of autism', www.autism-help.org, accessed 15 August 2020.
5. Nicola Davis, 'Leave those kids alone: "helicopter parenting" linked to behavioural problems', *The Guardian,* 18 June 2018.
6. Emma Gritt, 'Mother's Ruin: these are the three types of mums

most likely to raise a murderer ... is yours one of them?', *The Sun*, 30 August 2017.

7. Connor Garel, 'Social media makes mothers feel inadequate: Refinery29 Canada study', HuffPost Canada, 20 September 2019.

8. Michael Powell, 'Scientists blame working mothers for Britain's childhood obesity epidemic after study of 20,000 families', *Mail on Sunday*, 10 March 2019.

9. Emla Fitzsimons and Benedetta Pongiglione, 'The Impact of Maternal Employment on Children's Weight: Evidence from the UK', *SSM – Population Health*, Vol. 7, 100333 (2019): (March 2018). Section 6: Discussion

10. Powell, 'Scientists blame working mothers for Britain's childhood obesity epidemic'.

11. Ellie Cambridge, 'Mother of all claims: scientists blame working mums for UK's child obesity epidemic in shocking paper that claims their kids eat more and move less', *The Sun*, 10 March 2019.

12. Toby McDonald, 'Working mums have heavier children', *The Times*, 10 March 2019.

13. Amy Packham, 'Childhood obesity blamed on working mums – not dads – and people are furious', *Huffpost*, 11 March 2019.

14. Steve Doughty, 'Working mothers risk damaging child's prospects', Mail Online, accessed 12 August 2020.

15. Sarah Harris, 'Children of working mothers lag behind', Mail Online, accessed 12 August 2020.

16. Siofra Brenne, 'Psychotherapist warns that working mothers produce mentally ill children – and claims the problem is at an "epidemic level"', Mail Online, 2 March 2018,

17. John Bingham, 'Stay at home mothers "have the most worthwhile lives"', *Daily Telegraph*, 24 September 2014.

18. Carmen Nobel, 'Kids benefit from having a working mom', Harvard Business School, 15 May 2015.

19. Emily Oyster, *Cribsheet: A Data-Driven Guide to Better, More Relaxed Parenting, from Birth to Preschool* (London: Profile Books, 2020), p. 153.

20. Jonathan Cribb, Andrew Hood, Robert Joyce and Agnes Norris Keiller, 'In-work Poverty Among Families with Children', Institute of Fiscal Studies, 10 July 2017.

21. 'Families and the labour market, UK: 2019', Office for National Statistics, 24 October 2019.

22. 'British workers putting in longest hours in the EU, TUC analysis finds', www.tuc.org.uk, 17 April 2019.

23. 'Parents now spend twice as much time with their children as 50 years ago', *The Economist*, 27 November 2017.

24. Olivia Remes, Carol Brayne, Rianne van der Linde and Louise Lafortune, 'A Systematic Review of Reviews on the Prevalence of Anxiety Disorders in Adult Populations', *Brain and Behavior,* Vol. 6, 7 (2016): p. 1.

25. Stewart D. Friedman, 'How Our Careers Affect Our Children', *Harvard Business Review*, 14 November 2018.

26. Samantha Glass, 'Is "Me Time" selfish as a parent?', *HuffPost*, 7 August 2017.

27. Amanda R. Hair and Christi R. McGeorge, 'Negative Perceptions of Never-Married Custodial Single Mothers and Fathers: Applications of a Gender Analysis for Family Therapists', *Journal of Feminist Family Therapy*, Vol. 24, 1 (2012); Daphne E. Pedersen, 'The Good Mother, the Good Father, and the Good Parent: Gendered Definitions of Parenting', *Journal of Feminist Family Therapy,* Vol. 24, 3 (2012).

Chapter 4

1. Safia Samee Ali, '"Motherhood penalty" can affect women who never even have a child', NBC News, 11 April 2016.

2. Nina Pološki Vokić, Alka Obadić and Dubravka Sinčić Ćorić, *Gender Equality in the Workplace: Macro and Micro Perspectives on the Status of Highly Educated Women* (Cham, Switzerland: Palgrave Pivot, 2019).

3. Hannah Richardson, '"Girls outperform boys at school" despite inequality', BBC News, 22 January 2015.

4. 'School league tables: boys behind girls for three decades', BBC News, 6 February 2020.

5. Carrie Harding, Aline Simon, Lucy Evans, Lucy Joyce et al., 'Community Learning Learner Survey', Department of Business, Skills and Innovation, Research Paper Number 108 (2013): p. 94.

6. Christine Kawakami, Judith B. White, Ellen J. Langer, 'Mindful and Masculine: Freeing Women Leaders from the Constraints of Gender Roles', *Journal of Social Issues*, Vol. 56, 1 (2000): p. 49.

7. 'Annual Gender Pay Gap Estimates: 2022', Office for National Statistics, 24 November 2021.

8. 'Employment in the UK: August 2019', Office for National Statistics, 13 August 2019.

9. 'Gender Pay Gap in the UK: 2018', Office for National Statistics, 25 October 2018.

10. Lisa Martin, 'Gender pay gap: discrimination found to be most significant contributor to inequality', *The Guardian*, 21 August 2019.

11. Katherine Chapman, 'News: women continue to be hit hardest by low wages in UK', Living Wage Foundation, 10 November 2017.

12. 'Gender Pay Gap in the UK: 2019'.

13. Monica Costa Dias, Robert Joyce and Francesca Parodi, 'The gender pay gap in the UK: children and experience in work', Institute for Fiscal Studies, 5 February 2018: p. 13.

14. 'Working fathers get 21% "wage bonus", TUC study suggests', BBC News, 25 April 2016.

15. Ashley Wadhwani, '"Daddy bonus" common in B.C. workplaces, study finds', www.columbiavalleypioneer.com, 14 June 2018.

16. Monica Costa Dias, William Elming and Robert Joyce, 'Gender wage gap grows year on year after childbirth as mothers in low-hours jobs see no wage progression', Institute for Fiscal Studies, 23 August 2016.

17. Richard Breen and Giacomo Vagni, 'Earnings and Income Penalties for Motherhood: Estimates for British Women Using the Individual Synthetic Control Method', *European Sociological Review*, Vol. 37, 5 (2021).

18. Giselle Cory and Alfie Stirling, 'Pay and Parenthood: An Analysis of Wage Inequality Between Mums and Dads', www.tuc.org.uk, 2016: p. 5.

19. Damian Grimshaw and Jill Rubery, 'The Motherhood Pay Gap: A Review of the Issues, Theory and International Evidence', International Labour Office, 2015. Page 14, figure 2.1 shows that the pay gap between mothers with two children and non-mothers is 25 per cent.

20. Henrik Jacobsen Kleven, Camille Landais and Jakob Egholt Søgaard, 'Children and Gender Inequality: Evidence from Denmark', *American Economic Journal*, Vol. 11, 4 (2017): p. 181.

21. Martin Eckhoff Andresen and Emily Nix, 'What Causes the Child Penalty? Evidence from Same-sex Couples and Policy Reforms', www.econstor.eu, 2019.

22. Alysia Montaño, 'Nike told me to dream crazy, until I wanted a baby', *New York Times*, 12 May 2019.

23. Allyson Felix, 'Allyson Felix: My Own Nike Pregnancy Story', *New York Times*, 22 May 2019.

24. Stephen Morris, 'Women bankers criticise UBS over maternity leave cuts to bonuses', *Financial Times*, 11 March 2019.

25. Peter Hody, 'UBS Delivers on Gender Pledge', www.finews.com, 24 January 2018.
26. Carolanna Minashi, 'UBS is authentically committed to inclusivity', *Financial Times*, 14 March 2019.
27. Lucy Tobin, 'Entertainment giant Sony in the mother of all rows over sexism', *Evening Standard*, 15 May 2019.
28. Sian Fisher and Jane Portas, 'Solving Women's Pension Deficit to Improve Retirement Outcomes for All', www.insuringwomensfutures.co.uk, October 2018.
29. 'The Female Face of Poverty', Women's Budget Group, July 2018.
30. *Ibid.*

Chapter 5

1. Katharine Zaleski, 'Female company president: "I'm sorry to all the mothers I worked with, *Fortune*, 3 March 2015.
2. 'Employment Tribunal Decisions', www.gov.uk, accessed 13 August 2020.
3. 'Employment Tribunals, Case Number 3202214/2016', www.gov.uk.
4. 'Employment Tribunal Decisions'.
5. Bryan E. Robinson, 'How pregnancy discrimination affects health', *Psychology Today*, 11 July 2020.
6. 'Bosses are not hiring women because they "might start a family soon"', www.slatergordon.co.uk, 19 July 2018.
7. Shelley J. Correll, Stephen Benard and In Paik, 'Getting a Job: Is There a Motherhood Penalty?', *American Journal of Sociology*, Vol. 112, 5 (2007): p. 1316.
8. Correll, Benard and Paik, 'Getting a Job: Is There a Motherhood Penalty?': p. 1313.
9. 'Pregnancy and Maternity-Related Discrimination and Disadvantage: Experiences of Mothers', Equality and Human Rights Commission (2016).
10. 'Pregnancy and Maternity-Related Discrimination and Disadvantage: Experiences of Mothers': p. 40.
11. 'Pregnancy and Maternity-Related Discrimination and Disadvantage: Experiences of Mothers'.
12. Data by Pregnant Then Screwed of 2,600 pregnant workers in May 2020.
13. Oxford Population Health, 'Key Information on Covid-19 in Pregnancy', www.npeu.ox.ac.uk, 11 October 2021.

14. Tom Wall, 'Firms accused of putting workers' lives at risk by bending lockdown trading rules', *The Observer*, 16 January 2021.
15. 'The Management of Health and Safety at Work Regulations 1999', www.legislation.gov.uk, accessed 13 August 2020.
16. Email to Dr Samantha Decombel from the European Commission, Instagram, 29 November 2015.
17. Caroline Bolgona, 'Moms Rally Around Pregnant Scientist After She's Uninvited from Conference', *HuffPost*, 12 April 2015.
18. Tommy's, 'Miscarriage – information and support'.
19. Louisa Pritchard, 'Miscarriage: It's time for this secret club of women to break the taboo', *Daily Telegraph,* 5 August 2015.
20. Julia Carpenter, 'Miscarriages are common. But at work, a culture of silence keeps women quiet', www.edition.cnn.com, 10 January 2019.
21. Nosheen Iqbal, '"I lost my baby then I lost my job" – one mother's fight to change working rights', *The Guardian*, 18 August 2019.
22. Laura Bates, 'Third of breastfeeding mothers "forced to use toilet" to express milk at work', *The Guardian,* 21 Feburary 2019.
23. Bates, 'Third of breastfeeding mothers "forced to use toilet" to express milk at work'.
24. Bates, 'Third of breastfeeding mothers "forced to use toilet" to express milk at work'.
25. Anne Quito, 'A nursing mother was kicked out of TED's big conference about women for bringing her baby', www.qz.com, 31 October 2016.
26. Camilla Turner, 'Mothers banned from breastfeeding at breastfeeding conference', *Daily Telegraph*, 22 January 2015.
27. Daniel Boffey, 'KLM tells breastfeeding women they may be asked to cover up', *The Guardian*, 17 July 2019.
28. James Gallagher, 'UK "world's worst" at breastfeeding', BBC News, 29 January 2016.
29. Tom Powell, 'UK "one of Europe's worst countries for maternity leave"', *Evening Standard*, 24 March 2017.
30. Unicef, Office of Research – Innocenti 'Are the World's Richest Countries Family Friendly', Policy in the OECD and EU, Yekaterina Chzhen, Anna Gromada, Gwyther Rees, June 2019.
31. Author not named, 'One in four new parents get into debt and use credit to meet costs', www.moneyadvisor.co.uk, 27 April 2018. Research by credit report provider, Noddle.
32. 'Pregnancy and Maternity-Related Discrimination and Disadvantage: Experiences of Mothers', Equality and Human Rights Commission,

Notes

2016: p. 122. One per cent were made redundant while pregnant; 3 per cent while on maternity leave and 2 per cent on their return from maternity leave.

33. Pippa Crerar and Peter Walker, 'Commons leader says sorry to Jo Swinson for pairing pact error', *The Guardian*, 18 July 2018.

34. 'Pregnancy and Maternity Discrimination Research Findings', Equality of Human Rights Commission, 25 May 2018.

35. 'Pregnancy and Maternity Discrimination Research Findings'.

36. Stephen Benard and Shelley J. Correll, 'Normative Discrimination and the Motherhood Penalty', *Gender and Society*, Vol. 24, 5 (2010). A 2010 study by Harvard University examined normative workplace discrimination against mothers. In a behavioural experiment with 260 undergraduate students, female study-participants rated successful mothers as significantly less likeable and less committed compared to otherwise identical fathers. Highly successful fathers were seen as having more positive interpersonal skills than mothers.

37. 'Women negatively judged if they take maternity leave, and if they don't', *Science Daily*, 31 May 2017.

38. 'Pregnancy and Maternity Discrimination Research Findings'. Equality and Human Rights Commission, 25 May 2018. The first report, published in 2005 by the Equal Opportunities Commission, was called 'Greater Expectations'.

39. 'The Doom Clock', www.pregnantthenscrewed.com. This was a website we set up which has a formula embedded into a clock so it continuously counts how many women have lost their job through pregnancy or maternity discrimination since the EHRC 2015 report into the issue due to inaction by the Government.

40. Helen Miller, 'General election 2019: How much tax do British people pay?', BBC News, 19 November 2019. According to Helen Miller from the Institute of Fiscal Studies, in 2019: 'An employee earning £28,000 – a middle-income earner in the UK – will pay nearly £6,000 in income tax and NICs'. Per year. If 54,000 women are pushed out of their job each year and if each of them remained unemployed for 12 months, then that would be a total loss through income tax and NI contributions of £324 million per year. 324 million x 5.03 = £1.6 billion.

Chapter 6

1. 'Pregnancy and Maternity-Related Discrimination and Disadvantage: Experiences of Mothers', Equality and Human Rights Commission, 2016: p. 161.
2. Innes Clark, 'Employment Tribunal Awards Statistics 2018/2019', www.morton-fraser.com, 13 September 2019.
3. 'Employment Tribunal and Employment Appeal Tribunal Tables 2017 to 2018', Ministry of Justice, 2018.
4. Naomi Cunningham and Michael Reed, 'Supreme Court says ET fees are unlawful', www.etclaims.co.uk, 27 July 2017.
5. Jonathan Browning and Kaye Wiggins, 'Commerzbank told to train exec for promotion after bias suit', *Bloomberg*, 16 October 2018.
6. 'Liz Earle beauty firm ordered to pay £17k to sacked pregnant worker', BBC News, 9 January 2020.
7. Martin Bentham, 'Sexism in courts must be probed, top judge insists', *Evening Standard*, 19 February 2019.
8. Owen Bowcott, 'White and male UK judiciary "from another planet" claims Lady Hale', *The Guardian*, 1 January 2019.
9. 'Sexist Judges Allegations "Deeply Troubling"', *New Law Journal*, 30 March 2018.
10. 'Call out sexist judges, urges lord chief justice', *The Times*, 19 February 2019.
11. Ross Brannigan, Antti Tanskanen, Matti O. Huttunen, Mary Cannon et al., 'The role of prenatal stress as a pathway to personality disorder: longitudinal birth cohort study', *British Journal of Psychiatry*, Vol. 216, 2 (2020): p. 87.
12. 'Maternal Mental Health – Women's Voices', Royal College of Obstetricians and Gynaecologists, February 2017: p. ix.
13. Danielle Ayres, 'Discrimination causes depression in new mothers', www.gorvins.com, 14 May 2018.

Chapter 7

1. HM Government, 'Government response to the House of Commons Women and Equalities Committee report on pregnancy and maternity discrimination', January 2017.
2. TUC, 'The TUC response to the consultation on extending

redundancy protection for women and new parents', 5 April 2019.

3. Lauren Aratani, 'Harvey Weinstein bewildered as he abused women have their say', *The Guardian*, 11 March 2020.

4. Robert Mendick and Gordon Rayner, 'Non-disclosure agreements: everything you need to know about NDAs (and their misuse)', *Daily Telegraph*, 25 October 2018.

5. Rianna Croxford, 'UK universities face "gagging order" criticism', BBC News, 17 April 2019.

6. Rick Kelsey, 'Why do non-disclosure agreements matter?', BBC News, 12 February 2020.

7. Simon Murphy, 'Alzheimer's Society "paid out £750,000" to staff amid bullying claims', *The Guardian*, 21 February 2020.

8. 'Employment Tribunal Decisions', www.gov.uk, accessed 14 August 2020.

9. 'Banks at forefront of dropped discrimination claims', *The Times*, 11 September 2019.

Chapter 8

1. Laura Bates, 'Pregnant Then Screwed: How gagging contracts are used to silence sacked mothers, *The Guardian*, 22 January 2019.

2. Parliament, 'The use of non-disclosure agreements in discrimination cases', 11 June 2019.

3. Ylan Q. Mui, 'Study: Women with more children are more productive at work', *Washington Post*, 30 October 2014.

4. 'Do parents make better managers?', *Forbes*, 27 February 2007.

5. Catey Hill, 'Why parents may make better employees', www.marketwatch.com, 14 August 2015.

6. Kathleen Fuegen, Monica Biernat, Elizabeth L. Haines and Kay Deaux, 'Mothers and Fathers in the Workplace: How Gender and Parental Status Influence Judgments of Job-Related Competence', *Journal of Social Issues*, Vol. 60, 4 (2004): pp. 737–54.

7. 'Income and Tax by Gender, Region and Country', www.gov.uk, 1 January 2013.

Chapter 9

1. 'Bank of England "ready to act" as economy shrinks record 20%', BBC News, 12 June 2020.
2. Harriet Waldegrave and Lucy Lee, *Quality Childcare: Improving Early Years Childcare* (London: Policy Exchange, 2013), p. 59.
3. Craig Alexander and Dina Ignjatovic, 'Special Report: Early Childhood Education Has Widespread and Long Lasting Benefits', www.td.com, 27 November 2012.
4. Jedidajah Otte, 'Parents say childcare quality is falling', *Nursery World*, 14 February 2017.
5. Early Years Alliance, 'Freedom of Information Investigation Findings', www.eyalliance.org.uk
6. Megan Jarvie, 'Potential childcare shortages should cause concern for all', Coram Family and Childcare, 18 December 2020.
7. 'Joiners and Leavers in the Childcare Sector – July 2021', www.gov.uk, 16 August 2021.
8. Katy Morton, 'Number of childminders falls by a fifth', *Nursery World*, 19 November 2019.
9. Helen Penn, 'Why parents should fear childcare going the way of Carillion', *The Guardian*, 14 May 2018.
10. Sean Farrell, 'Busy Bees nursery set to go global after sale to Ontario Teachers' Pension Plan', *The Guardian*, 1 November 2013.
11. Lester Coleman, Mohammed Dali-Chaouch and Claire Harding, 'Childcare Survey 2020', Coram Family and Childcare, 2020.
12. 'Net Childcare Costs for Parents Using Childcare', www.oecd.org, accessed 14 August 2020.
13. '870,000 mums in England can't get the childcare they need', Save the Children.
14. Donald Hirsch, 'Cost of a Child', Child Poverty Action Group, 2020.
15. 'Net childcare costs', www.oecd.org, 2019.
16. Alexandra Topping, 'UK failing on childcare, finds survey of over 20,000 working parents', *The Guardian*, 12 September 2021
17. Hannah Parlett, 'Childcare Survey 2021', Coram Family and Childcare, 15 October 2021.
18. Claire Schofield, 'Most expensive regions for UK childcare revealed', www.inews.co.uk, 20 December 2018.
19. In 2019, minimum wage was £8.21 per hour.

20. Alison Andrew, Sarah Cattan, Monica Costa Dias, Christine Farquharson et al., 'Parents, especially mothers, paying heavy price for lockdown', Institute for Fiscal Studies, 27 May 2020.

21. Alison Andrew, Sarah Cattan, Monica Costa Dias, Christine Farquharson et al., 'How are mothers and fathers balancing work and family under lockdown?', Institute of Fiscal Studies, 27 May 2020.

22. 'Women shoulder the responsibility of "unpaid work"', Office for National Statistics, 10 November 2016.

23. 'Nursery Workforce Surveys and Reports 2019', National Day Nurseries Association, 2019.

24. Ceeda, 'Independent Research About and For the Early Years', www.aboutearlyears.co.uk, 2019: p. 18.

25. Sally Weale, 'One in eight childcare workers in England earn less than £5 per hour', The Guardian, 5 August 2020.

26. Ceeda, 'Independent Research About and For the Early Years, 2019'.

27. Hannah Crown, 'Childcare practitioners "living in poverty" – exclusive survey', Nursery World, 12 September 2019.

28. Christine Stephen, Lynn Ang, Liz Brooker, Kathy Sylva et al., 'Pre-school Quality and Educational Outcomes at Age 11: Low Quality Has Little Benefit', Journal of Early Childhood Research, Vol. 9, 2 (2011), pp. 109-24.

29. Rebecca Griffin, '£1 an hour wage increase makes good nurseries outstanding, new research finds', Coram Family and Childcare, 10 February 2016.

30. Rauch Foundation, 'A better start is a lifetime advantage' www.rauch-foundation.org/index.php, accessed 19 August 2020.

31. Paul Bolton, 'Education Spending in the UK', House of Commons Library, 9 October 2019: p. 11.

32. 'Public Spending on Childcare and Early Education', www.oecd.org, 2 April 2019: p. 1.

33. The Front Project, 'Economic Analysis: Investing in early childhood education doubles the return to Australia', www.readynationaustralia.org.au.

34. Hirokazu Yoshikawa, Christina Weiland, Jeanne Brooks-Gunn, Margaret R. Burchinal et al., 'Investing in Our Future: The Evidence Base on Preschool Education', Society for Research in Child Development and the Foundation for Child Development (2013).

35. 'A mother's place "is in the home"', BBC News, 10 July 2018.

36. Ravneet Nandra, '"The system does not support a working parent"', ITV News, 1 November 2021.

37. 'Child Care and the Growth of Love by John Bowlby', *Therapeutic Care Journal*, 1 May 2010.

38. H. Rudolph Schaffer and Peggy E. Emerson, 'The Development of social attachments in infancy', *Monographs of the Society for Research in Child Development*, Vol. 29, 3 (1964): p. 77.

39. Rudolph Schaffer and Peggy Emerson, in 1964, swiftly followed by Michael Rutter, in 1972, all determined that children show attachment for a variety of figures, not just the mother. In some cases, the same attachment was shown for pets and objects. Rutter concluded that temporary separation from the mother is not problematic as long as the child has an attachment bond with *someone*.

40. Barbara Tizard, 'The Making and Breaking of Attachment Theory', *The Psychologist*, Looking Back, Vol. 22, 10 (2009): pp. 902-3.

41. European Commission, 'Sweden: Early Childhood Education and Care', www.ec.europe.eu, 21 January 2020.

42. Department for Education, 'Childcare and Early Years Survey of Parents: 2017', www.gov.uk, 21 December 2017.

43. Phillip Inman, 'Gap between rich and poor grows alongside rise in UK's total wealth', *The Guardian*, 5 December 2019.

44. 'Care Giving and Child Care Average Salaries in Sweden 2020', www.salaryexplorer.com.

45. Exact conversion in pound sterling is £5,606.22, as of 19 August 2020.

46. 'Average Salary in Sweden 2020', www.salaryexplorerer.com

47. According to Statistica, the average per hour rate of pay for UK workers in 2020 was £15.14. Compared to a 2020 report by the Social Mobility Foundation, which found that the average pay for a childcare worker is £7.42 per hour.

48. Jerome De Henau, 'Costing and Funding Free Universal Childcare of High Quality', Women's Budget Group, 21 February 2017.

49. Rose Marcario, 'Patagonia's CEO Explains How To Make On-Site Child Care Pay For Itself', Fast Company, 16 August 2016.

50. Patagonia website, www.eu.patagonia.com/gb/en/family-business, accessed 19 August 2020.

51. Sara Reis and Lucie Stephens, 'Autumn Budget 2021: Childcare, gender and Covid-19', Women's Budget Group, 21 October 2021.

Chapter 10

1. Ellen Seidman, 'I am the person who notices we are running out of toilet paper, and I rock: A tribute to moms everywhere', www.lovethatmax.com, 5 May 2016.

2. 'Women shoulder the responsibility of "unpaid work", Office for National Statistics, 10 November 2016. The difference in the hourly rate between men's earnings and women's earnings is due to the weekly figures being aggregated from different forms of unpaid work. For example, the hourly wage-rate used for childcare is higher than that used for adult care as the wage-rates associated with similar market-based services is structured in that way. Overall, women's unpaid production is worth more than men's for two reasons: first, they do more of it; and, second, because they are doing types of unpaid work that are more expensive to contract out to a market service provider.

3. 'Men Enjoy Five Hours More Leisure Time Than Women', Office for National Statistics, 9 January 2018.

4. Elsa Vulliamy, 'Husbands "create extra seven hours of housework a week"', *The Independent,* 20 February 2016.

5. Ceri Parker, 'It's official: Women work nearly an hour longer than men every day', World Economics Forum, 1 June 2017.

6. 'Women shoulder the responsibility of "unpaid work"'.

7. Luke Messac, 'How women's unpaid work was nearly included in GDP calculations', *News Deeply*, 22 June 2018.

8. Jonathan Mulinix, 'Why Mother's Day Founder Anna Jarvis Later Fought to Have the Holiday Abolished', www.mentalfloss.com, 7 May 2019.

9. Amy Westervelt, *Forget 'Having It All': How America Messed Up Motherhood and How To Fix It* (New York: Seal Press, 2018), p. 78.

10. Evrim Altintas, Oriel Sullivan, 'Fifty Years of Change Updated: Cross-National Gender Convergence in Housework', *Demographic Research*, Vol. 35, 16 (2016): pp. 455–70.

11. Matt Krenz, Emily Kos, Anna Green and Jennifer Garcia-Alonso, 'Easing the Covid-19 Burden on Working Parents', www.bcg.com, 21 May 2020.

12. Alison Andrew, Sarah Cattan, Monica Costa Dias, Christine

Farquharson et al., 'How are mothers and fathers balancing work and family under lockdown?', Institute for Fiscal Studies, 27 May 2020.

13. Alexandra Topping, 'Working mothers interrupted more often than fathers in lockdown – study', *The Guardian,* 27 May 2020.

14. Richard Breen and Lynne Prince Cook, 'The Persistence of the Gendered Division of Domestic Labour', *European Sociological Review,* Vol. 21, 1 (2005), pp. 43–7.

15. Claudia Geist, 'Men's and Women's Reports About Housework', *Dividing the Domestic: Men, Women, & Household Work in Cross-National Perspective,* eds Judith Treas and Sonja Drobnič (Stanford: Stanford University Press, 2010).

16. Claire Cain Miller, 'Nearly half of men say they do most of the home schooling. 3 percent of women agree', *New York Times,* 6 May 2020.

17. Allison Daminger, 'How couples share "cognitive labor" and why it matters', *Behavioral Scientist,* 29 September 2019.

18. Kimberlee D'Ardenne, 'Invisible labor can negatively impact well-being in mothers', Arizona State University Department of Psychology, 22 January 2019.

19. Claire Cain Miller, 'Why Women, but Not Men, Are Judged for a Messy House', *New York Times,* 11 June 2019.

20. Sian Cain, 'Women are happier without children or a spouse, says happiness expert', *The Guardian,* 25 May 2019.

21. Melanie E. Brewster, 'Lesbian Women and Household Labor Division: A Systematic Review of Scholarly Research from 2000 to 2015', *Journal of Lesbian Studies,* Vol. 21, 1 (2016), pp. 47–69.

22. Claire Cain Miller, 'How same sex couples divide chores, and what it means about modern parenting', *New York Times,* 16 May 2018.

23. Gaëlle Ferrant, Luca Maria Pesando and Keiko Nowacka, 'Unpaid Care Work: The Missing Link in the Analysis of Gender Gaps in Labour Outcomes', www.oecd.org, December 2014.

24. Vivian Hunt, Richard Dobbs, Emma Gibbs, Anu Madgavkar et al., 'The Power of Parity: Advancing Women's Equality in the United Kingdom', www.mckinsey.com, 28 September 2016.

25. Malin Wiberg, 'Involved Fatherhood: An Analysis of Gendered and Classed Fathering Practices in Sweden', University of Gothenburg, June 2015.

26. 'Gender Equality Index: Index Score for European Union for 2019', www.eige.europa.eu, accessed 19 August 2020.

27. Maddy Savage, 'How Sweden is fixing the housework gender gap', BBC News, 4 March 2020.

28. 'Reflections on the Future of the Second Half of the Gender Revolution', Maryland Population Resource Center, accessed 19 August 2020.

29. Helen Lewis, 'Yes, there is one great contribution men can make to feminism: pick up a mop', *The Guardian*, 14 January 2016.

30. 'Is There a "Perfect Mum"?', www.dove.com, accessed 14 August 2020.

Chapter 11

1. Anna Machin, 'The marvel of the human dad', www.aeon.co, 17 January 2019.

2. Machin, 'The marvel of the human dad'.

3. Urmee Khan, 'Children who spend time with their fathers have a higher IQ', *Daily Telegraph*, 30 September 2008.

4. Dr Eyal Abraham, 'Fathers' Active Caring of Infants Changes Their Brains to be More Like Mothers', www.fatherhood.global/fathers-brains-mothers, 12 November 2016.

5. Colter Mitchell, Sara McLanahan, Lisa Schneper, Irv Garfinkel et al., 'Father Loss and Child Telomere Length', *Pediatrics*, Vol. 140, 2 (2017).

6. Allana Akhtar, 'Finland just gave both parents seven months of parental leave. Here's why it could drastically reduce postpartum depression in the country', *Business Insider*, 7 February 2020.

7. Maggie Redshaw and Jane Henderson, 'Fathers' engagement in pregnancy and childbirth: evidence from a national survey', *BMC Pregnancy and Childbirth*, Vol. 13, 70 (2013).

8. Rachel Hunter, 'COVID-19 has created a maternity mental health burden of £17.5 billion', *International Journal of Quality in Health Care & Economics*, 27 July 2021.

9. 'Poor mental health care for pregnant women and new mums costs £8bn', www.mind.org.uk, 20 October 2014.

10. 'State of the Worlds Fathers', www.men-care.org, 2019.

11. 'Two thirds of fathers are still not taking paternity leave', www.hrnews.co.uk, 5 August 2020.

12. Olivia Petter, 'Fewer than third of fathers take paternity leave, research suggests', *The Independent*, 8 July 2019.

13. TUC, 'One in four new dads missed out on paid paternity leave last year, says TUC', www.tuc.org.uk, 16 June 2019.

14. Katrin Bennhold, 'In Sweden, men can have it all', *New York Times*, 9 June 2010.

15. Simon Usborne, '"It was seen as weird": why are so few men taking shared parental leave?', *The Guardian*, 5 October 2019.

16. Kevin Peachey, 'How the UK's new rules on parental leave work', BBC News, 5 April 2015.

17. Mireille Silcoff, '"The Daddy quota": how Quebec got men to take parental leave', *The Guardian*, 15 June 2018.

18. Duncan Fisher, 'Want men to share parental leave? Just give them equality', *The Guardian*, 15 February 2018.

19. 'Length of maternity leave, parental leave and paid father-specific leave', www.oecd.org, accessed 14 August 2020.

20. 'Parental leave systems', www.oecd.org, 2019.

21. August Graham, 'Employers refuse fathers who want to spend more time with their kids', www.cityam.com, 20 May 2019.

22. Rachel Sharp, 'One in three flexible working requests turned down', *HR Magazine*, 3 September 2019.

23. 'Fathers working full-time earn 21 per cent more than men without children, says TUC', www.tuc.org.uk, 25 April 2016.

24. 'UK Labour Market: October 2015', Office for National Statistics, accessed 19 August 2020.

25. 'Piers Morgan mocks Daniel Craig for carrying baby', BBC News, 16 October 2018.

26. Mark Rice-Oxley, 'Hands-on fathers "less likely to break up with partners"', *The Guardian*, 30 September 2018.

27. Angela Henshall, 'Four ways paid paternity leave could boost family income', BBC News, 19 June 2016.

28. Helena Horton, 'Jacob Rees-Mogg: I have six children but have never changed a nappy', *Daily Telegraph,* 21 July 2017.

29. 'The Millenial Dad at Work', www.daddilife.com, May 2019.

30. David G. Allen, 'Retaining Talent: A Guide to Analyzing and Managing Employee Turnover', www.shrm.org, accessed 19 August 2020.

31. Sarah Young, 'The best companies for maternity and paternity pay, revealed', *The Independent*, 4 June 2019.

Chapter 12

1. 'Pregnancy and Maternity-Related Discrimination and Disadvantage: Experience of Mothers', Equality of Human Rights Commission, 2016, p. 88.

2. 'Denied and Discriminated Against', www.tuc.org.uk, 15 October 2021.

3. Killian Fox, 'It's a form of modern slavery: MPs on Ken Loach's film about the human cost of the zero-hours economy', *The Observer*, 6 October 2019.

4. 'Pregnancy and Maternity-Related Discrimination and Disadvantage: Experience of Mothers', Equality of Human Rights Commission, 2016.

5. Rachel Sharp, 'One in three flexible working requests turned down', *HR Magazine*, 3 September 2019.

6. Hannah Jordan, 'The benefits of senior job shares', *HR Magazine*, 30 July 2018.

7. Brigid Francis-Devine and Niamh Foley, 'Women and the Economy', House of Commons briefing paper CBP06838, 4 March 2020.

8. 'Women's employment in the EU', Eurostat, 6 March 2020.

9. 'Vodafone global survey reveals rapid adoption of flexible working', Vodafone UK News Centre, 8 February 2016.

10. 'The case to embrace flexible working is strengthening', *Financial Times*, 19 September 2018.

11. 'Nine in ten flexible working firms say it's been good for business', www.insider.co.uk, 7 October 2019.

12. Adrian Lewis, 'Flexible working could be more important than financial incentives', *HR Director*, 8 January 2018.

13. 'The Future of Work: Jobs and Skills in 2030', UK Commission for Employment and Skills, February 2014.

14. 'Big Demands and High Expectations: The Deloitte Millennial Survey', Deloitte, January 2014.

15. Jo Faraghar, 'Part-time parents missing out on promotion', *Personnel Today*, 4 February 2019.

16. 'Gender Pay Gap in the UK: 2018', Office for National Statistics, accessed 19 August 2020.

17. Stephen Clarke and Nye Cominetti, 'Setting the Record Straight:

How Record Employment Has Changed the UK', Resolution
Foundation, 14 January 2019: p. 52

18. 'The Timewise Flexible Jobs Index 2021', www.timewise.co.uk,
2021.

19. Mary Ann Siegheart, *The Real Gender Pay Gap*, Radio 4, 16 June
2019.

20. 'Families and the Labour Market, England: 2017', Office for
National Statistics, 26 September 2017.

21. 'Flexible Working in the UK', www.cipd.co.uk, 2019.

22. 'Presenteeism hits record high in UK organisations as stress at work
rises', www.cipd.co.uk, 2 May 2018.

23. Hilary Osborne, 'Home workers putting in more time since Covid,
research shows', *The Guardian*, 4 February 2021.

24. 'Presenteeism hits record high in UK organisations as stress at work
rises'.

25. 'The 2019 Workforce View in Europe Report', www.adp.com,
2019.

26. Chris Giles, 'Britain's productivity crisis in eight charts', *Financial
Times*, 13 August 2018.

27. Valentina Romei, 'French employees face challenge to short-hours
culture', *Financial Times*, 26 April 2019.

28. C. W. and A. J. K. D., 'Get a Life', *The Economist*, 24 September
2013.

29. Ashleigh Webber, 'Should we rethink our working hours to boost
productivity?', *Personnel Today*, 17 April 2019.

30. Clarke and Cominetti, 'Setting the Record Straight: How Record
Employment Has Changed the UK': p. 52.

31. Frank Chung, 'Why PepsiCo CEO asks his team to "leave loudly"',
www.news.com.au, 13 September 2017.

32. Hugh Schofield, 'The plan to ban work emails out of hours', BBC
News, 11 May 2016.

33. Phillip Inman and Jasper Jolly, 'Productivity woes: why giving staff
an extra day off can be the answer', *The Guardian*, 17 November
2018.

34. Phillip Inman, 'Growing number of Britons working from home,
says ONS', *The Guardian*, 18 June 2020.

35. 'Coronavirus and homeworking in the UK labour market: 2019',
Office for National Statistics, March 2020.

36. Lora Jones, 'I monitor my staff with software that takes screenshots',
BBC News, 29 September 2020.

37. Chris Newlands, 'Working from home: coronavirus pandemic has exposed the risks and rewards of remote working', www.inews. co.uk, 4 June 2020.

Chapter 13

1. 'NHS boosts support for black and ethnic minority women,' www. england.nhs.uk, 27 June 2020.
2. 'Pregnant women are not at greater risk of severe COVID-19 than other women, but most of those who have problems are in their third trimester', Nuffield Department of Population Health, University of Oxford, 18 May 2020.
3. Simonetta Longhi, 'The Disability Pay Gap', Equality and Human Rights Commission, 2017.
4. 'Ethnicity pay gaps in Great Britain: 2018', Office for National Statistics, 2018.
5. Valentina Romei, 'Ethnic minority pay gap in UK still stubbornly wide', *Financial Times*, 9 July 2019.
6. 'Ethnicity pay gaps in Great Britain: 2018'.
7. Sinead Butler, 'Closing the disability employment gap is an economic necessity', www.capx.co, 2018.
8. Gwyn Topham, '£3.2bn UK pay gap for black, Asian and ethnic minority workers', *The Guardian*, 27 December 2018.
9. Tim Wallace, 'White households earn £16,000 more than black families', *Daily Telegraph*, 23 June 2020.
10. 'Saving Lives, Improving Mothers' Care: Executive Summary', MMRRACE-UK, 2020.
11. Emma Kasprzak, 'Why are black mothers at more risk of dying?', BBC News, 12 April 2019.
12. H.M. Harb, F. Al-rshoud, R. Dhillon, M. Harb, A. Coomarasamy, 'Ethnicity and miscarriage: a large prospective observational study and meta-analysis', *Fertility and Sterility*, 1 September 2014.
13. Human Fertilisation and Embryology Authority, 'New figures show low uptake of fertility treatment among BAME communities', 2019.
14. Javaid Muglu, Henna Rather, David Arroyo-Manzano, Sohinee Bhattacharya, Imelda Balchin, Asma Khalil, Basky Thilaganathan, Khalid S. Khan, Javier Zamora, Shakila Thangaratinam, 'Risks of stillbirth and neonatal death with advancing gestation at term: A

systematic review and meta-analysis of cohort studies of 15 million pregnancies', *PLOS Medicine*, 2 July 2019.

15. 'Black babies are less likely to die when cared for by black doctors, US study finds', *British Medical Journal*, 21 August 2020.

16. 'Pregnancy and Maternity-Related Discrimination and Disadvantage: Summary of Key Findings', Equality and Human Rights Commission, 2016, accessed 19 August 2020.

17. House of Commons Women and Equalities Committee, 'Employment Opportunities for Muslims in the UK, Second Report of Session 2016–2017', www.parliament.uk, August 2016.

18. Nabil Khattab and Shereen Hussein, 'Can Religious Affiliation Explain the Disadvantage of Muslim Women in the British Labour Market?', *Work, Employment and Society*, Vol. 32, 6 (2017): pp. 1011–28.

19. Khattab and Hussein, 'Can Religious Affiliation Explain the Disadvantage of Muslim Women in the British Labour Market?'.

20. 'Employment Opportunities for Muslims in the UK, 2016–2017', www.parliament.uk, 11 August 2016.

21. Disability Living Foundation, 'Key Facts', www.dlf.org.uk.

22. Papworth Trust, 'Facts and Figures 2018: Disability in the United Kingdom', www.papworthtrust.org.uk, 2018.

23. Clare Kassa, 'The Extra Costs of Raising a Disabled Child', www.endchildpoverty.org.uk, accessed 19 August 2020.

24. Disability Rights UK, 'Nearly half of everyone in poverty is either a disabled person or lives with a disabled person', 7 February 2020.

25. 'Counting the Costs 2012: The Financial Reality for Families With Disabled Children Across the UK', www.contact.org.uk, 2012.

26. 'Helping Vulnerable Families', www.bestbeginnings.org.uk, accessed 19 August 2020.

27. 'Disabled Single Parents', www.gingerbread.org.uk (2019).

28. 'Pregnancy and Maternity-Related Discrimination and Disadvantage: Experience of Mothers', Equality and Human Rights Commission, 2016.

29. Tom Harris, 'The return of morality: the army of teenage mothers living off the state is a national catastrophe', *The Guardian*, 5 March 2009.

30. Ofra Koffman, 'Second thoughts: supporting teenage mothers', *The Guardian*, 7 October 2009.

31. Ellen Pugh, 'Student pregnancy and maternity: implications for higher education institutions', Equality Challenge Unit, 2010.

32. Suzanne Cater and Lester Coleman, '"Planned" Teenage Pregnancy: Views and Experiences of Young People from Poor and Disadvantaged Backgrounds', Joseph Rowntree Foundation, 2006.

33. Ermisch and Pavalin, 'The systematic review of long-term outcomes associated with teenage pregnancy within the UK', March 2010, pp. 14–17.

34. 'Half of young mums skip meals as they struggle to feed their children and a quarter have used a food bank, finds Young Womens' Trust', www.youngwomenstrust.org, 28 March 2017.

35. '#PowertotheBump unites young mothers in fight against pregnancy and maternity discrimination at work', Equality and Human Rights Commission, 17 May 2016.

36. 'Net Childcare Cost for Parents Using Childcare', www.oecd.org (2019).

37. Rebecca Cox, 'A letter to single mums: how to survive when it's all too much', *Harper's Bazaar*, 19 March 2020.

38. 'Single Parents: Facts and Figures', www.gingerbread.org.uk (2019).

39. Helen Barnard, 'UK Poverty 2018', Joseph Rowntree Foundation. The pay gap between lone parents and the second earner in couples was £2.14 an hour in 2018, compared with £0.31 in 2001–02. The pay gap between lone parents and the main earner in couples has increased from £3.59 to £5.86 an hour over the same period.

40. Barnard, 'UK Poverty 2018'.

41. 'Pregnancy and Maternity-Related Discrimination and Disadvantage', Equality and Human Rights Commission, pp. 79, 81, 84.

42. Emily Burt, 'Single working parents "bear financial burden of unsustainable, low-quality employment"', *People Management*, 22 February 2018.

43. Citizens Advice: https://www.citizensadvice.org.uk/family/education/discrimination-in-education/taking-action-about-discrimination-in-education.

Chapter 14

1. Rob May, 'Start-ups across the UK are going bust – they need more careful management for our economy to boom', *Daily Telegraph*, 24 January 2019.

2. 'Trends in Self-Employment in the UK: Analysing the Characteristics,

Income and Wealth of the Self-Employed', Office for National Statistics, 2018.

3. Katherine Ormerod, '2019 has not been a great work Year', www.workworkwork.co, 2019.

4. Heather Saul, 'Self employed mums say they are being forced to go back to work a day after giving birth', www.inews.co.uk, 15 November 2017.

5. Praseeda Nair, '"Six weeks support": Why self-employed mums deserve equal maternity pay', www.growthbusiness.co.uk, 4 December 2017.

6. 'Net Childcare Cost for Parents Using Childcare', www.oecd.org, 2019.

7. 'Women in Self-Employment Report', www.ipse.co.uk, 2020.

Chapter 15

1. Ashley May, 'Paid family leave is an elite benefit in the US', *USA Today,* 17 May 2017.

2. Abigail Hess, 'Here's how many paid vacation days the typical American worker gets', www.cnbc.com, 6 July 2018.

3. 'How many days of paid holiday is my US worker entitled to?', www.footholdamerica.com.

4. Adam Burtle and Stephen Bezruchka, 'Population Health and Paid Parental Leave: What the United States Can Learn from Two Decades of Research', *Healthcare*, 4, 2, (2016): p. 30.

5. C. R. Winegarden and P. M. Bracy, 'Demographic Consequences of Maternal-Leave Programs In Industrial Countries: Evidence From Fixed-Effects Models', *South Economic Journal*, 61, 4 (1995): pp. 1020–35.

6. Jody Heymann, Amy Raub and Alison Earle, 'Creating and Utilising New Data Sources to Analyze the Relationship Between Social Policy and Global Health: The Case of Maternal Leave', *Public Health Reports*, 126, 3 (2011): pp. 127–34.

7. Winegarden and Bracy, 'Demographic consequences of maternal-leave programs in industrial countries: evidence from fixed-effects models'.

8. Sharon Lerner, 'The Real War on Families: Why the US Needs Paid Leave Now', www.inthesetimes.com, 18 August 2015.

9. Jeff Hayes, Dallas Elgin, Ye Zhang, Sandeep Shetty et al., 'Paid Leave and Employment Stability of First-Time Mothers', www.impaqint.com, January 2017.

10. Christopher J. Ruhm, 'Parental Leave and Child Health', *Journal of Health Economics*, 19, 6 (2000): pp. 931–60.

11. 'The Child Development Case for a National Paid Family and Medical Leave Program', www.zerotothree.org, 17 December 2018.

12. Natalie Kitroeff and Jessica Silver-Greenberg, 'Pregnancy Discrimination Is Rampant Inside America's Biggest Companies', *New York Times*, 15 June 2018.

13. Hillary Hoffower and Taylor Borden, 'How much it costs to have a baby in every state, whether you have health insurance or don't', *Business Insider*, 9 December 2019.

14. Paulette Light, 'Why 43% of Women With Children Leave Their Jobs, and How to Get Them Back', *The Atlantic*, 19 April 2013.

15. 'The State of the Gender Pay Gap in 2020', payscale.com/data/gender-pay-gap#section02. Yekaterina Chosen, Anna Gromada and Gwyther Rees, 'Are the world's richest countries family friendly? Policy in the OECD and EU', Unicef, www.unicef-irc.org/publications/pdf/Family-Friendly-Policies-Research_UNICEF_%20 2019.pdf, June 2010. See also Mary Beth Ferrante, 'UNICEF Study Confirms: The U.S. Ranks Last for Family-Friendly Policies', Forbes, 21 June 2019, forbes.com/sites/marybethferrante/2019/06/21/unicef-study-confirms-the-u-s-ranks-last-for-family-friendly-policies/?sh=3e920de433ba.

16. Anders Chronholm, 'Fathers' Experience of Shared Parental Leave in Sweden', *Recherches Sociologiques et Anthropologiques*, 38, 2 (2007): pp. 9–25.

17. Simon Hedlin, 'Why Swedish men take so much paternity leave', *The Economist*, 23 July 2014.

18. Katrin Bennhold, 'In Sweden, men can have it all', *New York Times*, 9 June 2010.

19. Kate Doucet, 'Sweden's Maternity and Paternity Leave', Yale School of Medicine, 1 June 2018.

20. 'Expat Explorer Report 2019', www.expatexplorer.hsbc.com, accessed 14 August 2020.

21. 'How's Life in Sweden?', OECD Better Life Initiative, accessed 14 August 2020.

22. 'OECD Better Life Index: United Kingdom', www.oecdbetterlifeindex.org.

23. 'OECD Better Life Index: Work–Life Balance', www.oecdbetterlifeindex.org, accessed 14 August 2020.

24. 'Employment and Unemployment (Labour Force Survey)', Eurostat, 2019.

25. 'OECD Better Life Index: How's Life?', www.oecdbetterlifeindex.org, accessed 14 August 2020.

26. 'Child poverty in working households up by 800,000 since 2010, says TUC', www.tuc.org.uk, 18 November 2019.

27. 'Child poverty is falling in Sweden, but social gaps are growing', www.thelocal.se, 10 October 2018.

28. 'Child poverty is falling in Sweden, but social gaps are growing', www.thelocal.se, 10 October 2018.

29. 'OECD Better Life Index: Sweden', www.oecdbetterlifeindex.org. In Sweden, the average household net-adjusted disposable income per capita is US$31,287 a year, according to the OECD Better Life Index, while the average household net-adjusted disposable income per capita in the UK is US$28,715 a year.

30. 'World Happiness Report 2019', www.worldhappiness.report, 20 March 2019.

31. Maddy Savage, 'The "paradox" of working in the world's most equal countries', BBC News, 4 September 2019.

32. Savage, 'The "paradox" of working in the world's most equal countries'.

33. 'Half of Swedish mums want to stay home', Radio Sweden, 25 October 2011.

34. Savage, 'The "paradox" of working in the world's most equal countries'.

35. 'The Nordic Gender Effect at Work', www.norden.org.

36. 'The Urban Disadvantage: State of the World's Mothers 2015 – 2015 Mothers' Index Rankings', Save the Children, 2015.

37. Justin McCurry, 'Tokyo medical school admits changing results to exclude women', *The Guardian*, 8 August 2018.

38. Uptin Saiidi, 'Japan has some of the longest working hours in the world. It's trying to change', www.cnbc.com, 1 June 2018.

39. 'Women in the Workforce – Japan: Quick Take', www.catalyst.org, 2 October 2019.

40. Toko Shirakawa, 'Why paternity leave should be mandatory', *Japan Times*, 14 June 2019.

41. Justin McCurry, 'Japan shrinking as birthrate falls to lowest level in history', *The Guardian*, 27 December 2018.

42. Suzuki Wataru, 'Japan's Free Childcare Program No Panacea for Daycare Waitlists', www.nippon.com, 11 June 2019.

43. Motoko Rich, 'A Japanese politician is taking paternity leave. It's a Big Deal', 15 January 2020.

44. Joe Pinsker, 'Why Icelandic dads take parental leave and Japanese dads don't', *The Atlantic*, 23 January 2020.

45. 'How Much Could My Childcare Cost?', www.careforkids.com.uk, accessed 15 August 2020.

46. Dominique Allen, 'Pregnancy Discrimination in the Australian Workplace', Oxford Human Rights Hub, 24 June 2014.

47. Allen, 'Pregnancy Discrimination in the Australian Workplace'.

48. 'OECD Better Life Index: Work–Life Balance', www.oecdbetterlife-index.org, accessed 15 August 2020.

49. Laura Addati, Naomi Cassirer and Katherin Gilchrist, 'Maternity and Paternity at Work: Law and Practice Across the World', International Labour Organization, 13 May 2014.

50. Katie O'Malley, 'UK named among least family-friendly countries in new study', *The Independent*, 13 June 2019.

51. Rachael Kennedy, 'Switzerland and the UK ranked among the worst countries for families', Euronews, 13 June 2019.

52. Sif Sigmarsdottir, 'Once more, Iceland has shown it is the best place in the world to be female, *The Guardian*, 5 January 2018.

53. 'Gender Equality for Promoting Economic Development', Nordic Centre for Spatial Development, 2 March 2013.

54. Simon Rogers, 'Bobby Kennedy on GDP: "measures everything except that which is worthwhile"', *The Guardian*, 24 May 2012.

Chapter 16

1. 'Companies offering egg freezing', www.ivfbabble.com, 28 September 2017.

2. 'Child Poverty Facts and Figures', Child Poverty Action Group, July 2020.

3. 'Consultation on Setting the 2020 Persistent Child Poverty Target', www.gov.uk, June 2014.

4. Heather Stewart, 'Boris Johnson claimed children of working mothers "more likely to mug you"', *The Guardian*, 4 December 2019.

5. Francis Elliott, 'Boris Johnson criticised for attack on single mothers and their "ill-raised, ignorant" children', *The Times*, 28 November 2019.

6. 'A mother's place "is in the home"', BBC News, 10 July 2018.

7. J. Curtice, E. Clery, J. Perry, M. Phillips et al., 'British Social Attitudes 36', www.bsa.natcen.ac.uk, 2019: p. 86.

8. May Bulman, 'Closing gender gap could add £150 billion to UK economy', *The Independent*, 29 September 2016.

9. Bulman, 'Closing gender gap could add £150 billion to UK economy'

10. 'Whose time to care: Unpaid care and domestic work during Covid-19' data.unwomen.org/publications/whose-time-care-unpaid-care-and-domestic-work-during-covid-19, 25 November 2020.

11. Kim Slowey, 'By the numbers: Women in construction', www.constructiondive.com, 6 March 2019.

12. Jerome De Henau and Susan Himmelweit, 'A Care-Led Recovery from Coronavirus', Women's Budget Group, June 2020.

13. 'Creating a Caring Economy: A Call To Action', Women's Budget Group, September 2020.

14. 'Research Report 105: Estimating the Financial Cost of Maternity-Related Discrimination and Disadvantage', Equality and Human Rights Commission, October 2015.

15. Jane Gotts, 'Women Consumer Power', www.genanalytics.co.uk, 13 February 2017.

16. Sundiatu Dixon-Fyle, Kevin Dolan, Vivian Hunt and Sara Prince, 'Diversity in Leadership', McKinsey & Company, accessed 15 August 2020.

17. 'Women Matter: Ten Years of Insights on Gender Diversity', McKinsey & Company, 4 October 2017, p. 13.

18. Margaret McDonagh and Lorna Fitzsimons, 'Women Count 2020', The Pipeline.

19. 'Firms with more female executives "perform better"', BBC News, 27 July 2020.

20. 'Revealed: The worst explanations for not appointing women to FTSE company boards', www.gov.uk, 31 May 2018.

21. Damian Grimshaw and Jill Rubery, 'The Motherhood Pay Gap: A Review of the Issues, Theory and International Evidence', International Labour Office, 2015: p. 31. See also Wendy Olsen and Sylvia Walby, 'Modelling Gender Pay Gaps', Equal Opportunities Commission (2004), for a summary for the United Kingdom.

22. Alex Soojun-Kim Pang, 'Shorter Hours Make Stronger Business', Wall Street Journal, 27 February 2020.

23. Emma Jacobs, 'Can shorter working hours help avoid burnout and boost productivity?', Financial Times, 11 March 2020.

24. Robert Booth, 'Four-day week: trial finds lower stress and increased productivity', The Guardian, 19 February 2019.

25. 'Working in Denmark: Work–life balance', www.denmark.dk, accessed 15 August 2020.

26. Ashleigh Webber, 'Should we rethink our working hours to boost productivity?', *Personnel Today*, 17 April 2019.

27. 'Dare to Share: Germany's Experience of Promoting Equal Partnerships in Families', www.oecd.org (2017).

28. 'Part-Time Employment Rate', www.oecd.org (2019).

29. Flic Everett, '"I want a divorce": How lockdown tore us apart', *Daily Telegraph*, 3 June 2020.

30. 'An Unequal Crisis', Citizens Advice, 6 August 2020.

31. Grimshaw and Rubery, 'The Motherhood Pay Gap: A Review of the Issues, Theory and International Evidence': p. 1.

32. Andreas Kotsadam and Henning Finseraas, 'The State Intervenes in the Battle of the Sexes: Causal Effects of Paternity Leave', *Social Science Research*, 40, 6 (2011): pp. 1611–22.

33. 'State of the World's Fathers 2019 Report Finds that 85 Percent of Fathers Say They Would Do Anything To Be Very Involved in Caring for Their New Child, but Are Still Taking on Far Less Than Mothers', www.men-care.org, 5 June 2019.

34. Richard Kelly and Isobel White, 'All-Women Shortlists', www.parliament.uk, 7 March 2016.

35. Alice-Azania Jarvis, 'The timeline: maternity leave', *The Independent*, 23 October 2011.

36. Anne West and Philip Noden, 'Public Funding of Early Years Education in England: An Historical Perspective', London School of Economics and Political Science, 2016.

37. Analía V. Durán, 'Are Employment Quotas for Minorities the Right Way to Tackle Discrimination?', International Bar Association, 18 March 2016.

38. Oliver Staley, 'You know those quotas for female board members in Europe? They're working', www.qz.com, 3 May 2016.

39. Penny Wincer: '39 pence per hour if the person is doing 24-hour care, which full-time carers of disabled children are doing.'

40. 'Unpaid Carers save the UK £132 billion a year – the cost of second NHS', Carers UK, 12 November 2015.

41. 'Moms: We all know you're worth it. But how much is "it" really worth?', www.salary.com, accessed 15 August 2020.

42. Michael Savage, 'Stay at home mothers make a "lifestyle choice" says Osborne', *The Times*, 6 August 2013.

43. '870,000 mums in England can't get the childcare they need', www.savethechildren.org.uk, accessed 15 August 2020.

44. Thomas Deane, Trinity College Dublin, 'Countries with female

leaders suffer six times fewer Covid-19 deaths', *Medical X-press*, 29 May 2020.

45. 'New Fawcett data reveals that women's representation in local government "at a standstill"', 2 July 2019.

46. Devin K. Joshi and Ryan Goehrung, 'Mothers and fathers in Parliament: MP parental status and family gaps from a global perspective', *Parliamentary Affairs,* 7 February 2020.

Chapter 17

1. Mikey Smith, 'Boris Johnson declares "war" on coronavirus with new emergency "C-19 Committee"', *The Mirror*, 17 March 2020. Article lists the leaders of each of the four committees as: Michael Gove, Rishi Sunak, Matt Hancock and Dominic Raab, and states that the daily 'war cabinet' will be made up of the leaders of the four committees plus the prime minister.

2. Peter Walker, 'No 10's Covid briefings led exclusively by men for past six months', *The Guardian*, 16 December 2020.

3. Clare Wenham and Asha Herten-Crabb, 'Why we need a gender advisor on SAGE', *LSE Public Policy Review*, 28 January 2021.

4. The judgement can be found at https://www.doughtystreet.co.uk/sites/default/files/media/document/R%20%28The%20Motherhood%20Plan%29%20v%20HM%20Treasury%202021%20EWCA%20Civ%201703.pdf

5. André Zimmerman and Louisa Kallhoff, 'Covid-19 update: Germany to give working parents state-funded compensation claim during closure of childcare and schools', Orrick Employment Law and Litigation, blogs.orrick.com, 3 April 2020.

6. Tiago Vidal and Maria Eça, 'Government closes schools as pandemic worsens in Portugal', www.blogdeasuntospublicos.com, January 2021.

7. '"Scream or Shout": campaign group's voicemail service lets mothers rant', *The Guardian* podcast, 8 March 2021.

8. 'The Safety of Pregnant Women', www.pregnantthenscrewed.com, 22 July 2021.

9. Oxford Population Health, 'Key information on Covid-19 in pregnancy', www.npeu.ox.ac.uk, 11 October 2021.

10. Anna Mikhailova, 'Huge mental health toll that Covid restrictions have had on mothers-to-be laid bare in a landmark survey', Mail Online, 15 November 2020.

11. World Health Organization, 'Why having a companion during labour and childbirth may be better for you', www.who.int, 18 March 2019.

12. '7% of women have given birth on their own', www.pregnantthenscrewed.com, 18 June 2021.

13. Hannah Summers, 'UK women forced to wear masks during labour, charity finds', *The Guardian*, 14 May 2021.

14. Alexandra Topping, 'More than 75% of NHS midwives think staffing levels unsafe, says RCM', *The Guardian*, 16 November 2020.

15. '"We warned you" says RCM on shortfall in applications for midwifery degrees', Royal College of Midwives, 19 December 2016.

16. 'Nursing: Higher Education Investment', hansard.parliament.uk, Vol. 649, 21 November 2018.

17. Tom Lamont, '"I had no idea about the hidden labour": has the pandemic changed fatherhood forever?', *The Guardian*, 20 February 2021.

18. Heejung Chung, Hyojin Seo, Sarah Forbes and Holly Birkett, 'Working from home during the Covid-19 lockdown: changing preferences and the future of work', www.birmingham.ac.uk.

19. Adrienne Burgess and Rebecca Goldman, 'Lockdown fathers: the untold story', Fatherhood Institute, May 2021.

20. Mike Wade, 'After the pandemic, fathers are more likely to ask for flexible hours', *The Times*, 21 June 2021.

21. 'The Timewise Flexible Jobs Index 2021', www.timewise.co.uk

22. Geraldine Scott, 'Get back to the office to stop colleagues gossiping about you, PM tells workers', *Independent*, 5 October 2021.

23. Steven Swinford, Oliver Wright and Chris Smyth, 'Go back to office if you want to get on, says Rishi Sunak', *The Times*, 3 August 2021.

24. 'Conservative conference: "Get off your Pelotons and back to work", says Oliver Dowden', BBC News, 5 October 2021.

25. 'Women warned home working may harm their careers', BBC News, 12 November 2021.

26. Emma Powell, 'Women who work remotely will hurt their careers, says Bank of England's Catherine Mann', *The Times*, 11 November 2021.

27. Imogen Horton and Emer Scully, 'Women who work from home will damage their careers and could widen the gender pay gap, top economist warns', Mail Online, 12 November 2021.

28. Sean Fleming, 'Survey: 40% of employees are thinking of quitting their jobs', World Economic Forum, 2 June 2021.

29. 'Over a third of businesses report that employee mental health support has got better since the start of the pandemic', acas.org.uk, 2 September 2021.
30. 'Joiners and leavers in the childcare sector – July 2021', www.gov.uk, 16 August 2021.
31. 'Childcare costs rise by 4% as providers struggle to remain sustainable during the pandemic', www.coram.org.uk, 9 March 2021.
32. 'Childcare', hansard.parliament.uk, Vol. 700, 13 September 2021.
33. '"Baby shortage" could spell economic stagnation for UK', www.smf.co.uk, 20 September 2021.

Acknowledgements

On that blustery morning of International Women's Day 2015 when I sat down to teach myself WordPress so I could launch a website called Pregnant Then Screwed, I never expected that it would lead to this – a charity supporting thousands of women who experience pregnancy and maternity discrimination; Government lobbying; festivals for thousands of mums; marching through the streets to demand change; regular appearances on the TV and radio – and a book! A blooming book! My old English teacher would be so proud.

There have been many people who have made this possible – so many that to name every single one would take up half the book. You know who you are: the brilliant women who have given up their non-existent spare time to work on the Pregnant Then Screwed advice lines or to mentor a woman taking legal action against an employer, and those who have helped me unpick complex Government policy.

To Sarah, Celia, Gaby, Katie, Chloe, Sophia, Olga, Lauren, Analiese, Emily and Taryn: you're the beating heart of this campaign. To those who donated to the crowdfunder when I left my job and had to make Pregnant Then Screwed work financially; those who have volunteered at our events; those who have made invaluable introductions; my brilliant trustees; the small team of magnificent freelancers who were doing the heavy lifting while I was distracted by book-writing – Sarah Ronan, Tom Northey, Celia Venables and Heather Wong; Simon Canaway from Supanaught and Angela and Sammi from Design By Day, who lent me their creative skills and time when I had nothing to give in return.

Thank you to Chloe and Rosemary Kirton who came into my life unexpectedly and have brightened it up immeasurably with their incredible artistry – designing the illustration on the front of this book and most of the graphics on the Pregnant Then Screwed social media pages.

To Danielle Ayres, who's been with me from the beginning, giving thousands of vulnerable women free legal advice when they need it the most. You're the engine to my chassis. Pregnant Then Screwed would not exist without you. Your plain-speaking, no-nonsense attitude, generous heart and potty mouth have kept me smiling when it's felt impossible. Thank you, Danielle.

To Sue Coe, now working at the TUC but previously at the Equality and Human Rights Commission. It's superheroes like you, working tirelessly behind the scenes, who really make the world a better place. Thank you for supporting me and Pregnant Then Screwed over the past five years, and thank you for the commitment to always making me snort with laughter whenever we speak.

To Mills, co-founder of UsTwo, who genuinely cares about making the world a better place and believed in me from the get-go. And all the organisations who had been working in this world for a number of years when I burst onto the scene but who gave us a warm welcome. You know who you are.

Then there are all the magnificent humans who made

this book possible: my agent Marilia Savvides, who emailed one day out of the blue and told me I could write a book. She wasn't going to take no for an answer, so here we are. Thank you for not giving up. (Every woman should have a Marilia.) To my editor, Fritha Saunders, for her patience, attention to detail and kind words. To Philip McCabe and Alana Penkethman, who kindly read sections of the book that contained employment-law advice and made sure I wasn't saying anything that was nonsense. To every person who has provided a personal story or a quote: thank you – I hope you feel this book represents you and your experience.

And, finally, to the women who were there for me when I needed them the most: Kat, C, Laura, Kate and Kim. Your friendship and love kept me upright when everything around me collapsed. To my mum, Yvonne, and my sister, Kim, who are the greatest of all the humans.

To my partner and cheerleader, Tom, who just about puts up with my angry, feminist ranting and has been such a mental and physical support throughout the development of Pregnant Then Screwed. And, of course, to my boys, Theodore and Jack: no matter how shitty things are for mothers, you are most definitely worth it. I love you with every fibre of my being, and, now that I have finally finished this book, I promise to do some proper parenting. If, one day in the future, you decide that you would like to have children, I just hope the world has changed enough so that you can truly share the care, because being your mother will always be my greatest achievement.

Index

Index

Index

Index

Index

Index

Index